Asian Americans
in Higher Education
and at Work

Asian Americans
in Higher Education
and at Work

Jayjia Hsia

Educational Testing Service

LAWRENCE ERLBAUM ASSOCIATES, PUBLISHERS

1988   Hillsdale, New Jersey   Hove and London

Lawrence Erlbaum Associates, Inc., Publishers
365 Broadway
Hillsdale, New Jersey 07642

Library of Congress Cataloging-in-Publication Data

Hsia, Jayjia.
    Asia Americans in higher education and at work.

    Includes indexes.
    1. Asian Americans—Education (Higher)   2. Academic
achievement.   3. Asian Americans—Employment.   I. Title.
LC2633.6.H74   1988   378'.1982   87-13571
ISBN 0-8058-0089-1

Printed in the United States of America
10 9 8 7 6 5 4 3 2 1

Contents

v

Acknowledgments

This book was made possible by generous support from Educational Testing Service. ETS officers and board of trustees provided encouragement and time to explore the relatively neglected field of Asian American test performance and academic achievement. My colleagues in program and research areas searched their files and shared collections of program and research publications, research studies, and technical reports; as well as summary data collected during a decade of enormous change and growth in participation of Asian Americans in higher education. The library, ETS archives, and the ERIC Clearinghouse on Tests, Measurement and Evaluation were also rich mines of information.

The manuscript, with its many tables, was keyed with patience and good humor by Joanne Farr and Fran Livingston. The figures were produced by Richard Bondi. I am deeply grateful for all the help that was given me. The opinions expressed in the text, and any errors in fact or inference, however, are the sole responsibility of the author.

Jayjia Hsia

Foreword

Asian American students have become the fastest growing minority group enrolled in selective public and private institutions on both coasts of the United States. They also are tapping the resources of 2-year community colleges in major metropolitan areas. Yet, only limited information is available about the performance of Asian Americans in higher education.

Educational Testing Service is pleased to have supported the research reported in this book by my distinguished colleague, Jayjia Hsia. Written about Asian Americans by an Asian American, this volume brings together up-to-date information about the developed abilities, academic achievements, educational aspirations, and higher education and career attainments of Asian Americans in the aggregate, as well as separately by subgroups. The information presented here challenges some widely held beliefs about minorities in general, and Asian Americans in particular.

I believe that educators and policymakers will find this information useful. We also hope that this volume will be helpful to Asian American students and their families, as they make their plans and choices for higher education.

This is not a how-to book. Rather, the focus is on the reasons behind recent changes in the Asian American population. Presently just over 2% of the total United States population, Asian Americans are changing rapidly not only in numbers, but in racial and ethnic composition, socioeconomic status, educational attainment, and occupational levels. These changes happen not only through individual and cooperative efforts, but also via the dynamics of day-to-day interactions of Asian Americans as they encounter the myriads of social, economic, and political forces, international as well as domestic, of this complex society.

This volume is an expression of hope. It examines the range of choices available to individuals in a democratic, learning society. It describes the gains possible, in just one generation, among minority group members who—although limited in numbers and political influence—have a profound belief in the betterment of human lives through education.

Gregory R. Anrig
President
Educational Testing Service

1

Introduction

Asian Americans have become a significant presence on many college and university campuses. The varieties of distinctive Asian faces, their sheer numbers in highly selective as well as open-door institutions, and their tendency to concentrate in quantitative, scientific, and technological fields have attracted public attention. This review and analysis of recent literature about characteristics of Asian Americans and their aspirations and attainments in education and careers collects and analyzes a growing body of research related to Asian Americans.

Some current issues that face young Asian Americans when they begin to make college plans include their choice of institutions: public or private, 2- or 4-year, selective or less selective, within commuting distance or away from home and community. Will their high school records and test scores be good enough for their top choice schools? Can their families afford the tuition and other expenses at the college of their choice? What are their chances for obtaining financial aid in the form of grants, loans, or jobs? They must also decide on intended majors and the kinds of careers their major fields will allow them to pursue.

These decisions, in themselves, are no different in kind from those faced by all their college-bound classmates, black or white, rich or poor, highly able academically or just average. But Asian American college applicants are beginning to face additional hurdles. They must increasingly take into account the handicaps associated with their own ethnicity. Asians are now considered to be "overrepresented" in many institutions of higher education, and accepted at lower rates than other applicant groups, including the majority. Asian Americans are also more likely than all other college applicants to plan majors in science and technology fields, and more likely to be denied admission on account of their interests and abilities in mathematics, science, engineering, and medicine. More than one in four Asian American college-bound seniors admit English is not their best language. Poor ability to communicate in English is bound to work against any applicant. Yet, proportionately more Asian American youth do go on to college and stay through to graduation than all other Americans. Will the hurdles become increasingly higher as institutions try to balance the demands of many powerful interest groups with the press of Asian American applicants?

The institutions that are experiencing double, triple, even quadruple the numbers of qualified Asian American applicants during the past decade are also in a dilemma. Asian Americans are just over 2% of the total United States population in the mid-1980s. How can public higher education systems, private institutions, or individual faculties and departments justify admitting and educating 5, 10, 15, or even 20% or more Asian American students, even if standard, or more stringent, admissions criteria were being applied? Asian Americans present higher educations with the first instance of direct conflict between two goods in dealing with a minority group: that of equality of educational opportunity on one hand, and proportional representation on the other. Different institutions have responded differently, with a variety of rationales and justifications for their actions.

Other current issues include differences in developed abilities and achievement among various Asian ethnic groups, and differences in educational needs between recent immigrants and native-born or long-term residents. Differential patterns of developed abilities may explain the limited choice of fields observed among Asian Americans. These narrow areas of interest could, in turn, curtail Asian American access to selective institutions or to specific fields for graduate or professional studies and eventually block career paths. These issues have the potential of becoming divisive not only within the higher educational community but for American society as a whole. The goal of the present review is therefore to provide a balanced, up-to-date description of Asian Americans to interested educators and policymakers. This book can also provide information to Asian Americans, particularly the new-comers and their parents, to help them better understand higher education institutions and systems that have been instrumental in the advances Asian Americans have made to date and will undoubtedly continue to make in the future.

This book contains eight chapters. This chapter orients the reader to the organization of the book. In order to view critically and gain an understanding of the dialectical processes that the American concept of Asians, and Asian Americans, has undergone, it is important to know something about the history of ethnic Asians in America. Between 1850 and 1980, Asian Americans were transformed from the menace of "uneducable heathens" to the myth of the "model minority." It was not only the uninformed public that viewed all Asians as villains or unsung heroes, according to the temper of the times. Statesmen, educators, and popular media have all contributed to and continue to reinforce stereotypic views of vastly different peoples over more than a century.

Chapter 2 begins with some historical background and a demographic description of Asian Americans today, by describing where each ethnic group came from, when they began arriving in numbers, what made them decide to come to America, and how they were received when they landed on these shores. The primary sources of demographic information are the U.S. Bureau of the Census and population research studies based on census data. The chapter provides an overall picture of the diversity and complexity of peoples that are grouped under the generic classification of Asian Americans. The educational status of each of the major population subgroups is described. It is only in the light of historic, demographic, ethnic, and cultural diversity that we can begin to understand the differences among Asian groups in terms of interests and educational attainments. The special problems encountered by recent immigrants, who have limited proficiency in English, are discussed. Because data are seldom available by separate ethnic groups, this review uses available composite data, which can be about Asian Americans, Asian and Pacific Americans, or subgroups of Asians.

Chapter 3 reviews information about the developed academic abilities of Asian Americans, with the main focus on college, graduate, and professional school admissions tests scores that are used by institutions of higher education as one source of information to make admissions decisions. Most of the discussion on undergraduate admissions is based on data from two widely used college admissions testing programs: the American College Testing Program (ACT) and the College Board's Admissions Testing Program (ATP). In addition, there are data from the Graduate Record Examinations (GRE), the Graduate Management Admissions Test (GMAT), the Medical College Admissions Test (MCAT), and the Law School Admissions Test (LSAT). The intent is not to provide an exhaustive description of the test performance of Asian Americans, but to note whether there are consistent patterns of performance that have implications for Asian American students and their families as they make college plans; and for the higher education institutions that are receiving increasing numbers of Asian American applicants every year, and trying to deal fairly with many competing interest groups.

This chapter also reviews validity studies of widely used college admissions testing programs. Because interest in the performance of Asian Americans is relatively recent, the number of validity studies that have included Asian American subjects is limited. However, by including a variety of summary data and reliability and validity information about tests that are intended to measure the same underlying psychological dimensions, we can gain an understanding of the general consistency and trustworthiness of the available information on Asian American performance. Here, too, we look for patterns of performance that can explain observed relationships in the academic and career choices of Asian Americans.

Chapter 4 reports on a variety of information about academic achievement and extracurricular activities of college-bound Asian Americans. There are recent studies of achievement as well as of academic aptitude or developed abilities, but large-scale nationally representative studies are mainly lacking. The data available are used to draw inferences about Asian Americans, even though the information may be based on restricted samples of self-identified Asians or of specific ethnic subgroups. Here, too, the objective is not to obtain comprehensive coverage of the topic but to gain a sense of the areas and levels of achievement and interests among Asian Americans, and to relate these trends to observed patterns of developed abilities.

Chapter 5 discusses the historic and current situation of Asian Americans in terms of their aspirations, and changes in access to and enrollment in higher education. The level and quality of postsecondary aspirations and the realities reflected by actual enrollment figures are described. Choice of major fields and the special case of applicants whose English is faulty because of their recent arrival are discussed. In addition, recent questions raised by Asian American students in some highly selective institutions with regard to differential access are presented and so, too, are institutional responses. The implications of limiting access of qualified Asian American students to the most selective and prestigious higher education institutions are examined.

Chapter 6 summarizes overall achievement of Asian Americans in United States postsecondary education institutions. Degree award trends since the influx of Asian immigrants in the 1970s are described by levels and fields. Implications of the discrepancy observed between below-average attainment in fields that require mastery of the English language, and above-average attainment in science and mathematics related fields are explored.

Chapter 7 summarizes current information about Asian Americans and their work. Although the emphasis is on the careers of Asian Americans with postsecondary education, the special case of the newcomers with limited English is touched upon, in order to provide a balanced view of Asian Americans in the work place.

Chapter 8 includes a summary of the findings of the study, conclusions drawn from the information collected, and synthesis of the issues that confront Asian Americans with diverse backgrounds and aspirations as they make plans for higher education and beyond. Finally, recommendations are made for additional research necessary to understand the educational experiences among different Asian American subgroups, the implications for interpreting and using information for making selection, admission, and placement decisions, and the long-range implications of a variety of policy decisions in the context of a changing population.

2

Background and Demographic Factors: Implications for Higher Education

Two laws enacted in the 1960s, The Civil Rights Act of 1964 and the Immigration Act of 1965, freed Asian Americans from more than a century of severely curtailed access to education and work. Together, the impact of these laws upon the lives of Asian Americans has been far reaching.

The Civil Rights Act of 1964 banned discrimination on the basis of anyone's race, color, national origin, religion, or sex in the use of public facilities, the right to vote, or to seek work. It also forbade discrimination by any program that received monies from the federal government. The law further directed the Office of Education, now the Department of Education, to desegregate schools. In 1968, the Civil Rights Act was extended to prohibit discrimination in the sales or rental of housing.

The Immigration Act of 1965 amended the McCarran–Walter Act of 1952, which perpetuated a restrictive national origins system of the 1924 Immigration Act with tiny quotas for Asians. The 1965 amendments required one quota for the Western Hemisphere and one for the Eastern Hemisphere. With the change in Asian immigrant quotas, increasing numbers of Chinese, Koreans, Asian Indians, Filipinos, and other Asians have left their homelands voluntarily for the educational and economic opportunities in the United States.

In addition, since 1975, more than 800,000 Southeast Asian refugees, driven involuntarily from their homes, have arrived in North America through a series of parole authorizations granted by the Attorney General under the Immigration and Nationality Act (The Indochinese Refugee Panel, 1984). As a result, between 1970 and 1985, Asian Americans have almost quadrupled in number. From 1.4 million in 1970 to 3.5 million in 1980, Asian American population in September 1985, had grown to be an estimated 5.1 million, or just over 2% of the United States population. Gardner (1985) and his colleagues of the Population Institute, East–West Center, projected that by the year 2000 Asian Americans could reach a total of almost 10 million and approach 4% of the population.

The composition of the Asian American population has also changed. Today, there are more than 20 Asian American subgroups counted by the census, from Asian Indians and Bhutanese to Sri Lankans and Vietnamese. Asian Americans are the fastest growing minority in the United States. By taking advantage of changes in educational, residential, and employment practices brought about by the Civil Rights laws, and with increasing proportions of Asian immigrants holding college degrees, Asian Americans have become the best educated Americans. As for those who have lived in the United States for several generations, or who arrived with strong credentials and a command of English, they now are more likely to have good jobs, earn above-average incomes, and live in affordable housing in communities with academically strong schools for their children. Many newcomers, however, particularly those from preliterate cultures and those with little education or lacking proficiency in English, remain among the poorest of the poor. Their children are the most likely to attend center-city schools with other disadvantaged, non-English-speaking classmates.

Table 2.1 summarizes the numbers and percentages of Asian Americans in the total United States population in 1980, specified by age group, and by enrollment in elementary and secondary schools and in higher education. There are data from two separate sources for higher education enrollment, from the 1980 census, and from the National Center for Education Statistics (NCES) of the Department of Education. Although the numbers are somewhat different from the two sources,

TABLE 2.1

Percent of Asian Americans and Asian/Pacific Americans in the U.S. Population, by Age Groups; and Enrollment in Elementary and Secondary Schools and Higher Education in 1980

	N (000s)	Percent	Asian and Pacific Americans (%)	Asian Americans (%)
U.S. Population[a]	226,545	100	1.6	1.5
Age Distribution[a]				
5–9	16,655	100	2.0	1.8
10–14	18,285	100	1.6	1.5
15–19	21,179	100	1.4	1.3
20–24	21,294	100	1.6	1.5
Enrollment in Public Elementary and Secondary Schools (Fall, 1980)[b]	39,832	100	1.9	—
Enrollment in Higher Education Institution[b]	12,088	100	2.4	—
College Enrollment[a]	12,379	100	3.1	2.9

Sources: [a]From U.S. Department of Commerce, Bureau of the Census, 1983b
[b]From Grant and Eiden, 1982

both sets of data showed that about twice the expected proportion of college-age Asian Americans, compared with all Americans of the same age group, were enrolled in some kind of higher education. The NCES data on elementary and secondary school enrollment also showed a high rate of school enrollment among Asian Americans. The data for 1980 from both sources included Pacific Americans (Hawaiians, Guamanians, and Samoans) with the count of Asians. However, because Pacific Americans constitute less than 7% of the Asian and Pacific Islanders population and enroll in college at somewhat lower rates than Asian Americans, the inclusion of Pacific Islander data would not have influenced the Asian American participation rate very much—generally in the neighborhood of one to two tenths of 1%, as shown in Table 2.1.

Most Asian Americans have been slow to adopt the rhetoric of civil rights activitists. Only recently, in emulation of the political consciousness of other minority groups, have some Asian American voices been raised about past wrongs and current injustices. These have been primarily in the areas of denial of access to quality education, closed or split labor markets, or underutilization in terms of work not commensurate with abilities, qualifications, and experience. Many of the Asian Americans' concerns have focused upon the relevance and validity of standardized tests, developed for the majority, for making admission and selection decisions about minority individuals and for formulating public policy with regard to Asians or Asian Americans in education and employment (Sue, 1983).

This report summarizes a growing body of evidence about abilities, motivation, and achievements among Asian Americans. It also describes current and past climates in American society, which may have facilitated or hindered educational and career development in certain directions among various Asian American groups. But first, we need to define more specifically who Asian Americans are and what kinds of data are available about them.

WHO ARE ASIAN AMERICANS?

The answer depends on who is asking the question and to whom it is addressed. In the 1980s, an Asian American can be a fourth or fifth generation Japanese American whose native tongue is English, or a Southeast Asian refugee who arrived no more than a couple of years ago, who still has trouble communicating in English, and whose native language may not have had a written form.

With the exception of a handful of students from gentry or merchant backgrounds, Asians did not originally emigrate for an education. Most left their homelands in order to escape war, poverty, famine, unemployment, overcrowding, political, religious or caste/class persecution, and other human misfortune. They shipped for America because it was a new land with many jobs for willing hands.

Sojourners from coastal regions of China came first, until their flow was cut off by the Chinese Exclusion Act of 1882. Japanese laborers were next. Rural emigrants came initially to Hawaii as plantation workers. More urban Japanese immigrated to the United States mainland during the decades around the turn of the century. The flow from Japan was then voluntarily curtailed by the Japanese government after the Gentleman's Agreement of 1908 between Japan and the United States. The agreement was negotiated by President Theodore Roosevelt to forestall unfriendly relations with a growing Pacific power that would have been inevitable, with the imminent passage of exclusionary legislation, directed specifically against the Japanese, that was being demanded by Californians. Laborers from other Asian countries then came to take on work done earlier by the Chinese and Japanese. Each group, in their turn, became unwelcome guest workers. The 1924 National Origins Act barred immigrants from Asia altogether, with the exception of Filipinos. Until the Philippine Independence Act of 1934, Filipinos could enter the country freely as nationals. Thereafter, Filipino immigration was limited to 50 each year (Daniels, 1976).

During periods of racial tension and violence, many Asian sojourners returned to their homelands. Some chose to stay on. Shut out of the primary labor market, some worked as domestics or farm hands, others started small service businesses. Most depended on family or ethnic associations for mutual support in a racially hostile environment. These businesses provided jobs for others within their ethnic enclaves (Bonacich, 1972).

Most Asian Americans were denied fundamental civil rights by federal or state laws and local statutes. They could not join unions, obtain occupational or professional licenses, testify in court, own land, form families by marrying local women or importing wives from home, or live outside ethnic ghettos. Their businesses were subject to special taxes and license fees. Chinese, Japanese, Filipinos, and other Asians were ineligible to become United States citizens through naturalization (Daniels, 1976; Nee & Nee, 1972).

Native-born Asian American children were denied entrance to public schools, or relegated to segregated, inferior schooling in many states. Many of these discriminatory laws remained on the books until the 1950s. Yet, Asian Americans persevered without losing their faith in education. They worked through legal and administrative channels to enroll their children in public schools, founded private schools if public schools were not available, and sacrificed their own immediate comforts to invest in education for the next generation (Low, 1982).

The McCarran Act of 1952 ended all racial bars to naturalization and gave token immigrant quotas of about 100 each year to most Asian nations. The Immigration Act of 1965 ended all racial and ethnic quotas. Asians again began to emigrate in numbers with the United States as their destination.

Changing Structure of Asian American Population

In 1960, the census counted under 900,000 Asian Americans, only about one-half of 1% of the total United States population. By 1970, Asian Americans had increased to almost a million and a half, about seven-tenths of 1% of the total population.

In 1985, there were more than 5 million Asian Americans, 2.1% of the United States population. The growth came about not through natural increase, but as a result of the fundamental change in immigration policy. If present trends continue, Asian Americans could reach almost 10 million, or about 4% of the total United States population by the turn of the century (Gardner, Robey, & Smith, 1985).

Immigrants from many Asian countries arrived in numbers from 1968 onwards, when liberalized Eastern Hemisphere quotas set by the Immigration Act of 1965 took effect. These new immigrants were no longer the unskilled contract laborers of the 19th and early 20th centuries. Sixty-four percent of Asian immigrants have had some college education. Many arrive with a working knowledge of English. Most were sponsored by Asian American relatives because immigration policy had changed in favor of family reunification. Others were professionals, skilled workers, and technicians given preferential status because their expertise was needed in the labor market. They left their homelands for a higher standard of living, to pursue advanced degrees, to seek better jobs; but above all, to give their children better opportunities by investing in quality higher education. Between 1980 and 1985, nearly half of the 2.8 million legal immigrants to this country came from Asia.

Since 1975, waves of Southeast Asian refugees have also landed through a series of parole authorizations granted by the Attorney General under the Immigration and Nationality Act. The early refugees were socioeconomically and educationally advantaged. The most recent "boatpeople" tended to come from much less privileged backgrounds.

The national origins, ethnic identities, and socioeconomic characteristics of the newer Asian immigrants and refugees have not only influenced the numbers and proportions of Asian Americans in the total United States population, they have profoundly altered the structure of the Asian American population itself, in terms of demographic characteristics. Today, Asian Americans are much more heterogeneous, better educated, and younger. Many arrive with marketable skills. On the whole, the newcomers are perhaps less patient, docile, and frightened than the landless peasants of the first generation Asian immigrants in the 19th century.

As late as the 1960s, Korean Americans and the handful of Indochinese were classified by the census as "Other." Until 1980, Asian Indians were counted as Caucasians by the census. The number of Asians counted by each census depended on the definition of Asians for that census. Other federal agencies defined the United States (with or without Hawaii) or grouped Asians differently. As a result, data on Asians varied from one source to another. Since 1975, the numbers of Asian immigrants have increased substantially as shown in Table 2.2 and Fig. 2.1. The larger groups, in descending rank order, are Filipino, Chinese, Japanese, Asian Indian, Korean, Vietnamese, Laotian, and Thai. Filipinos overtook the Chinese as the largest ethnic group in 1986. Overall, Asian Americans concentrate in metropolitan areas in the West and Mid-Atlantic states, although the 1980 census reported Asian Americans as being less regionally concentrated than they were a decade earlier (U.S. Department of Commerce, 1983f). The rapid rise in numbers, and increasing ethnic

TABLE 2.2
1960, 1970, 1980, and September, 1985 Estimates of Asian American Subpopulations

Ethnic Group:	Chinese	Filipino	Japanese	Asian Indian	Korean	Vietnamese	Total
Year							
1985	1,079,400	1,051,600	766,300	525,600	542,400	634,200	5,174,900
1980	806,027	774,640	700,747	361,544[a]	354,529	261,714[b]	3,466,421
1970	435,062	343,060	591,290	——	70,598[c]	——	1,429,562
1960	237,292	175,494	464,332	——	——	——	877,934

Note: From U.S. Department of Commerce, Bureau of the Census, 1983a; Gardner et al., 1985
[a]Asian Indians were counted as an Asian American ethnic group for the first time for 1980 census.
[b]Vietnamese were counted as a distinct ethnic group for the first time in the 1980 census.
[c]Koreans were counted as a distinct ethnic group for the first time in the 1970 census.

diversity of Asian Americans will have direct impact on the numbers and hetero-geneity of ethnic Asians who will be entering college and the job market.

Not only do boundaries of national origin and ethnicity divide Asian Americans, but generations of American residence, degree of acculturation to American society and concomitant deculturation from their Asian past, regional and religious loyalties, homeland political affiliations, differences in caste and social class, and language and dialect differences pose multiple barriers to a sense of shared interests as members of a pan-Asian American community. The designation, Asian American, came into use only recently among government agencies for grouping and sorting Americans by race or ethnicity, and was taken up for reporting purposes by a variety of agencies and institutions. Even more recently, various groups of Americans of Asian descent have begun to form coalitions and to use the term *Asian American* as a means of achieving common educational, political, and economic goals.

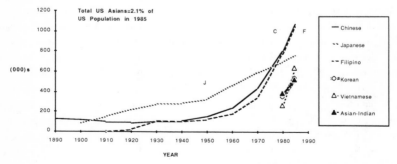

FIG. 2.1. A century of Asian American population growth (from Gardner, Robey, & Smith, 1985; U.S. Department of Commerce, Bureau of the Census, 1983a).

EARLY EXPERIENCES WITH AMERICAN EDUCATION

The demographic changes have been particularly dramatic in the past 2 decades, but each wave of immigrants from Asia has been received by the majority of Americans with mixed feelings.

Over the past century, American opinion of the abilities and characters of Asians, Asian immigrants and their American-born children has waxed and waned (Isaacs, 1958). In California, for example, Chinese Americans were reported as "one of the most worthy classes of our newly adopted citizens" by Governor Bigler of California in 1852 (Low, 1982, p. 1). Only 10 years later, Governor Leland Stanford described the same group as "a degraded and distinct people . . . who must exercise a deleterious influence upon the superior race" (Low, 1982, p. 18). Changes had occurred in the political economy of the State of California, that resulted in an about-face in public regard for Chinese Americans. As subsequent waves of Asian immigrants arrived—the Japanese, Filipinos, and others—each was at first welcomed by a labor-starved developing region and then reviled by local residents who resented poorly paid Asian competition in the labor market.

Education for Asian Americans in the earliest days was rarely at issue. Asian children seldom had access to public schools, even though their parents, the Asian laborers, involuntarily supported public schools at higher rates than other Americans through a series of repressive taxes. In 1861, San Francisco school superintendant George Tait visited the single, sporadic public school in Chinatown and recorded that he "became conscious of the patience and aptness with which the Chinaman acquired knowledge" (Low, 1982, p. 35). This observation by an educator, however, had little influence upon educational policies or the political system. Only a year later, Governor Stanford declared "it will afford me great pleasure to concur with the Legislature in any constitutional action, having for its object the repression of the immigration of the Asiatic races" (Low, 1982, p. 18). Politics notwithstanding, the sole teacher of the San Francisco Chinese school reported that "his little Celestials were very apt at learning. The younger ones knew nothing whatever of the English language on entering, but they picked it up with marvelous facility. Writing they learned with even greater ease than Yankees" (Low, 1982, p. 35). Over the next few years, the *San Francisco Daily Alta California* reported:

> We are reliably informed that the children learn with great facility and give promise of reasonable improvement if encouraged. . . .
>
> Many of the pupils . . . make surprising progress in the branches taught, considering the dissimilarity in our language and that of their native land. (Low, 1982, p. 36)

Despite their desire for education, Chinese pupils were not accepted in California's public schools. The Chinese, and later the Japanese and other minority groups, resorted to the courts to gain access to schools for their children. The courts generally responded favorably to their arguments. In 1885, after the courts ruled that there was no legal basis for excluding Chinese children from San Francisco schools, a separate school was established in Chinatown. Subsequently, "Asiatic Schools" were established in several other California communities. The California legislature removed the last of the *de jure* segregation provisions from the state Education Code in 1947 (Wollenberg, 1978).

The Japanese did not become a concern to California educators until they began to arrive in large numbers during the first decade of the 20th century. The Japanese shared the prejudice and hostility directed against the Chinese, but the Japanese were a better educated and more stable group of immigrants. Free public education was already available for 8 years in Japan, and at least 4 years was obligatory. Moreover, the Japanese also tended to arrive as families, rather than as single, male sojourners.

The Japanese were committed to seek a sound public education for their children, who were able to attend local schools until the earthquake and fire of 1906. Anti-Asian sentiments increased, and Japanese and Korean children were required to attend the Oriental public school originally built to keep Chinese children apart. Japanese parents boycotted the decision and precipitated an international crisis by rallying public opinion in Japan and obtaining support against school segregation from the Japanese government, a "most favored nation." The issue was settled temporarily in 1907 by President Theodore Roosevelt, who made a commitment to negotiate a "gentleman's agreement" with Japan to end immigration of Japanese laborers, and to issue an executive order to prohibit migration of Japanese laborers from Hawaii, in return for the San Francisco delegation's promise to rescind the segregation policy.

Anti-Japanese sentiment fluctuated between the two World Wars. In 1921, the California legislature amended the Education Code to include Japanese as a group eligible for segregation. However, the actual number of Japanese American pupils affected was small. By 1929, even V. S. McClatchy, a leading spokesman on behalf of Japanese exclusion, was convinced that young Japanese Americans were "fine specimens physically and mentally, a credit to their race and to this country." Nevertheless, he considered them to be "American citizens in rights but a group set apart" (Wollenberg, 1978, p. 74).

By 1930, the typical Japanese American over 20 had completed 12 years of schooling, a higher figure than for the general population. Social scientists began to report that Nisei (second generation, native-born, Japanese Americans) high school students earned better grades than other students. In standardized tests of intelligence, such as the Stanford–Binet, Nisei performance was found to be inferior to white children's only in tasks "based on meanings or concepts represented by the verbal symbols of the English language." In other tasks, the Nisei children were "at least equal and possibly superior" (Darsie, 1926, p. 85). The incarceration during World War II of West Coast Japanese Americans and Japanese aliens in "relocation camps" without anyone being charged with crimes was an unprecedented miscarriage of justice. College students were among the first to be resettled out of camps in the Midwest or East. They maintained good, even outstanding, records in the face of adversity (Daniels, Taylor, & Kitano, 1986; Petersen, 1971).

Since the first two groups, each wave of Asian immigrants has undergone similar experiences when asking for quality education for their children. Today, the immigrants and refugees from Southeast Asia are the focus of public concern. These diverse ethnic groups, Cambodians, Hmong, Laotians, Vietnamese, and others, also look to the school to help their children learn English and acquire knowledge and skills that will be necessary to become self-sufficient citizens. Preliminary reports of research on "boat refugee" families have indicated that, although the children still encountered difficulties in mastering English, they have adjusted well to their schools and are holding their own academically (Caplan, Whitmore, Bui, & Troutman, 1985).

Since World War II, opportunities for postsecondary education have become widely available. Asian Americans have been historically among the most committed to higher education. The right to any sort of education has been so dearly won by each of the Asian immigrant groups that most still regard a college education as a privilege, albeit one essential for their full acceptance and success in American society.

EDUCATION OF CONTEMPORARY ASIAN AMERICANS

Asian Americans are the best educated Americans. The 1980 census figures on median years of schooling for men and women 25 years old and over recorded that among the six main Asian American groups, every group except Vietnamese has had more years of schooling than other Americans. Table 2.3 shows that the median years of schooling completed by Vietnamese newcomers, 12.4 years, were very close to the white population's 12.5 years. Male high school graduation rates were higher among all six Asian ethnic groups than white men's 69.6%. The highest was among Korean males. Ninety percent of them had graduated from high school. Among adult Asian American women, the high school completion rates of Filipino, Japanese, Asian Indian, and Korean Americans were higher, and of Chinese and Vietnamese, lower than white women's 68.1%.

Among white men and women, rates for completing 4 or more years of college were 21.3 and 13.3% respectively. Asian American males, with the exception of Vietnamese, had higher college completion rates. More than 68% of Asian Indian men held at least a college degree, 3 times the proportion of white males with college degrees. Chinese and Korean males, with more than 52% having completed 4 years or more of higher education, doubled the white male rate. Japanese and Filipino American male college completion rates were about 1.5 times higher than

TABLE 2.3

Educational Levels of Six Asian American Ethnic Groups and of White Men and Women 25 Years Old and Over in 1980[a]

	White		Chinese		Filipino		Japanese		Asian Indian		Korean		Vietnamese	
	M	F	M	F	M	F	M	F	M	F	M	F	M	F
Percent High School Graduates	69.6	68.1	75.2	67.4	73.1	75.1	84.2	79.5	88.8	71.5	90.0	70.6	71.3	53.6
Percent Completed 4 or More Years of College	21.3	13.3	52.8	29.5	32.2	41.2	35.2	19.7	68.5	35.5	52.4	22.0	18.2	7.9
Median Years of School Completed by Persons 25 Years Old or Over	12.5		13.4		14.1		12.9		16.1		13.0		12.4	

[a]From U.S. Department of Commerce, Bureau of the Census, 1983b

that of white males. Substantial numbers of Asians received their degrees from Asian universities.

The most highly educated Asian women were Filipino Americans. Forty-one percent, triple the proportion of white women, had completed 4 or more years of college. Filipinos are the only Asian group in which women were better educated than men. Asian Indian, Chinese, Korean, and Japanese women also reported substantially higher college completion rates than white women. Among Vietnamese women, 7.9% had at least 4 years of college. The educational level among Vietnamese has probably become lower since 1980, due to the arrival of later waves of refugees and boat people. Other Southeast Asian refugees also would be likely to have lower educational levels.

The disparities in educational levels among Asian Americans are the result of historic, structural, and cultural differences among groups. Each wave of Asian immigrants has landed at a different period in American history. They arrived with different educational backgrounds that reflected the forces that drove them from their native lands and drew them to America.

Chinese laborers began to work on the West Coast after the 1849 gold rush. They were for the most part unschooled sojourners, barred from permanent settlement in the United States by the Chinese Exclusion Law of 1882. Fathers, sons, even grandsons were born in the same villages on the south coast of China and spent most of their working lives in America. The successful men with savings returned to China to start families, and eventually retired to their villages (Nee & Nee, 1972). Second generation, American-born Chinese did not become of college age until the 1920s and 1930s. Higher education was regarded as a way out of the hard life of laborers, service workers, and small shopkeepers. The usual progression of immigrants through skilled blue-collar jobs was barred by strong anti-Asian policies of labor unions.

Japanese immigrants, who began arriving in Hawaii and the West Coast in the late 1880s, typically came with 4 to 8 years of schooling as a result of the Meiji reform in Japan. They came as families, or started families soon after settling in this country. Second generation, native-born, Japanese Americans (Nisei) also began enrolling in American colleges at about the same time as Chinese Americans (Chan, 1981).

Filipinos began work in Hawaiian sugar plantations at the turn of the century. Between 1898 and 1934, they moved freely between the Philippines, Hawaii, and Mainland United States as United States nationals. All immigration slowed during the Depression and World War II. Since 1960, the number of Filipino immigrants has exceeded that of all other countries except Mexico (Gardner et al., 1985). The more recent Filipino immigrants have more marketable skills and better education than the early plantation workers, whose children and grandchildren are now also enrolling in colleges, but at slower rates than those of other Asian Americans.

After the Immigration Act of 1965 took effect in 1968, restrictive "national origins" quotas were relaxed. Many Asian immigrants were admitted as skilled professionals and technical personnel, the third and sixth preferential categories for admitting immigrants. Filipinos, Chinese from Taiwan, Hong Kong, and the People's Republic of China, Koreans, Asian Indians, and other Asians arrived with high school, college, or professional degrees. The Filipinos and Asian Indians, for the most part, also had the advantage of being proficient in English. Higher education for these new immigrants' children is considered a means for maintaining or improving their families' socioeconomic standing, or for regaining family status that had declined after immigration from multiple causes: lack of proficiency in English, barriers to transfer of professional credentials, underemployment or unemployment, and a host of cultural and economic difficulties that have confronted all immigrant groups.

The first wave of Vietnamese refugees arrived in 1975. These early Indochinese refugees were better educated than the later waves of boat people from Vietnam and refugees from Laos and Cambodia. By 1985, more than 700,000 Indochinese refugees had settled in this country.

Although education and job skills varied among and within each group of Asians who came to America, all came with the hope of better lives for themselves and their children. More than other Americans, Asian Americans are convinced that investment in education will bring them optimal returns.

Number of years of schooling alone fails to convey information about the quality of education. There are variations in the quality of education among and within Asian countries as there is in the United States. It is possible to draw some inferences about the quality of prior schooling of Asian immigrant students by examining their developed abilities and academic performance after enrolling in American high schools and colleges. Chapter 3 analyzes the developed academic abilities of Asian Americans.

3

Asian American Abilities

The American public is aware of a mounting challenge to United States dominance in science and technology from Pacific Rim nations, even though most of them are insignificant in comparison to the United States with respect to natural resources, military strength, or population size. Popular media have speculated about the causes of growing competition from Japan, Korea, Hong Kong, and Singapore (Chira, 1986). Could the well-educated and highly motivated, although often socially and politically docile, labor forces, along with the lower wage scales, be the key to these Asian nations' increasing prosperity? Business literature abounds with reports of the culture of Asian work places. There are many studies describing Asian management–labor relations and the salubrious influence of rigid, systematic quality control. What are the human factors that might have contributed to higher productivity? Do these factors apply to Asian Americans as a group as well as to Asians?

A polite debate is also being waged in the social science literature about abilities and personality characteristics among diverse Asian groups. At issue are questions such as "Are Japanese more intelligent, as measured by standardized instruments developed in the West?" (Lynn, 1977) and "Could the Confucian ethic be the driving energy behind the Asian thirst for education and work ethic?" (Cordes, 1984) or "Are Asian children simply better prepared for school than children in industrialized Western societies?" (Stevenson, Lee, & Stigler, 1986; Stevenson et al., 1985).

United States policymakers have recently joined industry's alarm and have been studying the threat of lagging abilities and educational achievement among American youth (National Commission on Excellence in Education, 1983; National Science

Board Commission on Precollege Education in Mathematics, Science and Technology, 1983). How have these debates impinged upon the lives of Asian Americans? Do Asian American youth show the same kinds of abilities as their Asian contemporaries? Or do the lives of all young Americans have so much in common that Asian Americans are becoming more American than Asian in their abilities, values, and behavior? What are the characteristics, perceived by others, that cause other Americans to call Asian Americans a "model minority"? Are these the very characteristics that have led to their exclusion in the past from the mainstream of American society?

To be the focus of public approbation, after more than 100 years of less than benign neglect, has been a source of some discomfort to various segments of the Asian American population. One group after another, Chinese, Japanese, Filipino, and other Asian Americans have disclaimed their new label, *the model minority*. They have learned valuable lessons from observing the struggles of other American minority groups to achieve equity in education and work. Today, increasing numbers of Asian American activists question the validity of standardized test scores reported for Asian Americans, declare tests to be tools for barring them from access to higher education, particularly, to the most selective colleges and professional schools (Asian American Law Students' Association, 1978). Even traditional, conservative Asian Americans wonder aloud about the motives that lie behind sudden praise after a long century of calumny or neglect (Gee, 1976).

Asian Americans are becoming concerned about proliferating reports of their superior cognitive abilities (Vernon, 1982), which could cause divisiveness among minority groups and work against the interests of Americans of Asian descent. The fact is, there has been increasing attention to the study of abilities and achievement among Asian Americans in general, as well as special problems or achievements among particular ethnic and linguistic subgroups. Some of these empirical data could shed light on potentially damaging debates.

Early studies of cognitive behavior among Asian Americans usually concentrated on one group, such as Chinese, Japanese, or Filipino Americans in some specific community, state, or region. Since the 1960s, studies have reported data about "Orientals" or "Asians" without detailed descriptions of the ethnic composition of the study population. This chapter summarizes information now available about Asian Americans' developed abilities in general, as well as studies about the performance of specific subgroups.

It is important to recognize that inferences about the behavior of one Asian ethnic group cannot be automatically generalized to another group, unless there are very good reasons to believe that the two groups have strong cultural, linguistic, historical, and educational ties and share common experiences that warrant such comparisons. Nor can data about Asian Americans at one period of United States history be generally applied to another time, because the composition of Asian American groups has shifted structurally over time.

ASIAN AMERICAN ABILITIES: PRECOLLEGE AND COLLEGE ADMISSIONS TEST SCORES

The Available Data and Their Quality

Reports about cognitive behavior among Asian Americans fall into several categories:

1. Historical anecdotal records of Asian immigrants and sojourners.
2. Small-scale field studies of specific Asian American subgroups.
3. Well-designed, statistically and/or physically controlled studies of Asian American subgroups.
4. National data bases of excellent quality, in terms of reliability and validity, of self-selected and self-identified Asian Americans.
5. National surveys of Americans, with a category labeled Orientals or Asian Americans, a category which may or may not constitute a biased sample, depending on sampling design and methodology. Because Asian Americans are not much more than 2% of the population and have historically been concentrated in a few states, the numbers sampled have been necessarily limited even in the most thorough national surveys. Subgroup information is virtually never available.

An example from each of these categories can serve to illustrate the range of relevance, quality, and interpretability of available information. Anecdotal historical information is available about each of the Asian ethnic groups who arrived on American soil in the 19th century. There are anthologies of such writings collected for university courses in Asian American studies, such as *Counterpoint* (Gee, 1976), monographs such as *The Unimpressible Race*, which described the early education experiences of Chinese Americans (Low, 1982), and journal articles, many of which have appeared in *Amerasia*. Although these records are limited in terms of scientific validity, and generalizability, they often provide a rich flavor of the educational climate of a particular period, and illuminate our understanding of how the same people are perceived in terms of character and educability at different times and places in the history of the United States (Isaacs, 1958).

Small-scale field studies about specific groups of Asian Americans vary in quality. Sometimes, these are the only data available about a particular group. Chao's study (1977) about Chinese immigrant children in New York's Chinatown is an example. Kim's (1980) monograph, which gives a detailed picture of life among foreign-born Korean Americans in the Midwest, is another.

Well-designed, replicated, or longitudinal studies are rare. However, reliable and valid findings from a few studies can act as the foundation for developmental models that can lead to a more solid understanding of the cognitive behavior of particular ethnic groups. Studies on young Chinese children by Lesser, Fifer, and

Clark (1965) and on the various ethnic groups on the island of Kauai by Werner, Simonian, and Smith (1968) fall under these categories.

Large-scale data bases of self-selected, self-identified Asian American populations include summary statistics from national assessment programs such as the American College Testing Program (ACT) high school and college profile reports, and similar data from the College Entrance Examination Board's Scholastic Aptitude Test (SAT) and other Admissions Testing Program (ATP) tests, the Graduate Record Examinations (GRE) and Graduate Management Aptitude Test (GMAT). Data about each candidate group can be considered reliable only for that cohort, although trends of Asian American performance over time can provide insight into changing demographics, which in turn influence group performance.

Finally, only national educational surveys have had the resources for collecting reliable data from random samples of the United States population. Sometimes, Asian Americans are left out because their numbers are small and unevenly distributed across the nation or just not considered interesting enough to warrant a separate category. Because the definition of Asian Americans has changed over time, comparison of data from one survey to another is not always meaningful. However, some information about Asian Americans, whatever their demographic composition at the time, is available from large-scale surveys such as Project TALENT (Backman, 1972), the Equal Educational Opportunity Survey (Coleman et al., 1966), National Longitudinal Study (Taylor, Stafford, & Place, 1981), and High School and Beyond (Peng, Owings, & Fetters, 1984; Rock, Ekstrom, Goertz, & Pollack, 1985; Rock, Ekstrom, Goertz, Pollack, & Hilton, 1984).

Each of these types of studies has its own uses and shortcomings. However, the aggregated weight of evidence from a variety of studies, based on different populations at different times, can enhance the credibility of conclusions about an ethnic group or Asian Americans as a whole (Light & Pillemer, 1984). This review includes studies of widely different scales and quality but draw strong inference only in those instances where the body of evidence seems to point unequivocally in some direction.

The reliability and validity of standard instruments for assessing Asian American performance are included, primarily because there have been references to test bias against Asian Americans in the Asian American studies literature. The nature of the criticism has been similar to those voiced by other American minorities. Asian Americans assume there are inherent biases built into cognitive measures developed for the mainstream culture for assessing minority performance (Gross & Su, 1975). In fact, there has not been any significant amount of test bias research done among Asian Americans. This is an area that deserves more attention.

Generally, reliabilities of test batteries and subtests that have been reported for Asian Americans appear similar to those of whites and within professionally acceptable limits. Reliability, however, is only one aspect of validity. This review, by gathering together a variety of information about the cognitive performance of diverse ethnic groups at different educational levels and with varying degrees of familiarity with English, will allow a kind of quasi multi-trait, multi-method approach to assess the construct validity of several types of assessment instruments.

In order to understand the meaning of typical performance among Asian Americans or for particular subgroups, comparisons of Asian American performance is usually made with the total population or with white performance. The majority group score ranges and means are the customary yardsticks for measuring minority performance. Comparison with other minority groups is made only when some particular educational or measurement purpose can be served.

Abilities Important for Access to College

How Asians and Asian Americans perform on general intelligence, academic aptitude, or developed abilities tests has depended on who was assessing whom, at what period of United States domestic history, as well as on the cordiality of United States relations with particular Asian countries at that specific period. For the purposes of this section, developed abilities are viewed as process structures, relatively stable constellations of psychological processes developed through learning over time (Messick, 1983). These are the abilities considered important for doing well in school and subsequently for gaining access to colleges and universities.

Early assessments of Asian immigrant children and adults tended to report lower typical performances than do findings from more recent studies. These differences observed over time might have been found not only because English language profiency and access to education have improved, but also because public perceptions have changed and Asian immigrants' educational background and social economic status have been improving. The increase in educational level of immigrants came about in part as a result of United States immigration policies but also in response to political and social forces in Asia which have encouraged the "brain drain."

Precollege Academic Abilities

The proliferation of group administered, standardized academic aptitude tests was a post-World War II phenomenon, so relatively little information about the developed abilities of Asian Americans can be found between the Chinese Exclusion Act of 1882 and the Civil Rights Act of 1964, when public attention turned once more to the performance of minority groups.

A number of national surveys and innumerable state and local studies have been conducted to provide information for government and institutions to make policies about access to and progress of minority students in higher education institutions. The abilities, plans, aspirations, motivations, and interests of precollege youth have been the subject of the most important national surveys. The purpose and objectives of each survey varied, but they shared an interest in equal educational opportunities for all American youth.

To understand the role Asian American abilities and achievement have played in higher education and vice versa, it is necessary to look at the pool of precollege Asian Americans in high school, in particular those who planned to go on to higher education. There have been several national surveys that included Orientals or Oriental Americans: Project TALENT in 1960, The Equality of Educational Opportunity Survey of 1965, The National Longitudinal Study in 1972, and High School and Beyond in 1980.

Asian Americans have not been included as a separate category in every major survey. The National Assessment of Educational Progress, for example, has not routinely collected, analyzed, or reported Asian American data. Even when Asian Americans have been included in the sampling frame, their geographic clustering by subgroups in a few states and metropolitan areas may have yielded biased Asian American samples in some national surveys. Nevertheless, enough data have accumulated since the 1960s to allow some reasonably reliable descriptive statements to be made about Asian Americans' academic abilities in comparison with the performance of their peers.

Typically, Asian American high school juniors and seniors have performed about as well as or better than white classmates in tests of mathematical reasoning. They have not done as well as whites, but did about as well as all students at their grade level, in a variety of tests of verbal abilities. Data on the performance of disadvantaged Asian Americans were not consistent. Some groups did no better than other disadvantaged minorities, particularly in verbal tasks. Other groups, according to more recent reports, have shown lower average levels, but the same patterns of low verbal and high mathematical performance as more advantaged Asian Americans.

With the influx of new immigrants since the late 1960s, there has been an increase in the number of Asian American youth whose first language was not English. This demographic change has been reflected by falling verbal abilities scores beginning in the mid-1960s, which seemed to have leveled off by the late 1970s. At the same time, average Asian American mathematical scores have remained above mean white scores. Table 3.1 summarizes data from a number of surveys and national data bases. A discussion of each of these studies of precollege youth follows in chronological order, except when interpretation of trends over time can be facilitated by grouping related data bases.

Project TALENT. In Spring of 1960, Project TALENT surveyed 4.5% of the United States high school students, about 100,000 in each grade from 9 through 12. The data for Grade 12 Asian Americans shown in Table 3.2 were obtained from among the 2,925 original subjects who responded to a 5-year postgraduation follow-up survey, when information was collected on ethnic background (Backman, 1972). The 150 Orientals who participated in the follow-up were about 5% of the respondents, a much higher proportion than that of Asian Americans in the population in 1960, and therefore may not have been typical of the original Project TALENT

TABLE 3.1

Asian American High School Students' Mean Developed Abilities Scores in Comparison with Total or White Performances 1960–1984

Year	Source	Level	Subjects	N	Comparison Group	Score Difference[a]		
						Verbal	Mathematical	Nonverbal
1960	Project TALENT[b]	Grade 12	Orientals	150	Total	−0.10	+0.91	
					Non-Jewish white	−0.29	+0.70	
1965	Equality of Educational Opportunity Survey[c]	Grade 12	Oriental Americans	999	Total	−0.04	—	+0.16
					Whites	−0.28	—	−0.04
1970	ACT[d]	Enrolled college freshmen[e]	Disadvantaged Oriental Americans	91	Disadvantaged whites	(English) −0.77	−0.36	
1972	College Board SAT[f]	College-bound seniors	Asian/Pacific Americans	10,098	Total college-bound seniors	−0.04	+0.36	
					Whites	−0.29 (Vocabulary)	+0.11	
1972	National Longitudinal Study[g]	High school seniors	Asian-Americans	182	Total	+0.04	+0.41	
					Whites	−0.09 (Vocabulary)	+0.29	
1980	High School and Beyond[g]	High School seniors	Asian-Americans	365	Total	+0.05	+0.50	
					Whites	−0.10 (English)	+0.37	
1983	ACT[b]	High School	Asian-Americans	1,140	Whites	−0.54	+0.14	
1984	College Board SAT[i]	College-bound seniors	Asian/Pacific Americans	37,294	Total college-bound seniors	−0.25	+0.40	
					Whites	−0.46	+0.28	

[a] In standard deviation units
[b] Backman (1972)
[c] Coleman et al. (1966)
[d] American College Testing Program (1972)
[e] Tested as high school juniors and seniors
[f] Hsia (1983)
[g] Rock et al. (1984)
[h] American College Testing Program (1983b)
[i] Arbeiter (1984)

TABLE 3.2
1960 Project TALENT Grade 12 Oriental and White Students' Mean Factor Scores by Sex and
Socioeconomic Status (SES)

Sex/SES/Ethnic Group	N	Verbal Knowledge		Mathematics	
		Mean	SD	Mean	SD
Males: Upper middle SES					
Oriental	31	53.2	2.5	72.5	4.3
White[a]	280	56.2	0.9	65.0	2.0
Lower middle SES					
Oriental	37	50.2	1.5	62.7	6.6
White	227	51.7	2.0	61.5	0.5
Females: Upper middle SES					
Oriental	30	47.2	3.2	52.2	4.9
White	282	52.2	0.5	42.5	0.5
Lower middle SES					
Oriental	52	45.5	1.0	49.0	1.4
White	262	47.5	1.0	39.2	1.7

Note: From Backman, 1972
[a]Non-Jewish white

representative sample. The study was conducted before the increase of immigrants toward the end of the 1960s.

Comparisons were available among four ethnic groups, Jewish and non-Jewish whites, Negroes and Orientals; and two socioeconomic status (SES) groups, upper and lower middle class. Two of the six major Project TALENT mental ability factors reported were verbal knowledge and mathematics. Factor scores were reported on a scale with mean of 50 and standard deviations of 10 for high school students from Grades 9 through 12 combined. Backman (1972) reported that analysis of variance showed that sex accounted for 69% of the total variance, a much larger proportion than accounted for by ethnicity (13%) or SES (7%). It should be noted that SES was restricted to middle class. Orientals in Grade 12 attained a mean verbal knowledge factor score of 49, and mean mathematics score of 59.1. There were differences within the Oriental and white groups by sex and SES, as shown in Table 3.2. However, within each group, mean Oriental mathematics scores were higher and verbal knowledge, lower, than white mean scores.

Equality of Educational Opportunity Survey. This landmark survey (EEOS) of students in public schools was mandated by Title IV of the Civil Rights Act of 1964. The survey was carried out by the National Center for Educational Statistics (NCES) of the U.S. Office of Education. The sample consisted of students in selected grades in 5% of the public schools, stratified according to the proportion of nonwhite students in each school so as to yield more than a 40% minority among the 650,000 students studied in the fall of 1965. A report of the findings, *Equality of Educational Opportunity* (EEO) widely known as the Coleman Report, was submitted to the President and Congress in the summer of 1966.

The student test scores were scaled with a mean of 50 and standard deviation of 10. Scores were reported by ethnic groups as well as by region. Among the students tested were about 1,000 Grade 12 Oriental students. Their mean verbal ability score was reported to be 49.6, and nonverbal ability score, 51.6. These average scores were below those of white classmates, particularly those in the Northeastern region of the United States. Oriental ability scores were close to the average of all public school seniors. The EEOS was conducted just before the changes in immigration laws that allowed greater numbers of Asians to land in the United States. From this time onwards, interpretation of verbal test scores among Asian Americans became more complex because there were increasing numbers of Asian newcomers whose mother tongue was not English.

Scholastic Aptitude Test, 1972. Beginning in 1971–1972, The Admissions Testing Program (ATP) of the College Entrance Examination Board provided student candidates with an opportunity to indicate their ethnic group identity and other personal information in the Student Descriptive Questionnaire (SDQ). The SDQ became one of the major components of the ATP, which also included the Scholastic Aptitude Test (SAT), a multiple-choice test of developed verbal and mathematical reasoning abilities related to success in college, and the achievement tests that assess knowledge in specific subject areas. Students who register for the ATP are distributed unevenly across the nation, with most from New England and middle states, fewer from the South and West, and the lowest proportions from the Midwestern and Southwestern regions. Among the more than 800,000 high school seniors who took the SAT that academic year as a prerequisite for admission to many selective colleges and universities, there were more than 10,000 who identified themselves as Orientals, about 10% were not United States citizens. The average Verbal and Mathematical SAT scores of Grade 12 Oriental SAT candidates, compared with those of whites and all college-bound seniors in 1972, and 1983 are shown in Table 3.3.

The performance of Oriental seniors who took the SATs showed that, on the average, they were below white means in verbal ability, but close to the average of all college-bound seniors. In mathematical ability, Orientals were slightly above the average of whites, and about a third of a standard deviation above all seniors. These data were not estimates for the larger population from performance by a representative sample, but constituted the total population of college-bound seniors who took the SAT during that academic year. The similarity of SAT scores to score estimates from smaller randomly selected samples of Grade 12 Orientals in the Project TALENT and EEO surveys lends support to the trustworthiness of the data.

TABLE 3.3
Mean Scholastic Aptitude Test (SAT) Scores of College-Bound High School Seniors 1971–1972,
1983–1984[a]

	Academic Year 1971–1972		
	Orientals	Whites	All seniors
SAT-Verbal	442	474	446
SAT-Quantitative	517	505	477
	Academic Year 1983–1984		
	Asian/Pacific Americans	Whites	All seniors
SAT-Verbal	398	445	426
S.D.	130	103	110
SAT-Quantitative	519	487	471
S.D.	127	114	113

[a]From Arbeiter, 1984; Hsia, 1983

The National Longitudinal Study, 1972. **During the same academic year as the 1972 ATP data from select, college-bound high school seniors just reported, NCES began the National Longitudinal Study of the High School Senior Class of 1972 (NLS). In the Spring of 1972, 18 randomly selected seniors in a sample of 1,200 randomly selected high schools were given a battery of tests and detailed questionnaires to collect data for the base year study. Follow-up studies of these 1972 seniors were to be conducted for an unspecified length of time as they continued their education or pursued other post-high school plans.**

Among the 1972 sample of 16,683, who represented more than 3 million seniors, 193 identified themselves as Orientals, who represented a weighted total of 27,740 Asian Americans or just under 1% among the nation's 1972 seniors. The data from NLS are particularly useful, because 68% of the cognitive test items used in 1972 were repeated to test high school seniors in 1980 for the base year survey of NCES's High School and Beyond (HS&B) Study. Rock et al. (1984) have equated mathematical, vocabulary, and reading test scores from 1972 and 1980, using item response theory (IRT) methods that permitted comparisons to be made across populations over time. The student questionnaires from NLS and HS&B also covered much of the same material and had many items repeated verbatim. It is therefore possible to compare cross-sectional test performances of specific population subgroups between 1972 and 1980, across diverse subgroups for one academic year, as well as examine background, family, school, and community characteristics that relate to test scores for each group.

The 182 Orientals with NLS cognitive test scores in 1972 represented an academically less select group than 1972 college-bound seniors who took the SAT. The NLS seniors' mean scores in IRT scaled units are shown for whites, Asian

Americans, and the total national sample in Table 3.4. Grade 12 Asian American mean IRT scores for each of three cognitive tests—vocabulary, reading, and mathematics—were higher than total senior average scores. Asian Americans' mean mathematics test score was also higher than that of their white classmates, but their vocabulary and reading scores were lower. The difference in mathematics scores between Asian Americans and the total group tested was about four-tenths of a standard deviation unit, similar to the SAT mathematical score difference reported for college-bound seniors in 1972.

From NLS and the SAT test scores obtained through completely different data collection methods, it would be reasonable to infer that in 1972, for both the college-bound and the general high school senior populations, the direction and size of test score differences between Asian American and white twelfth grade students seemed to have been consistent. Inferences made from two data sets for the same year would be further strengthened if the same relationships were to hold over time. The NCES's High School and Beyond Study, begun in 1980, permitted cross-sectional comparisons to be made between high school seniors in 1972 and 8 years later, in 1980.

High School and Beyond. In the Spring of 1980, NCES began collecting base year data from high school seniors for the High School and Beyond (HS&B) Study, a longitudinal study similar in purpose to NLS. HS&B replicated many of the NLS test and questionnaire items verbatim. The design called for 36 randomly chosen seniors to be surveyed from each of 1,200 United States high schools. Item Response Theory (IRT) was used to score and equate the 1972 and 1980 tests so that the

TABLE 3.4

IRT Vocabulary, Reading, and Mathematics Formula Scores of Asian Americans, Whites, and Total National Longitudinal Study of High School Seniors, Class of 1972[a]

	Sample N	Weighted N	Mean	S.D.
IRT Vocabulary Score:				
Total	25,696	2,860,348	6.55	4.0
White	12,174	2,383,015	7.08	3.9
Asian American	182	25,667	6.72	4.2
IRT Reading Score:				
Total	15,713	2,863,482	9.89	5.0
White	12,180	2,384,253	10.56	4.8
Asian American	182	25,667	10.14	5.2
IRT Mathematics Score:				
Total	15,705	2,862,252	12.94	7.3
White	12,179	2,334,219	13.95	6.9
Asian American	182	25,667	15.96	6.7

[a]From Rock et al., 1984

1980 seniors' mathematics, vocabulary, and reading scores were put on the 1972 score scale (Rock et al., 1984).

The 320 Asian Americans with complete data who participated in the HS&B survey represented a national Asian American senior population of 33,726, or 1.3% of the total weighted number of the HS&B study sample. Table 3.5 summarizes the mean scaled scores for vocabulary, reading, and mathematics tests among Asian American, white, and all seniors in 1980, and also shows, in the last columns, the difference in mean performance between the 1980 and 1972 cohorts for each group. The 1980 average performance in each area was lower than that of the 1972 group. Rock and his associates reported the differences were significant for Total and white seniors, but the sample size of Asian Americans was too small for statistically significant differences to be found between the mean scores of the two cohorts. The magnitude of Asian American score differences were the same as white and Total differences.

ACT High School and College Freshmen Norms, 1982–1983. The American College Testing Program (ACT) is an assessment program that provides evaluation, guidance, and placement services for youth in transition from high school to college. ACT is widely used in the Midwest, the Rocky Mountains, the Great Plains, and the South. ACT academic tests measure abilities in four subject areas: English, mathematics, social studies, and natural sciences. Periodically, the American College Testing Program publishes summary student information for high school and college institutional users. The High School Profile Report describes a 10% national sample of

TABLE 3.5

IRT Vocabulary, Reading, and Mathematics Formula Score of Asian American, White, and Total High School and Beyond Study of High School Seniors, Class of 1980

	Sample N	Weighted N	Mean	S.D.	1980–1972 Score Difference[a]
IRT Vocabulary Score:					
Total	24,936	2,666,481	5.70	3.7	−0.22
White	17,862	2,110,778	6.24	3.6	−0.23
Asian American	320	33,726	5.87	3.9	−0.21
IRT Reading Score:					
Total	24,864	2,658,958	8.84	5.1	−0.21
White	17,816	2,105,217	9.60	5.0	−0.20
Asian American	320	33,695	9.11	5.0	−0.20
IRT Mathematics Score:					
Total	24,758	2,650,446	11.90	7.2	−0.14
White	17,756	2,099,886	12.98	6.9	−0.14
Asian American	317	33,116	15.50	7.2	−0.07

Note: From Rock et al., 1984
[a]Standard Deviation Units

TABLE 3.6

ACT College Student Profiles, Fall 1982 and High School Profiles, 1982–1983 (Based on 10% Samples of ACT Assessment Program Participants)[a]

	English	Mathematics	Social Studies	Natural Sciences	Composite Scores
College Freshmen Enrolled in Fall, 1982					
Oriental Americans					
N = 352					
Means	17.1	20.5	16.5	21.0	18.9
S.D.	5.6	7.5	7.7	6.8	5.9
Whites					
N = 33,217					
Means	19.2	18.8	19.0	22.3	19.9
S.D.	5.0	7.6	7.0	5.8	5.4
Total					
N = 42,563					
Means	18.2	17.4	17.8	21.2	18.8
S.D.	5.4	8.0	7.4	6.2	5.9
High School Students Tested in 1982–1983					
Asian Americans					
N = 1,140					
Mean	16.8	19.9	16.6	21.0	18.7
S.D.	6.3	8.2	7.8	6.8	6.3
Whites					
N = 67,214					
Means	18.6	17.9	18.1	21.8	19.2
S.D.	5.1	7.9	7.0	6.1	5.6

[a]From ACT, 1983a, 1983b

high school students who took the ACT Assessment. In Spring, 1980, 22.4% of Asian American high school seniors had taken the ACT assessment that year, their junior year, or both years (National Center for Education Statistics, 1984). The College Student Profiles provide norms for the ACT Assessment by aggregating information from individual Class Profile Reports of enrolled freshmen at the more than 1,000 participating institutions. The College Student Profiles describe a smaller and more select group of youth than the high school reports, since they were actually enrolled in college, rather than being in high school and planning to enroll in college. There were 352 Asian Americans in the college freshmen sample, and 1,140 in the high school sample, each a one-tenth random sample of all ACT participants. Table 3.6 shows Asian American and white groups' scores for successive years.

Enrolled college freshmen in 1982 were slightly more able than college-bound high school students in 1982–1983. Asian American high school students and college freshmen ACT scores were consistent with SAT data in their performance, below white means in English and social studies, and above white means in mathematics.

ATP College-Bound Seniors, 1985. Among the 1 million graduating seniors in 1985 who registered for the ATP, more than 42,000 or 4.2% identified themselves as Asian/Pacific Americans. This proportion is almost 4 times higher than the 1.2% of Asian American population ATP registrants in 1972, and double the percentage in 1975. The proportion of Asian Americans who registered for the ATP has been rising steadily. In 1980, 65% of the Asian American high school seniors reported they had taken the SAT in their junior and/or senior years (National Center for Education Statistics, 1984). The 1985 Asian American college-bound seniors represented more than half of all Asian American 18-year-olds, about double the proportion of college-bound seniors among all American 18-year-olds. The Scholastic Aptitude Test (SAT) and Test of Standard Written English (TSWE) scores of Asian/ Pacific Americans and comparison groups are shown in Table 3.7. Scale scores of SAT-Mathematical (M), SAT-Verbal (V), and the ATP achievement tests range in value from 200 to 800. TSWE scores range from 20 to 60 + .

The TSWE scores were about six-tenths of a standard deviation below white means, and more than a third of a standard deviation below all seniors. The SAT-Verbal scores were also well below white and all senior means. These figures reflect, in part, the fact that Asian/Pacific Americans participate at double the national rate and represent a less select proportion of the Asian American population.

In 1985, 26.6% of Asian/Pacific American college-bound seniors reported English was not their best language, in comparison with 4% of all seniors and less than 2% of white students. There was a difference of 162 score points, more than one standard

TABLE 3.7
Mean Scholastic Aptitude Test (SAT) and Test of Standard Written English (TSWE) Scores of 1985 College Bound Seniors

		Ethnic Group[a]		
		Asian/Pacific Americans	Whites	All Seniors
N		42,637	705,147	1,020,442
SAT-Verbal	Mean	404	449	431
	S.D.	131	104	111
SAT-Mathematical	Mean	518	490	475
	S.D.	128	113	119
TSWE	Mean	38.8	44.6	42.7
	S.D.	12.0	10.0	10.8
Percent who considered English as best language		73.4%	98.3%	96%

Note: From Ramist and Arbeiter, 1986
[a]Who responded to SDQ item on ethnic background

deviation, between the median SAT-V score of Asian Americans who reported their best language to be English and those whose best language was not English. The distribution of SAT scores among 1985 Asian American college-bound seniors classified by their proficiency in English is shown in Fig. 3.1. When English was not their best language, 9 out of 10 Asian American SAT-Verbal scores fell in the two lowest score intervals (between 200 and 400). Sixty-three percent had scores between 200 and 300. The score distribution of Asian Americans whose best language was

(a)

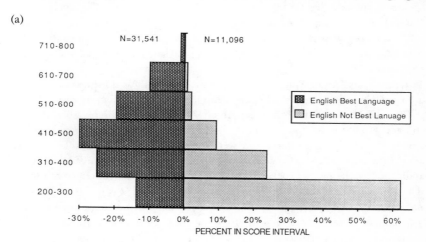

(b)

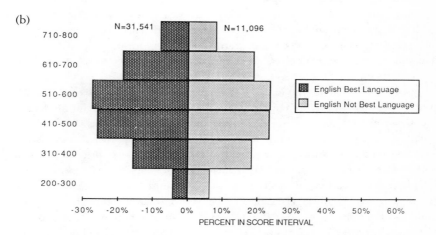

FIG. 3.1. (a) SAT verbal scores of 1985 Asian American college-bound seniors by English language proficiency and score interval (based on 6% random sample; from College Board Programs, 1986). (b) SAT mathematics scores of 1985 Asian American-bound seniors by English language proficiency ad score interval (based on 6% random sample; from College Board Programs, 1986).

English spread more normally across the score range. Asian American performance on SAT-Verbal showed a bimodal distribution when the test takers were classified according to whether English was their best language.

In contrast to the very substantial gap in verbal performance, typical scores of the two Asian American groups on SAT-Mathematical were alike. The distribution of scores was different between the groups. There were proportionately more students whose best language was not English at both the high and low ends of score intervals, and fewer in the middle. Their frequency distribution graph was flat, compared to the English proficient Asian Americans'. The median SAT-Mathematical scores were only one score point apart. The less English proficient Asian American students had median SAT-M scores of 522. The English was best language group's median SAT-M score was 521.

In recent years, Asian Americans whose best language was not English have had SAT-M median scores slightly above their English proficient Asian American brethren. The SAT-M means of both Asian American groups were higher than those of whites and of all college-bound seniors. Variability was higher in Asian American test performance. Standard deviations were larger for both SAT-Verbal (131) and Mathematical scores (128) of Asian Americans than for their white and all classmates, an indication of the heterogeneity of the college-bound Asian American seniors.

The performance of students who reported that English was not their best language suggests that the majority of them have not yet acquired the necessary proficiency and communicative skills to allow them to pursue with ease college-level studies in subjects that require full mastery of the English language. At the same time, their typical mathematical performance showed they were quite ready to pursue college-level studies in quantitative areas. They represented more than a fourth of Asian American college-bound seniors. The difference between their developed quantitative and English communicative abilities constitutes not only a serious scholastic challenge to themselves but an instructional challenge to the institutions that serve them.

College-bound seniors who identify themselves as Asian Americans are indeed a diverse group. They differ in terms of ethnic identity, language and culture, length of residence in the United States, citizenship and immigration status, family background, access to and quality of prior education, and a host of other characteristics. Their SAT-Verbal scores are more related to their parents' level of education and family income than are their SAT-Mathematical scores. Since 1980, median SAT scores have decreased for students from low-income families and increased for those from high-income families. The difference between median scores of students from families with income below $6,000 and those from families with income of $50,000 or more each year has increased by 66 score points on SAT-Verbal and by 29 points on SAT-Mathematical tests (Ramist & Arbeiter, 1986). Family income, length of residence in the United States, and English language proficiency are closely linked to each other. Newcomers are likely to be less proficient in English and therefore have a harder time finding well paying jobs. The SAT-Verbal performance of low-income students is confounded with the effect of limited English proficiency.

Asian American SAT Score Trends Over Time by Declared Major Fields

The SAT score decline, which gave impetus to demands for academic excellence through reform of educational policies, was also observed among Asian American test takers. Figure 3.2 shows the trends in average performance of SAT scores of Asian American and white ATP participants with declared college major since 1975. Grandy (1984a) reported that those ATP participants who declared intended college majors on their SDQs earned about the same or marginally higher average scores than the total ATP population. The average scores of Asian American participants who intended to major in the humanities, related social sciences, and all other fields are shown in Table 3.8. No matter which major field, average Asian American SAT-Mathematical scores were consistently higher, and SAT-Verbal scores, lower than their white peers'.

Asian Americans who intended to major in the humanities earned average SAT-V scores that were higher; and SAT-M scores, lower than Asian Americans who declared other major fields. The students who declared related social sciences majors had average SAT-V scores higher than other Asian Americans, and until 1979, SAT-M scores that were lower. However, since 1980, Asian Americans who planned to specialize in related social sciences earned higher SAT-M scores than all other Asian American candidates. These typical scores indicated not only that capable Asian Americans were planning to study social sciences, but that they are probably either native born or early immigrants who have a command of English. The Others majors category, which is numerically the largest group each year, included most of the quantitative major fields. Asian Americans who planned Other majors earned average SAT-M scores that were about average or a point or two higher and SAT-V scores a little lower than all Asian American candidates'.

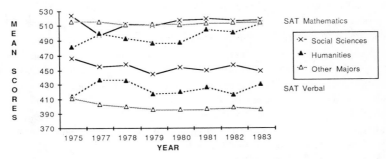

FIG. 3.2. Mean SAT Scores of Asian American college-bound seniors by declared major fields, 1975–1983 (from Grandy, 1984a, 1984b).

TABLE 3.8
SAT Averages of Asian Americans Classified by Declared Major Fields 1975–1983

Year	1975	1976	1977	1978	1979	1980	1981	1982	1983
	SAT-Verbal								
Total means	—	414	405	401	396	396	397	398	395
With declared majors	413	—	405	401	396	397	398	399	396
Humanities[a]	414	—	437	436	418	420	426	416	430
Related social sciences[b]	467	—	455	458	444	454	449	457	448
Other majors[c]	411		403	399	395	395	396	398	395
	SAT-Mathematical								
Total means	—	518	514	510	511	509	513	513	514
With declared majors	515	—	515	510	512	510	514	515	515
Humanities	482	—	500	493	487	488	505	501	513
Related social sciences	523	—	498	512	510	518	520	517	519
Other majors	516	—	516	511	512	511	514	515	515

Note: From Grandy, 1984a, 1984b

[a]Humanities: Art History, English and Literature, Ethnic Studies, Foreign Languages, History, Philosophy, and Religion.

[b]Related social sciences: Anthropology, Government/Politics, International Relations, Political Science, and Sociology.

[c]Other majors: Agriculture, Architecture and Environmental Design, Biological and Physical Sciences, Business, Engineering and Computer Science, Education, Health and Profession Mathematics, Psychology, and Others.

Wainer (1984) used methods of exploratory data analyses (EDA) to decompose the performance of various ethnic groups on the SAT from 1976 to 1982. EDA was used to show the nature of changes in group performance across time and the interaction between ethnicity and time. Wainer exposed layers of the complex data structure by successively removing the arbitrary origin (median) of the SAT-V and -M, the ethnic group effects, and the overall time trend in order to isolate separately the trend for each ethnic group. The estimated ethnic group effect for Asian American average SAT verbal score was minus 28 score points over the period of 1976–1982, while their average SAT-M score gained 44 points. When the overall time trend was also removed, the residuals for the model, interpreted as ethnic group specific time trends, showed that Asian Americans' average SAT-Verbal scores had dropped steadily from 1976 to 1979 and has risen slightly since 1980. SAT-Mathematical scores of Asian Americans, after EDA, showed a slight drop from 1976 to 1978, and then a rise to original levels.

These trends were observed over a 6-year period of decreasing selectivity among Asian American SAT test takers. The proportion of Asian American ATP candidates had doubled since 1975 to include about half of all Asian American 18-year-olds. Even the downturn observed during 1976 to 1978 could have been, at least in part, a manifestation of less self-selectivity among the test takers. Nevertheless, the observed downward trend of SAT-V was probably also related to the growing proportions of immigrant Asian American test takers for whom English was a second or third language. Between 1980 and 1985, SAT-Verbal mean scores of Asian Americans has increased by 8 points and Mathematical mean by 9 points, an increase comparable to national increases of 7 and 9 points, respectively (Ramist & Arbeiter, 1986).

Abilities of Disadvantaged Asian Americans.

Like everyone else, Asian American youth from well-established, middle-class families enjoy educational opportunities and social advantages seldom available to their economically disadvantaged peers. The EEO survey of 1965 had reported that Asian Americans were more like white classmates than other minority students in terms of their school environments and academic abilities. However, the surge in Asian immigrants and consequent increase in low-income, limited-English-proficiency students did not begin until after 1965. Recently, Berryman (1983) reported that unlike all other Americans, whites or minorities, Asian Americans persisted in the educational pipeline and chose major fields, particularly in quantitative areas, in ways that seemed to be "insensitive" to variations in parental educational levels.

Scrutiny of available data shows a more complex picture of the characteristics of disadvantaged Asian Americans, their academic abilities as measured by admissions tests, and access to higher education. The two testing programs that have been used widely for selection, admissions, and placement in college are the ACT and the ATP. Data are available for a 10% sample of disadvantaged Asian Americans who took the ACT assessment in 1970–1971 and enrolled as college freshmen (American College Testing Program, 1972), and for all Asian/Pacific ATP candidates by family income level since 1980–1981. The category, disadvantaged, was used by the ACT program for enrolled freshmen who reported family income of less than $7,500 a year. The two lowest income groups in the College Board's SDQ summary reports— under $6,000 and $6,000 to $11,999—were used to define low-income college-bound seniors for the purpose of this study. The ACT and SAT data presented quite different ability profiles for disadvantaged Asian American college-bound students, separated by a decade in time.

Disadvantaged Asian Americans, ACT 1972. In 1973, the ACT assessment program published *The Technical Report for the ACT Assessment Program.* National norms were published in 1972. The report included scores and personal information for "disadvantaged" students in five racial/ethnic categories with reported family income below $7,500 a year. One of these was Oriental Americans. The norms were based on a 10% random sample of the more than one-half million 1970–1971 ACT high school student participants who were enrolled as freshmen in 1971. They attended more than 1,000 ACT participating institutions, many of them public colleges and universities and community colleges in the Midwest, the Rocky Mountains, and the South. About 1 in 5 students was classified as disadvantaged on the basis of family income. Altogether, there were 9,850 low-income freshmen in the norms sample. There were 95 Oriental Americans, or just under 1%, among the disadvantaged freshmen.

The typical low-income Asian American college freshmen scored about three-fourths of a standard deviation below equally disadvantaged white classmates in English. The average Asian American English score was also below mean scores earned by all other low-income minority freshmen: blacks, American Indians, and Hispanic Americans. In mathematics, disadvantaged Asian Americans attained mean scores about a third of a standard deviation below whites. Table 3.9 shows mean ACT subject and composite scores for disadvantaged freshmen by ethnic groups.

These data on the test scores and related personal characteristics of disadvantaged Asian Americans were not consistent with information collected through Project TALENT, the EEO survey, the National Longitudinal Study nor with SAT data from 1972. Possible explanations for the discrepancy could be that the 95 Oriental Americans in the ACT disadvantaged student norms constituted a biased sample of Asian American freshmen in ACT colleges. Alternatively, they could have been representative of the 1970–1971 ACT low-income cohort, but were not typical of low-income Asian Americans nationally. A third possibility is that they were, in

TABLE 3.9

ACT Assessment Program Mean Scores of Disadvantaged White and Minority Freshmen Who Reported Family Income under $7,500, 1970–1971.

	Afro-Americans	American Indians	Oriental Americans	Spanish Americans	Caucasian Americans
Sample N	855	143	91	376	8,385
English					
Mean	13.1	14.6	13.0	14.2	17.9
S.D.	5.4	5.4	5.3	5.4	5.1
Mathematics					
Mean	13.9	15.7	16.7	15.1	19.0
S.D.	5.5	5.7	6.4	5.8	6.4
Social Studies					
Mean	13.1	15.8	13.7	15.5	19.0
S.D.	6.5	6.5	6.4	6.8	6.8
Natural Sciences					
Mean	15.1	17.1	16.5	16.1	20.3
S.D.	5.2	4.8	5.5	5.4	6.0
Composite					
Mean	14.0	15.9	15.1	15.3	19.2
S.D.	4.5	4.3	4.9	4.8	5.1

Note: From American College Testing, 1972, 1,169 colleges and a 10% random sample of 9,850 students

fact, typical of disadvantaged Asian Americans, whose academic abilities, as for other poor minority students, had been negatively influenced by their families' socioeconomic condition. At least the first of these possibilities can be reasonably ruled out. Documentation for the ACT technical report was so comprehensive and detailed, that the likelihood of having drawn a biased sample of Asian Americans from the disadvantaged ACT population of 1970–1971 would be low, even though the total number of Orientals was not large.

Examination of the descriptive information available from the Student Profile Section of the ACT program tended to support one of the alternate explanations, that this particular cohort of low-income Asian Americans was a self-selected and somewhat atypical group, different in important ways from other college-bound Asian American high school seniors. Economically, this group was more like disadvantaged whites in that they were better off than other minority groups. More than half of them reported family incomes in the highest "disadvantaged" range, from $5,000 to the $7,499 ceiling. Men outnumbered women 2 to 1. Relatively higher percentages among them planned to major in health and engineering fields than among other disadvantaged groups. Unlike all other disadvantaged groups, fewer than half of the Asian Americans planned to apply for financial aid. Most of the low-income Asian Americans planned to live at home or with relatives and commute to school rather than live in college housing (American College Testing Program, 1972).

The description of disadvantaged Asian American college freshmen who were ACT participants in 1970–1971 can be compared with later SDQ profiles of low-income Asian American students who participated in the ATP program of the College Board.

Low-Income Asian/Pacific American SAT Scores, 1980–1985. Since 1981, the College Board has published profiles of college-bound high school seniors by racial/ethnic groups. These annual profiles included information about family income, and the SAT performance within income ranges. The two lowest income categories included students with family income reported to be below $6,000 and between $6,000 and $11,999 a year. In 1980, the federal interagency definition of poverty threshold for a typical family of four was $7,412. The census also reported data on families near poverty, below 125% of poverty, which would have been $9,265. Since 1980, when these data became available, the proportion of self-identified Asian/Pacific Americans in the two lowest income categories have fluctuated between 21 and 22.5%, which was almost 3 times higher than the proportion of low-income white college-bound seniors, but substantially lower than among other minority groups. Overall, low-income Asian/Pacific Americans were about 1% of the total SAT population. The proportion of males to females was about the same as in the general Asian American age group.

The SAT performances of 1980 to 1985 Asian/Pacific and all college-bound seniors from the lowest income level is shown in Fig. 3.3. Figure 3.4 shows 1985 Asian

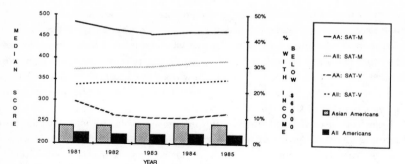

FIG. 3.3. Median SAT scores of Asian American and of all college-bound seniors whose reported family income was below $6,000 per year, 1981–1985 (from Arbeiter, 1984; College Entrance Examination Board, 1982; Ramist & Arbeiter, 1984a, 1984b, 1986).

American and white median scores by income levels. The median SAT verbal and mathematical scores rose for all groups with each higher level of income. Figure 3.4 shows that the 22% of Asian Americans, who were in the two lowest income levels, earned much lower median SAT-Verbal scores, but higher SAT-Mathematics scores than the 8% of whites who fell in the same two lowest income groups. In these two lowest categories, Asian American mean Verbal scores were lower than Verbal scores of blacks, Mexican Americans, Puerto Ricans, and American Indians. In the highest income range, over $50,000, Asian American median scores were higher than whites' of the same income group in both SAT-Verbal and Mathematical. The rise, particularly in verbal scores, is steeper with higher family income among the Asian Americans. Differences in median scores between the highest and lowest income white students was about 50 points in verbal and 70 in mathematical. It

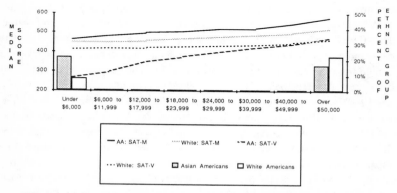

FIG. 3.4. Median SAT verbal and mathematics scores of Asian American and white college-bound seniors classified by parental income, 1985 (from Ramist & Arbeiter, 1986).

was more than 200 points in verbal and 115 points in mathematical between Asian Americans (Arbeiter, 1984; Ramist & Arbeiter, 1984a, 1984b, 1986).

Since 1980, SAT median scores, particularly the verbal scores, have decreased for Asian American students from low-income families, and increased for those from high-income families. Between 1980 and 1985, the median SAT-Verbal score of students with family income under $6,000 has decreased by 23 points, and by 2 points on SAT-Mathematical. For those from family incomes of $50,000 or more, the SAT-Verbal median score increased by 43 points, and by 27 points on the SAT-Mathematical. The poorest families were likely to be recent immigrants or refugees with limited education and English proficiency. The higher income families were likely to be acculturated and very well educated whether they were earlier Asian immigrants or native-born Asian Americans. SAT-Verbal scores were more related to income and parental education levels than SAT-Mathematical scores (Ramist & Arbeiter, 1986).

Unlike other high school seniors, low-income Asian American students typically had discrepancies of about 200 score points between their SAT Verbal and Mathematical tests. The median SAT-Mathematical scores of the most disadvantaged Asian Americans were very close to the national averages, while their median Verbal scores were more than one standard deviation below the national average. In 1985, SAT-Verbal median score was 271 for Asian American seniors with family income under $6,000, and 301 for income between $6,000 and $11,999. The SAT-Mathematical medians were 464 and 483 respectively.

The discrepancy between verbal and mathematical performance can be explained in part by the verbal performance of Asian Americans for whom English was not the best language. In 1984, 28.3% of all Asian American SAT candidates did not consider English their best language. The percentage was 26.6 in 1985. Because new immigrant families are the most likely to be among the less English proficient as well as the economically disadvantaged, the proportion of limited English proficient Asian Americans in the two lowest income groups was probably higher than in the total Asian American college-bound seniors population. If, on the other hand, immigrant Asian American seniors received at least part of their basic mathematics training in their countries of origin, it was possible they benefitted from the more rigorous elementary and secondary mathematics curricula in their countries of origin (Stevenson et al., 1986).

The pattern of performance among low-income, college-bound Asian American seniors who took the SAT in the 1980s was different from that of disadvantaged Oriental Americans reported for ACT's 1972 norms. The disadvantaged Oriental Americans who took the ACT assessment program in 1970–1971 were not only performing below whites and other minorities in English, but below average in Mathematics as well. The 1985 low-income SAT candidates, like the 1972 ACT disadvantaged Asian Americans, were a self-selected group. Many also planned to enroll in 2-year institutions. A decade separated data of different Asian American subpopulations from the two sources. Although ACT and SAT institutional users and test takers overlap in membership and are not mutually exclusive, the two testing programs served different regions. ACT serves most institutions and students in the Midwest. Most Asian Americans and more than half of the Asian/Pacific American SAT candidates live in the West (55% in 1984), and in the Middle states (20%). Only about 7% of the Asian American SAT candidates come from the Midwest. However, Midwestern Asian American SAT candidates of all income groups have consistently been the most able group among Asian Americans from all regions. The norms information from the SAT and ACT programs a decade apart cannot be compared directly, particularly because a great influx of Asian immigrants occurred during the interim. However, the consistency of the Asian/Pacific American SAT data over 5 years provides support for the earlier hypothesis that the disadvantaged Asian American freshmen of the 1972 ACT norms may have been a self-selected, and somewhat less academically able group of Midwestern, Asian American youth, whereas the Midwestern Asian Americans who have taken the SAT have been a self-selected and relatively more academically capable group. Figure 3.4 also shows that the average Verbal score of Asian Americans rose more steeply than whites' with each higher level of family income, so that in the highest income categories, Asian American and white Verbal scores were very close.

Summary

A series of reports on precollege youth was reviewed, beginning with Project TALENT in 1960. The reports were reasonably consistent in recording the pattern of Asian American high school student performance in tests of academic abilities. Asian Americans performed differently from whites and all other minority classmates. Asian American developed verbal abilities were generally lower, and mathematical abilities, higher, than those of their white peers. The variations in Asian American performance were also greater than among whites. Although levels of performance was related to family income and parental education, the pattern of relatively high mathematical and low verbal abilities held for every cohort of Asian Americans. Because twice the proportion of Asian American seniors make college plans in comparison with all other classmates, and an increasing proportion have limited English proficiency, they are a less highly selected group than general college-bound seniors. The Asian Americans' performance in college entrance tests is different from but does not compare unfavorably with the performance of white and other high school seniors. There was consistent strength shown in performing tasks requiring developed quantitative abilities. Only the socioeconomically advantaged Asian American students performed as well as white peers in verbal tasks.

These data support the notion that test scores, in themselves, could not act as barriers to Asian American access to college. More than 8 out of 10 among the 1980 Asian American high school seniors followed in the HS&B study had enrolled in postsecondary education, more than half in 4-year colleges by 1982 (Peng, 1985). Their range of test scores, and their typical performance suggest that Asian Americans would be able to pursue a broad array of opportunities in higher education. However, socioeconomically disadvantaged students with limited English proficiency would need continuing development and remediation in English communicative skills to succeed in subjects that required high-level verbal abilities.

Does the fact that most Asian American students' performance on verbal and quantitative abilities tests has been within ranges that would allow them access to higher education institutions mean that academic aptitude tests are both reliable and valid for Asian Americans? Can their test scores be considered unbiased estimates of their true abilities? There have been several studies that addressed these issues directly.

Reliability, Validity, and Fairness

An examination of reports of Asian American high school students' academic abilities over the past 25 years has revealed a remarkable consistency in the levels and patterns of their performance. This configuration of relatively high quantitative ability and lower verbal ability has held up despite structural changes that have altered the composition of the Asian American college-bound population—changes in American society, in education as well as in educational measurement.

Environmental changes included changing rates of college attendance in the general population, shifting educational policies that led to elementary and high school curriculum revisions, differences in the sampling frames for national surveys carried out at different times, differences in the instruments used to measure academic abilities, and the Civil Rights laws that have changed patterns in housing and school attendance.

Over the past quarter of a century, the Asian American population has risen in numbers through immigration rather than by natural increase. Asian American women bear fewer children than all other groups, although there are differences among the diverse Asian subgroups (U. S. Department of Commerce, Bureau of the Census, 1983b). Not only has the demographic composition of Asian Americans changed, but there are greater proportions of young people who do not consider English to be their best language. Yet, more than ever before, higher proportions of Asian Americans are making plans for college.

Does the observed consistency in test performance among Asian Americans over time mean that the standardized, norms-references, tests used to assess academic ability among college-bound high school students are reliable, valid, and fair, or unbiased estimates of Asian American performance? Reliability refers to the consistency of test scores earned by the same individuals upon retest with the same instrument, or a parallel form of the test, under varying examining conditions, rather than the consistency of performance by population groups over time described above. Validity refers to whether, and how well, a test measures what it is supposed to measure. Test fairness among academic abilities measures is related to the usefulness of a test for predicting future performance of particular groups. In the case of a testing program such as the ATP, the key issue would be whether test scores relate to the performance of the test takers after they have enrolled in college, or whether the tests introduce systematic error, or bias, in the prediction of future performance.

Reliability

Large-scale national surveys and national testing programs, which were described previously, routinely reported the reliability of their test batteries, although not always with separate estimates for each subpopulation. One carefully documented study was the construct validity study of the SAT across populations, by Rock and Werts (1979).

Split-half reliabilities were reported by student populations for SAT-Verbal (V), Mathematical (M), and the Test of Standard Written English (TSWE) factors. These validity coefficients are summarized in Table 3.10. Each of the reliability coefficients reported for the Asian American candidates was about 0.9, higher than the corresponding coefficients for whites. Asian American SAT-V factor reliability was also higher than those of all other minority candidate groups. For SAT-M, Asian American factor reliability coefficients were higher than other minorities with the exception of American Indians,' and for TSWE, higher than all other minorities but Puerto Ricans. For Asian American candidates, the SAT, which is typical of large-scale, carefully designed, college admissions testing programs, is as reliable as for other American high school students.

Validity and Bias

The national surveys and testing programs described earlier have published extensive reports on the validity of their test batteries. For Asian Americans interested in access to institutions of higher education, the relevant types of validity include content validity, predictive validity, and construct validity.

Test makers and test users tend to agree that the abilities assessed by the verbal and mathematical reasoning problems in college admissions tests such as the ACT and SAT constitute academic work samples, like the work in high school and college courses (Manning & Jackson, 1984). For Asian American students who are limited

TABLE 3.10
Reliabilities of SAT-V, -M, and TSWE Factors by Population[a]

	American Indians	Blacks	Mexican-Americans	Asian Americans	Puerto Ricans	Whites
Verbal	.9131	.8811	.8950	.9229	.9032	.8947
Mathematical	.9157	.8600	.8971	.9091	.8974	.9047
Test of standard written english	.9087	.9018	.8977	.9105	.9148	.8620

[a]From Rock and Werts, 1979

in their English proficiency, and who may have received a substantial portion of their precollege education abroad, the generally accepted assumption of content relevance may not be warranted. The difference between Asian American Verbal and Mathematical scores provides support for the possibility; so do other analyses of item and test performance.

Do tests such as ACT and SAT measure the same underlying psychological traits for Asian Americans as for other groups who seek college admissions? The construct validity of virtually all widely used college assessment and admissions tests have been extensively studied by factor analytic methods. Rock and Werts (1979), for example, used analysis of covariance structure methodology to study the structure of correlations among SAT-V, M, and TSWE factors for six ethnic groups.

Mathematics scores of Asian American SAT candidates showed lower relationships with the two verbal factors. In other words, mathematics and verbal skills were shown to be more differentiated within the Asian American candidate populations, with high mathematics ability less related to high verbal ability and vice versa, than among all other groups. This phenomenon was considered by the authors to be a true population difference. With the increased numbers of limited English proficiency, high mathematical ability Asian immigrant candidates during the 1980s, the differences between verbal and quantitative performance would be expected to, and indeed has, continued to be pronounced.

Two recent statistical reports (Bleistein & Wright, 1985; Kulick & Dorans, 1983) used a statistical method called *standardization* to study whether or not there were unexpected differences in SAT item performance between Asian Americans and white candidates and Asian Americans and white candidates for whom English was not the best language. An item is defined as exhibiting unexpected differential item performance (UDIP) when the probability of correctly answering the item is lower for examinees from one group than for examinees of equal ability from the standard group. The standardization method had been used for a series of studies on item bias, and had identified no group, females or minorities, with large numbers of unexpected differential performance items in any specific direction on the SAT forms studied when the standardization group was white SAT takers or white male SAT takers (Donlon, 1984).

The first instance of consistent UDIP was found among Asian American test takers who declared that English was not their best language. When their performance was compared with white examinees for whom English was not the best language or with Asian American and white candidates who stated that English was their best language, there was fairly extensive evidence of systematic unexpected differential item performance on SAT-V, TSWE, and SAT-M. For SAT-V and TSWE items, the investigators reasoned that unexpected differential item performance was found when the items covered verbal skills that the limited English Asian American test takers had not yet mastered. Unexpected differential item performance for SAT-M was more surprising because Asian Americans whose best language was not English have consistently performed better than all other groups of SAT candidates on this test. The investigators hypothesized that mathematical items with verbal content may be differentially difficult for this group of examinees. The items were independently sorted into three groups: "verbally loaded," "neutral," and "pure" mathematical problems. Reanalysis of the three categories of items resulted in the verbally loaded category having the most unexpected difficult items, while the pure math category had the most unexpectedly easy items for the limited-English Asian American candidates. The investigators concluded that for Asian Americans whose best language is not English, SAT-M was a multidimensional test.

Despite the fact that the statistical report was based on a limited number of Asian American subjects, these findings should serve as a caution to test score users that the high SAT-M scores of many Asian Americans, whose best language is not English, could still be an underestimate of their true developed mathematical reasoning abilities. There is no evidence that SAT scores of Asian Americans whose best language was English showed unexpected differential item performance when white candidates were the standard group. The SAT-M scores of limited-English proficient Asian American candidates should be considered possible underestimations of their true mathematical abilities. The superior developed mathematical abilities of newcomers could explain, at least in part, how the group has managed to achieve in qualitative fields in college despite very low SAT-Verbal scores.

Information from construct validity studies such as factor analysis that reported greater than expected differentiation between verbal and mathematics test performance of Asian Americans and from standardization method for UDIP that found unexpectedly difficult mathematical items with high verbal content is fundamental to test quality. Predictive validity is more important for higher education application and admissions decisions. The possibility of bias in the use of standardized tests scores to predict future academic performance of Asian American students has been raised by concerned student activists (Asian American Law Students' Association, 1978). Specifically, Asian Americans have been concerned with the possibility of using regression equations based on majority students' data that may systematically underpredict Asian American college and university performance. This type of test bias, if demonstrated, might result in the denial of access to Asian American students who would otherwise have succeeded in higher education. The possibility of underprediction is particularly salient to the academic development of recent Asian immigrants with strong quantitative skills and limited English proficiency.

Breland and Griswald (1981) reported a concurrent validity study of a number of admissions and placement measures for six subject groups. Scores of each group on the SAT, TSWE, and four subtests of the English Placement Test (EPT), including an essay, were analyzed. Correlational analyses showed there were close relationships among SAT-V, TSWE, and EPT non-essay components for all groups, including Asian Americans. However, scores from SAT-V, TSWE, and the non-essay components of EPT tended to overpredict Asian American performance in essay writing. Essays written by Asian Americans were not scored as highly as their multiple-choice test scores would have predicted. Writing well is important not only for college and postgraduate studies. A recent survey of faculty members reported that even in engineering and the physical sciences, writing effectively was important not only to academic success, but even more crucial for professional success after graduation (Bridgeman & Carlson, 1983).

The SAT is the admissions testing program most widely used by Asian American students, largely because regions of Asian American concentration and of institutional uses of the ATP program coincide. Institutional users of the SAT most often choose first-year college grade point average (GPA) as the criterion for predictive validity studies. The median value for validity coefficients for predicting freshman GPA from more than 800 institutional validity studies was .41 and .58 respectively for SAT and for high school records and SAT scores combined (Manning & Jackson, 1984).

A predictive validity study by ethnic groups of students from four University of California campuses was reported by Goldman and Hewitt (1976). Among the 50 states, the University of California system enrolls the largest numbers of Asian Americans. The authors reported validity coefficients at UCLA of .43 among 4,000 white students, and of .42 for 852 Asian Americans. The four campuses studied were highly selective institutions with similar admission standards. The observed correlations were undoubtedly restricted by the limited range of abilities of the students (Weitzman, 1982). Goldman and Hewitt (1976) reported that the regression systems for the four ethnic groups enrolled during 1973–1974 were, for all practical purposes, parallel. The academic predictors yielded regression systems that were virtually identical. White-derived regression equations were used to predict mean GPAs for other groups. Asian Americans' mean GPAs were predicted with less accuracy than blacks', but more accurately than Chicanos'. Differences between the predicted and actual GPAs among Asian American students at the four campuses were small, from −.01 to −.06 of one grade point. There was slight underprediction of actual GPAs. College grades of whites and Asian Americans were generally more accurately predicted from high school records and SAT scores than were the college GPAs of black and Chicano students.

The College Board launched an SAT validity study of Asian American freshmen who entered the UC system in the Fall of 1985 (Lee, 1985). UCLA psychologists Stanley Sue and Nolan Zane, who carried out the study, classified Asian American students by ethnic groups. Criterion was freshman year grade point averages. According to Robert Cameron, executive director of research for the College Board, the large and diverse Asian American enrollment in the UC undergraduate system facilitated analysis by subgroups. Some differences were observed among Asian ethnic groups, but validity coefficients were all well within the middle range of values reported for white students. The most notable finding was that SAT-M was a better predictor than SAT-V of first year college grades earned by Asian Americans at UC (personal communication, March 24, 1987).

The SAT validity studies just cited found relationships between predictors and criteria that were similar for all ethnic groups. However, Asian American performance on essays tended to be slightly overpredicted by objective multiple-choice test scores, whereas college grades were reported to have been very slightly underpredicted by objective test scores and high school records. The Goldman and Hewitt study (1976) used as criterion the average grades earned by groups of students at four campuses, in a variety of courses taught by different instructors, while the Breland and Griswald (1981) study's criterion consisted of blind ratings of short essays by at least two trained readers. The observed difference could have been associated with differences in reliability and validity between criteria, as well as the imperfect predictive validity of test scores and other predictors.

Instructors' grades, even averaged over a semester, a year, or more, represent less than perfect measures of college performance. The lack of reliability of grades would limit the predictive validity of test scores and other variables used in predicting academic performance. Particularly among disadvantaged Asian Americans whose verbal test scores cluster toward the low end of the scale, restriction of range of the predictors would also limit the relationship between predictors and grades.

Sawyer (1986) used racial/ethnic subgroups' membership dummy variables as additional predictors in a large-scale predictive validity study of the ACT Assessment Program. The dummy variables of subgroup membership were used as proxies for many complex background, socioeconomic, and educational characteristics that are related to performance in college. Separate subgroups' equations were also used to estimate predictive validity.

The relationships of high school grades and ACT scores to college freshmen grades of more than 300,000 students in ACT Validity Studies Service institutions were studied by separate group prediction equations and with racial/ethnic subgroupings as dummy variables. Changes in colleges' mean grades, the criterion, over time were found to be the most important source of prediction bias. For racial/ethnic subgroups, dummy variables and separate subgroup equations were more often than not less accurate than total group equations, upon cross validation.

ABILITIES FOR PURSUING GRADUATE AND PROFESSIONAL STUDIES

Most applicants to postgraduate faculties and graduate professional schools are required to submit scores earned on specific admissions tests, undergraduate records, and other personal information for consideration (Oltman & Hartnett, 1984). In recent years, changing attitudes and values, shifting demographic patterns, and labor market conditions have reduced the demand for places in graduate schools and even professional schools (Maeroff, 1985). Asian Americans, however, are staying in school beyond college. In 1980, more than half of Chinese American 22- to 24-year-olds, and 4 out of 10 Japanese, Asian Indian, and Vietnamese Americans in the same age group were in school compared to 17% in the general population (U.S. Department of Commerce, Bureau of the Census, 1983a, 1983b). Asian American GRE test takers were younger than all other groups of students by about 2 years. They had allowed less time to elapse between receiving their bachelor's degrees and applying to graduate studies (Smith, 1984).

Abilities considered important to succeed in postgraduate schooling vary by subject areas, but highly developed verbal and mathematical reasoning abilities remain important. There are recent data available on the performance of Asian Americans in a variety of graduate admissions testing programs. The levels and patterns of abilities among Asian American college graduates who plan to continue in higher education were remarkably consistent with the performance reported for precollege youth.

The Graduate Record Examinations

Since 1976, the Graduate Record Examinations Board has released summary GRE data by ethnic groups annually. Figure 3.5 shows the average GRE verbal (V) and quantitative (Q) test scores for Asian American and white test takers who were United States citizens and who declared intended graduate major fields from 1976 to 1984. A comparison of the GRE verbal and quantitative score trends and patterns in Fig. 3.5 to SAT trends in Fig. 3.2 demonstrates the similarity in Asian American verbal and quantitative performance in relation to white peers for both college and postgraduate studies. The distribution of undergraduate academic major fields varied by ethnic groups, so that intervening educational experiences on even a single campus would not be alike for all students. Asian Americans were more likely to choose physical and biological sciences or business majors and planned to continue in graduate and professional schools in quantitative areas. Their different interests and

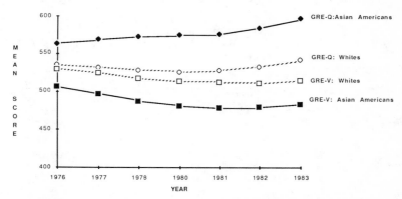

FIG. 3.5. Mean GRE verbal and quantitative scores of Asian American and white U.S. citizens who declared graduate major fields, 1976–1983. Data for 1979 not available (from Grandy, 1984a, 1984b).

college experiences were reflected by typical GRE scores with relatively larger differences between quantitative and verbal ability scores in comparison with those of their white peers than had been the case among college-bound youth.

In 1977, a restructured version of the GRE General Test was introduced. In addition to the two familiar measures of verbal and quantitative abilities, a third test for analytical ability (A) was added. The analytical test was the result of several years of developmental research (Wild, Swinton, & Wallmark, 1982). An initial report of the analytical test's validity was prepared by Wilson (1982). The report was based on first-year graduate GPAs from more than 100 graduate departments at 36 universities. Because the students had been admitted without direct consideration of their analytical scores, the range of scores tended to be less restricted. Earlier concurrent validity studies had shown that the analytical measure was substantially related to both the verbal and quantitative measures, and also significantly related to undergraduate GPAs. Wilson concluded that in verbal fields, the predictive value of GRE A was similar to V, while in quantitative fields, the analytic scores paralleled the predictive value of quantitative scores.

Average Asian American performance compared with that of whites and all test takers on the restructured GRE in 1982–1983 is shown in Table 3.11, and Asian American mean scores grouped by graduate major fields is shown in Fig. 3.6. Compared with white test-takers, Asian Americans who sought entrance to graduate schools showed a profile with higher quantitative scores and lower verbal and analytical scores in every field of study. The average quantitative and analytical scores of Asian Americans across all fields was higher than for all test takers. Average score levels of Asian Americans in different fields were similar to whites' in the same field, but the relative rankings of V, Q, and A remained the same among Asian Americans.

Asian American test takers were 1.95% of all GRE candidates. The numbers and GRE scores of Asian Americans who applied for graduate studies did not suggest

TABLE 3.11

Average GRE Verbal, Quantitative, and Analytical Scores of Asian American, White, and All U.S. Citizen Test Takers, 1982–1983[a]

		Asian American	White	Total
N		2,715	117,686	141,465
Scores				
Verbal	Mean	483	514	502
	S.D.	125	110	117
Quantiative	Mean	596	542	529
	S.D.	126	125	133
Analytical	Mean	532	542	528
	S.D.	127	119	125

[a]From Smith, 1984

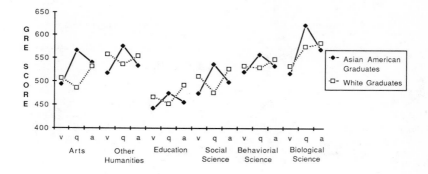

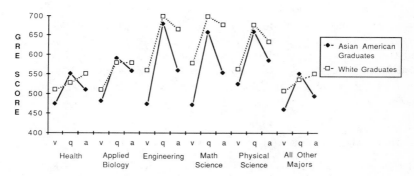

FIG. 3.6. Average GRE quantitative, analytical, and verbal scores by graduate majors of Asian American and white test takers (U.S. citizens only), 1983–1984 (from Smith, 1985).

a potential problem due to demand exceeding supply of places in graduate schools. Most Asians in United States graduate schools were and are foreign nationals (National Science Foundation, 1981a). However, the distribution of Asian American candidates by planned graduate major fields showed that relatively smaller proportions of Asian Americans had declared plans to study humanities and social sciences and double the expected proportions planned to study physical sciences and engineering, as shown in Table 3.12. Baird (1982) has found the GRE scores were used by white students and by minority students for decisions to make applications to more or less prestigious departments, for the numbers of applications they make for admissions and assistantships or financial aid, and for decisions on whether they will attend graduate school full time and enter a doctoral program.

Even though Asian American students who plan graduate studies tended to concentrate in a limited number of major fields, their sparse numbers in any individual department have not permitted predictive validity studies of GRE test scores

TABLE 3.12

Percent of Asian American GRE Test Takers who Declared Major Fields for Graduate Study
Compared with All GRE Test Takers, 1982–1983[a]

	Asian Americans	GRE Candidates
N	2,655	136,004
Humanities	8.2%	11.3%
Social Sciences	26.3%	40.9%
Behavioral Sciences	21.7%	19.7%
Physical Science/Engineering	33.7%	16.4%

[a]From Smith, 1984

by classical statistical methods. Braun and Jones (1985) investigated empirical Bayes methods to address the constraints imposed by small numbers of subjects. The authors compared experimental Bayesian and least squares models for estimating validity of GRE scores and other predictors of first-year graduate school grade point averages of whites, Asians, Asian Americans, and other minorities. On the basis of half sample cross validation, the authors did not find reasons to use separate prediction planes for the three groups. They noted a tendency for the observed first-year grade point averages of Asian and Asian American students to be somewhat higher than those of other students with the same predictor scores.

Graduate Management Admission Test

Management has been a growing profession. A number of surveys of graduate business school enrollment, conducted since the early 1970s, tracked the steady increase in minority enrollment. Asian Americans' participation in graduate management studies has grown from under 1% in 1970–1971 to 1.7% by 1976 (Willingham & Breland, 1977).

Member schools of the Graduate Management Admission Council sponsor the Graduate Management Admission Test, which is required of applicants to selective institutions. In 1980–1981, the proportion of Asian American GMAT test takers had risen to 2.2%. Asian American GMAT test takers typically scored lower than white test takers. The average GMAT scores, verbal, quantitative, and total, for Asian American, white, and all GMAT test takers in 1980–1981 are shown in Table 3.13.

The typical Asian American GMAT candidate earned a total score about a third of a standard deviation below white candidates' mean total score. Although the quantitative scores were about the same, Asian American verbal scores were about a half a standard deviation lower than whites'. When undergraduate major subjects were taken into account, economics majors contributed most of the high scores that resulted in a slightly higher average quantitative score among Asian American test takers. Undergraduate majors in science, humanities, and business who took the

TABLE 3.13
Average GMAT Verbal, Quantitative, and Total Scores of Asian American, White, and All Test Takers, 1980–1981[a]

		Asian American	White	Total
	N	3,508	127,569	156,591
GMAT Scores:				
Verbal	Mean	25.04	28.98	28.29
	S.D.	8.83	7.79	8.22
Quantitative	Mean	27.68	27.38	26.79
	S.D.	8.56	7.80	8.06
Total	Mean	458	487	478
	S.D.	105	94	99

[a]From Leary and Wrightman, 1982.

GMAT earned lower average verbal and quantitative scores (Leary & Wightman, 1982). GMAT candidates are a self-selected group. It is possible that among Asian Americans who planned to pursue professional degrees, management schools were not the first choice of the most able students, who were most likely to apply to medical schools.

A detailed study of performance by groups on GMAT verbal and quantitative item types was reported by Sinnott (1980). For five groups of applicants classified by ethnicity, Sinnott found differential performance among them according to item types. Asian and Asian American males were ranked tops in problem-solving and data sufficiency items from GMAT sections that assessed quantitative abilities. They were ranked third among five groups in Reading Compehension and Practical Business Judgment items and fourth in Language Usage items.

Medical College Admission Test

In 1980–1981, 18,797 Asian/Pacific Americans received Bachelor's degrees (Grant & Snyder, 1984). They obtained 2.01% of all bachelor's degrees conferred. That same year, 3,370, or 18% of Asian/Pacific American college graduates, took the Medical College Admission Test (MCAT), required for admission to medical schools (Association of American Medical Colleges, 1981). Asian Americans constituted 7% of MCAT candidates. Clearly, a substantial proportion of Asian American college graduates aspired to medicine as a profession.

The average MCAT assessment area scores reported for Asian/Pacific American, white, and Total MCAT test takers during 1981 are shown in Table 3.14. Relative to white and total test takers, Asian Americans had higher mean scores in subject area tests, and lower mean scores in the two skills analysis areas. In Biology, Chemistry, Physics, and Science Problems, average Asian American scores were higher than total means, and higher than white means in all except Biology. In

TABLE 3.14

Average Medical College Admission Test Assessment Area Scores of Asian/Pacific Americans, White, and Total Test Takers, 1981[a]

		Asian/ Pacific Americans	White	Total
N		2,254	38,018	48,203
Percent		7.0	78.9	100
Area Scores:				
Biology	Mean	8.22	8.52	8.13
	S.D.	2.56	2.31	2.51
Chemistry	Mean	8.66	8.23	7.94
	S.D.	2.58	2.42	2.52
Physics	Mean	8.81	8.38	8.07
	S.D.	2.68	2.47	2.60
Science Problems	Mean	8.37	8.17	7.83
	S.D.	2.58	2.39	2.52
Skills Analysis:	Mean	6.68	8.04	7.50
Reading	S.D.	2.72	2.12	2.52
Skills Analysis:				
Quantative	Mean	7.35	7.90	7.45
	S.D.	2.42	2.24	2.56

[a]From Association of American Medical Colleges, 1981

Skills Analysis, Reading, however, Asian American test takers' mean score was two-thirds of a standard deviation below whites', and one-third of a standard deviation below total means. The differences in Skills Analysis, Quantitative, were smaller.

Like the students who chose to take GRE and GMAT, MCAT test takers were a self-selected group. A higher proportion of Asian American college graduates took the MCAT, which made the Asian American MCAT population a less select group than other test takers. The course-related, subject area test scores of Asian Americans were as high as or higher than their white peers'. The dramatic difference in performance was in Reading Skills Analysis, a difference that may reflect the increasing proportion of Asian American college students whose mother tongue was not English, as well as the pattern of lower than average verbal reasoning abilities found among all but the most socioeconomically advantaged Asian Americans.

Predictive validity of MCAT scores by racial/ethnic groups is available for black and white examinees and medical school matriculants (Jones & Mitchell, 1986). The predictive validity of MCAT for Asian American examinees and matriculants is not yet available from the Association of American Medical Colleges. The increasing numbers of Asian Americans in medical schools suggest that predictive validity studies may be feasible in the near future.

Law School Admission Test

Asian American law school applicants as a group did not perform as well as white applicants in the Law School Admission Test program during the 1975–1976 application year, as shown in Table 3.15. However, the record showed that relatively greater proportions of Oriental applicants were accepted by at least one law school. The 64% of Oriental candidates admitted to law school was almost twice the proportion of Asian American MCAT candidates admitted into medical school during the same year. There are relatively fewer Asian American lawyers but more physicians than expected in the total United States population. With greater acceptance rates than those of whites, the imbalance may begin to be redressed (Hsia, 1983).

Success in law schools demands verbal as well as analytical abilities. Asian American performance in all the testing programs reviewed have shown lower verbal ability scores than those of their white peers. A meta-analysis of the predictive validity results and data from 1981–1982 LSAT Validity Study Service applicants and accepted students to 154 law schools was conducted by Linn and Hastings (1984). The mean observed validity was .38 for LSAT, .24 for UGPA, and .46 for the two predictors combined. Differences in selectivity between law schools accounted for over half of the variability in validity of the LSAT or UGPA alone or in combination. The investigators concluded that the validity of LSAT and UGPA for predicting first-year grades in law school was higher than those found in several other educational admissions situations, and was highly generalizable across law schools.

The University of California, Berkeley law school's Asian American Law Students' Association (1978) reported that for Asian students at Boalt Hall, the length of time to attain a bachelor's degree predicted law school performance better than the LSAT in 1976. Particularly for economically disadvantaged Asian Americans, access to law school may still be difficult, due to their previous educational experience as well as to low LSAT scores. This was the argument set forth by the Boalt Hall Asian American Law Students Association in favor of a focused affirmative action program for recent immigrants and low-income Asian Americans.

TABLE 3.15

Number and Percent of Candidates at or Above Select LSAT Score Levels and Percent Who Received at Least One Offer of Admission to an LSDAS-ABA Law School, 1975–1976[a]

	Oriental			White & Unidentified		
Score	N	%	% Accepted	N	%	% Accepted
LSAT ≥ 600	206	25	84	24,468	37	85
LSAT ≥ 500	520	63	78	51,307	77	77
LSAT ≥ 450	647	78	75	59,359	89	65
Total	829	100	64	66,994	100	59

[a]From Hsia, 1983

CONCLUSIONS AND DISCUSSION

The academic abilities of Asian Americans, assessed through national surveys and admissions testing programs at every level of higher education, showed a consistent pattern of high quantitative reasoning relative to verbal reasoning abilities. This pattern held without regard to the level of tests, major fields of study planned, selectivity of the test taking cohorts, the socioeconomic levels of the test takers, or their familiarity with the English language.

This pattern of relatively higher quantitative and lower verbal reasoning abilities than their white peers' has been reported again and again over the past 20 years, and verified through validity studies. The levels of Asian American performance, like those of all other test takers, varied according to the type and difficulty of the test, selectivity of the test-taking populations, past educational experience and anticipated major fields of study, socioeconomic background, and proficiency in English.

For each of the data bases reviewed, the typical level of Asian American performance was closest to that of white test takers but generally lower than white peers' in verbal and higher in quantitative scores. The changing demographic composition of the Asian American population, with increasing proportions of recent immigrants from Asia, was reflected by lower average verbal scores during the 1970s and some leveling off in recent years. At the same time, the quantitative ability of Asian Americans has remained high. For example, from 1980 to 1985, Asian American SAT candidates whose best language was not English attained median average SAT-M scores higher than those of Asian Americans whose best language was English. The SAT-M medians of English and non-English proficient Asian Americans were higher than white students' and all test takers'. Because Asian Americans take the SAT at almost double the rate of other high school seniors, they constituted a less select group of students than other college-bound seniors. The higher SAT-M performance is all the more notable and suggests that the prior mathematics education of most Asian immigrants was not of lower quality than that of Asian Americans who were born and reared in the United States. Indeed, international comparative studies have agreed that mathematics education in several Asian countries produce the best math students in the world (Crosswhite et al., 1985; Stevenson et al., 1986; McKnight et al., 1987; Travers & McKnight, 1985).

Among economically disadvantaged Asian Americans, test score data were not as consistent. In 1970–1971, an Asian American ACT norms sample of college freshmen who were classified as disadvantaged reported average ACT English and Mathematics scores below those of disadvantaged whites and other minorities. More recent SAT data summaries since 1980 have reported academic ability patterns among low-income Asian Americans to be more like other Asian American students', high in mathematical, but lower in verbal abilities. Since 1980, SAT median scores, particularly verbal scores, have decreased for students whose parents have a low income, and increased for students whose parents have a high income. SAT-Verbal scores of Asian Americans are more related to the level of their parents' education and income than are SAT-Mathematical scores. The gap between low-income Asian Americans' verbal and mathematical scores was greater than that of any other group, as much as 200 score points.

In SAT-Mathematical tests, Asian Americans in the two lowest income groups have typically done as well as or better than all college-bound seniors, including white classmates. In SAT-Verbal tests, the same low-income Asian Americans had median scores between one and one-and-one-half standard deviations below scores of white students in the same income groups. Their verbal scores were also lower than those of all other minority groups in the same income ranges. The lowest SAT scores were reported for Asian Americans who planned to enroll in a 2-year program. Although the data on low-income Asian Americans from the SAT and ACT norm reports were not in close agreement; more than a decade had separated the test takers described. Time and changing demographics could explain the difference, particularly in mathematical ability. However, self-selection in the choice of college admissions testing programs cannot be ruled out. Asian American students' choices of undergraduate and graduate admissions testing programs and types of institutions, as well as their planned major fields of study, lend support to the notion that as a group, Asian Americans have acted with considerable deliberateness in decision making with respect to choice of institutions and major fields in higher education.

Asian Americans took tests in a variety of admissions testing programs at successive levels of higher education in numbers commensurate with or higher than their proportion in the United States population. Their average levels of test scores in most testing programs were close to their white peers', although their patterns of abilities were different. Given Asian American test performance and current enrollment figures, it would be difficult to argue that admissions tests, in themselves, constituted significant barriers for most Asian Americans in their desire for higher education. Choice of majors and professional specialties may contribute to the perception of great competitiveness among Asian Americans in specific fields, such as medicine. Low-income, limited English proficiency Asian Americans, particularly immigrants from very different cultures, are increasing, and they perform verbal tasks at levels that suggest they could benefit significantly from special consideration in the interpretation and use of test scores for admissions decisions, and from support services as matriculants.

4

Academic and Extracurricular Achievements

Data for specific Asian American ethnic groups are still sparse. The increasing numbers of Asian Americans at all levels of education have permitted reports of aggregated data across groups. There is agreement from different sources that Asian American precollege youth go to school regularly, stay in the educational pipeline longer, and take their academic studies seriously.

HIGH SCHOOL ATTENDANCE, RETENTION, AND HOMEWORK

The relatively high educational levels of Asian Americans, particularly among immigrants, will probably be surpassed by their second-generation American offspring. For most American minority groups, excessive high school dropout rates are a root cause of limited college enrollments. The dropout rate among Asian American high school students is, however, the lowest in the nation.

The National Center for Education Statistics (NCES) of the Department of Education has sponsored two longitudinal studies of high school students. The National Longitudinal Study (NLS) began in 1972, when the number of new immigrants from Asia was still relatively low. High School and Beyond (HS&B) collected base year data in 1980, when the Asian American population had more than doubled, more through immigration than through natural increase. Among more than 75,000 high school sophomores and seniors sampled in the 1980 longitudinal study, about 400 in each class identified themselves as Asian Americans. The uneven distribution of Asian Americans across the states may have resulted in some undersampling of

56

the group in carrying out the highly stratified national probability sampling design of HS&B.

The first follow-up survey was conducted in the Spring of 1982. During the 2-year interval, almost 14% of the 1980 sophomores had dropped out of school. More than 12% of the white sophomores had left school before graduation. Among Asian American sophomores, 3.1% had dropped out (Peng, 1983). Rock, Ekstrom, Goertz, and Pollack (1985) conducted independent analyses of NCES's longitudinal data and reported that sophomores who later left school without graduating differed in significant ways from their classmates who stayed on in school. Dropouts had lower test scores and school grades as sophomores, did less homework, had lower self-esteem and sense of control over their lives, had more discipline problems at school, dated more and spent more time driving and riding around, and had parents who were less likely to know what the students were doing. Other students have reported that low socioeconomic status (SES) and enrollment in nonacademic programs were also related to dropout rates.

There is evidence of growing dropout rates among some Southeast Asian refugee students who entered high school over age, with learning lags due to limited exposure to formal education in refugee camps or their war torn homelands, understanding little or no English, and without the economic and emotional support of intact families. A summary report from the Boston Public Schools (1986b) recorded that for the first time, dropouts from high schools with substantial Southeast Asian enrollment had almost doubled over all Asian American 4-year cumulative dropout rates to 27% for the graduating class of 1985. Four years earlier, 1982 Asian American cumulative drop out rate was 14%. Asian Americans, particularly Kampuchean and Laotian students,˙were dropping out of Boston public schools at rates that were increasing faster than those of all other groups in Boston. Neverthless, overall Asian American dropout rate remains the lowest among all groups (Boston Public Schools, 1986a). Sege (1987) described Boston area high schools that enrolled substantial numbers of Southeast Asian refugee students as having many Asian names on their honor rolls (mostly earlier arriving Vietnamese) as well as on their dropout lists (mostly Kampuchean and Laotian newcomers).

Problems with retention among Hmong youth have been reported by high schools in communities with substantial numbers of Hmongs. Special dropout prevention programs have been developed for these newcomers. Lack of professional or para-professional staff members who can communicate in Khmer, Hmong, and Laotian languages has been a main problem in serving the educational needs of recent Southeast Asian refugees (Podeschi, 1987).

Although Asian American students in the HS&B sample enrolled more frequently in college preparatory programs than other students, they were not of higher social status than white classmates. A composite SES measure showed that 22% of Asian American and 18% of white sophomores were in the lowest SES quartile, 47% of Asian American and 52% of white students were in the two middle quartiles, and 32% of Asian American and 30% of white students were in the upper quartile. In the Asian American sample, 2% more fell in the upper quartile and 4% more in the lowest quartile when compared with their white classmates. Asian American academic achievement test scores were similar to white students', but Asians, a heterogeneous group, consistently manifested greater variations in performance than white classmates did (Peng, Owings, & Fetters, 1984). Not only did Asian American high school students attend school more regularly, enroll in college preparatory programs, and stay on through graduation, they also spent more time each week on homework. In 1980, more than half of the Asian American seniors surveyed in the HS&B study reported they spent 5 to 10 hours, or more than 10 hours each week on homework. Less than a fourth of their white classmates did so (National Center for Education Statistics, 1984a). Peng et al. (1984) reported that almost half of Asian American high school sophomores reported in 1980 that they spent at least 5 hours each week on homework, compared to 3 out of 10 white classmates. The 1982 followup of 1980 HS&B sophomores found that, other things being equal, students who did more homework showed greater achievement score gains between their sophomore and senior years (Rock et al., 1985).

Asian American high school students also went to school more regularly than their classmates. In 1980, 45% of the Asian American sophomores reported they were never absent from school, and 42% said they were never late. The comparison figures for white sophomores were 36% and 46% respectively. Peng et al. (1984) reported weak, negative relationships between absence and tardiness and achievement measures.

The high retention rate of Asian Americans through high school means that Asian American high school graduates are a less select group within their population than high school graduates of all other groups.

ACADEMIC ACHIEVEMENT

Dramatic changes have taken place in the composition of the Asian American population since the beginning of the 1970s. Any observed changes in typical academic achievement, as measured by standardized tests, grades, academic credits earned, or other criteria, must be understood not only in terms of temporal and cohort changes common to all Americans but also in terms of structural changes in the Asian American population itself. The most significant difference, from an educational viewpoint, is the increased proportion of Asian American students who have limited proficiency in the English language. According to the 1980 census, the proportion of Asians residing in the United States, age 5 or older, who speak English "not well" or "not at all" was 22.3%. There were differences among ethnic/language groups in the proportion of limited English proficient individuals. Differences were related to SES, educational levels, proportion of new immigrants, length of residence in the United States, former colonial status of country of origin, and the use of English as a medium of instruction in the schools, as shown here:

Language Group	Percent of Persons 5 Years or Older with Limited English
Asian Indian languages	8.4
Chinese	29.7
Japanese	17.5
Korean	28.9
Filipine languages	9.3
Thai	35.5
Vietnamese	37.8

Have demographic changes in the Asian American population since 1970 been accompanied by changes in student achievement in school? There are data to suggest that although changes have occurred, they have been in the same direction and magnitude as the majority of their classmates.

CHANGES IN ACADEMIC ACHIEVEMENT OVER TIME

Boardman, Lloyd, and Wood (1978) analyzed achievement data of a sample of 1,324 twelfth-grade Asian American students of the 1965 Equality of Educational Opportunity Survey. Achievement depended on participation in a college preparatory program and belief in the student's own ability to control his or her environment. The investigators concluded that Asian American high school seniors had a complex but logical view of their educational process. They formed academic self-concepts based on their past achievement, perceptions of their teachers' evaluations of their potential, and of family attitudes and expectations. Teacher characteristics proved to be important to achievement. Inexperienced female teachers with high verbal ability raised achievement levels. Classroom and school characteristics did not affect achievement. Nor did the SES of their families influence achievement, expectations, or sense of control. Speaking a foreign language at home, however, lowered achievement and sense of control but raised aspirations and expectations.

Because a fourth of Asian Americans are handicapped by limited proficiency in English, it would be reasonable to consider whether or not overall academic achievement levels have been adversely affected. Comparison of the academic performance of high school seniors is possible between 1972, the base year of NLS, when there were relatively few new Asian immigrants; and 1980, the base year of HS&B, when immigrants and refugees had doubled the number of ethnic Asians in America.

Rock, Ekstrom, Goertz, Pollack, and Hilton (1984) have analyzed NCES data from both NLS and HS&B longitudinal studies. Because 68% of the achievement test items were common to both studies, item response theory (IRT) was used to score and equate vocabulary, reading, and mathematics tests across populations. IRT formula scores of a national probability sample of high school seniors in 1972 were then compared to formula scores of seniors in 1980.

Table 4.1 summarizes the achievement test results of total, white, and Asian American high school seniors across these 2 years. It can be seen that vocabulary, reading, and mathematics test scores declined across all three groups from 1972 to 1980. The score declines ranged from a low of minus 7% of a standard deviation (S.D.) in mathematics for Asian Americans, to minus .23 S.D. in vocabulary for white seniors. Average achievement score differences between years were statistically significant at the .05 level or less for total and white students. The magnitude of Asian American test score declines in vocabulary and reading were about the same as among white students but were not statistically significant. The sample sizes for Asian Americans were small, particularly in 1972. The lack of significance may have been due to the small numbers. The findings for Asian Americans between 1972 and 1980 would be strengthened if other data were available to support this report of absence of differential decline in achievement among Asian American students despite structural changes in the population.

Cross-sectional comparisons of mean achievement test formula scores for high school seniors classified by ethnicity in 1972 and 1980 are shown in Table 4.2. In 1972, Asian American seniors typically achieved vocabulary scores .09 S.D. below their white classmates'. Their mean score was .1 S.D. below white scores in 1980. The difference over the 8-year interval was −0.01 S.D. Mean Asian American reading score difference from white classmates' also increased by −.01 S.D. in the interval. Mathematics formula score differences also increased during the interval but were larger than vocabulary and reading score differences and in the opposite direction. In 1972, the average Asian American mathematics score was .29 S.D. above white classmates' and .41 S.D. above all seniors'. By 1980, the gap had increased to .37 and .50 S.D.s respectively. Mean scores of Asian Americans were

TABLE 4.1
IRT Vocabulary, Reading, and Mathematics Formula Score Differences of High School Seniors, 1972–1980

	NLS 1972		HS&B 1980		Score Difference[a]		
	Sample N	Weighted N	Sample N	Weighted N	Vocabulary	Reading	Mathematics
Total	15,696	2,860,438	24,936	2,666,481	−0.22*	−0.21*	−0.14*
White	12,174	2,383,015	17,862	2,110,778	−0.23*	−0.20*	−0.14*
Asian American	182	25,667	320	33,726	−0.21	−0.20	−0.07

Note: From Rock et al., 1984
*Significant at .05 or less
[a]In Standard Deviation Units

TABLE 4.2

Asian American High School Seniors' Average Achievement Scores in Relation to Total and White Average Achievement Scores in 1972 and 1980

Year	Source	Level	N	Comparison Group	Vocabulary	Reading	Mathematics
1972	National Longitu-dinal Study	High School Seniors	182	Total	+0.04	+0.05	+0.41
				White	−0.09	−0.09	+0.29
1980	High School and Beyond	High School Seniors	320	Total	+0.05	+0.05	+0.50
				White	−0.10	−0.10	+0.37

Note: From Rock et al., 1984

[a]In Standard Deviation units

above total means in 1972 and 1980 in vocabulary and reading tests as well. The modest decrease in reading and vocabulary score differences from white seniors' and the considerable increase in a positive direction in mean mathematics score differences may reflect the quality of immigrant Asian American seniors' prior education in English and mathematics, as well as the courses they took in high school.

In addition to the cross-sectional comparisons of two cohorts of high school seniors reported by Rock et al. (1984), Peng et al. (1984) reported on the results of the first longitudinal follow-up survey of HS&B high school sophomores in 1982, when the 1980 sophomores who stayed in school had become seniors. The score scales and combinations of tests chosen for the longitudinal analyses were different from the cross-sectional analyses reported previously for 1972 and 1980 seniors.

Peng and his NCES colleagues considered examining the performance of Asian American students by subgroups: Chinese, Japanese, Korean, and so on. However, they reported that preliminary examination of the Asian American data indicated that subgroup differences were not large, and could be attributed to length of residence in this country. Table 4.3 shows the average scores of verbal skills, mathematics, and science tests, taken by Asian American students as sophomores in 1980 and again as seniors in 1982, in comparison with the scores of their classmates. When the performance of all Asian American students is compared with their white classmates', Asian Americans scored lower than white students at both the tenth and twelfth grades in verbal skills. Asian American students scored higher than white classmates in mathematics, but the differences were not statistically significant. Nor were differences between groups statistically significant in science scores. By senior year, more than 12% of the white 1980 sophomores had left school, whereas only 3% of Asian Americans were dropouts. Average scores are therefore not totally comparable.

The standard errors reported for average scores of Asian Americans, either classified by their length of residence in the United States or as a group, were substantially higher than for white students, so that comparisons should be made with caution. However, only Asian American tenth and twelfth graders who have resided in this

TABLE 4.3

Average scores in Verbal Skills, Mathematics, and Science in Grades 10 (1980) and 12 (1982) of White
Students and of Asian American Students Classified by Length of Residence in U.S.

Ethnic Group	Length of Residence	Verbal Skills[a]		Mathematics[b]		Science[c]	
Grade		10	12	10	12	10	12
White	—	27.8	32.9	15.5	17.6	10.3	11.3
		(.24)[d]	(.23)	(.18)	(.19)	(.08)	(.08)
Asian Americans	—	25.2	29.8	16.6	18.8	9.2	10.8
		(1.48)	(1.24)	(.86)	(.91)	(.43)	(.50)
	All or almost all life	27.6	32.4	17.2	18.7	10.1	11.3
	More than 10 years, less than all	30.6	31.6	17.1	17.3	10.2	11.6
	6 to 10 years	29.7	35.4	16.6	21.3	9.9	11.7
	1 to 5 years	16.1	20.6	15.6	18.4	6.6	9.0

Note: From Peng et al., 1984
[a]Vocabulary, reading, and writing tests
[b]Computational and curriculum specific tests (e.g., geometry)
[c]Maximum scores: Verbal skills, 57; Mathetmatics, 37; Science, 20
[d](Standard errors)

country from 1 to 5 years achieved verbal skills scores considerably below their white classmates'. Asian American tenth graders with 6 years to less than lifetime residency had higher verbal scores than their native-born Asian and white classmates. The highest average mathematics scores among twelfth graders were reported for Asian Americans with 6 to 10 years of residence. Highest average science scores were reported for Asian American twelfth graders with 6 to less than lifetime residence.

There could be many explanations for the observed differences in average performance among Asian Americans classified by length of residence in this country. The newcomers with 1 to 5 years in the United States have not yet become proficient in English, so their low verbal scores could be due to lack of mastery of abilities needed to perform tasks requiring verbal skills. Their mathematics scores, higher than white scores in tenth and twelfth grades, could be related to the quality of mathematics instruction in their countries of origin as well as to their choice of mathematics courses between 1980 and 1982. Nevertheless, these scores may be an underestimate of their true mathematical ability, because they would have been at a disadvantage in performing mathematical tasks with verbal content.

Peng also reported student performance in terms of cognitive growth rates: percent of incorrect answers and nonresponses by sophomores in 1980 that were answered correctly by them in 1982 as seniors. Growth rates of Asian Americans classified by length of residence are shown in Table 4.4. Again, it is necessary to take into account the larger standard errors of estimate for Asian American growth rates. The differences between white and Asian American cognitive growth rates were not statistically significant. The relatively slow growth rate in verbal skills of Asian American students with 1 to 5 years of residence in this country over the 2-year interval, in comparison with Asian Americans who had lived here 6 years or more, suggests that the newcomers have not yet mastered the necessary basic verbal skills to make progress in learning vocabulary, reading, and writing at the same pace as their Asian classmates with 6 or more years in this country. Despite their limited verbal skills, the newcomers had kept up with the pace set by white and Asian classmates in mathematics and science.

The 1980 HS&B survey also questioned high school seniors about their plans after graduation. Among Asian American seniors, 85% replied that they planned to continue in some kind of postsecondary education. Fifty-seven percent of the white students reported similar plans. There was a substantial difference between the two groups in the proportion that expected to attend a 4-year college. Sixty-two percent of Asian American and 38% of the white seniors expected to go on to a 4-year college. In anticipating college admissions requirements, 65% of Asian American and 38% of white seniors had taken the College Board's SAT at least once, and about 22% of white and Asian American students took the ACT assessment (National Center for Education Statistics, 1984a). While test takers were self-selected, and not representative of all college-bound seniors, Asian American college admissions test takers number in the tens of thousands each year and represent the majority of 18-year-olds. An examination of recent performance on subject-specific ATP achievement tests and ACT subject area tests provides a picture of the academic preparation of Asian American college-bound students. More than 1 in 4 reported that English

TABLE 4.4

Growth Rate: Average Percent of Items on the Verbal Skills, Mathematics, and Science Tests Incorrectly Answered or Omitted by Sophomores in 1980 that Were Correctly Answered in 1982, for White and Asian American Students Classified by Length of Residence in U.S.

Ethnic Group	Length of Residence	Verbal[a]	Mathematics[b]	Science
		%	%	%
White	—	48 (.41)[c]	44 (.42)	40 (.39)
Asian Americans	—	47 (1.23)	45 (1.52)	43 (1.49)
	All or almost all of life	50	45	41
	More than 10 years less than all	46	41	45
	6 to 10 years	49	50	45
	1 to 5 years	39	46	41

Note: From Peng et al., 1984
[a]Vocabulary, reading, and writing tests
[b]Computational and curriculum specific tests
[c]Standard error

is not their best language, a fact that needs to be taken into consideration in evaluating performance in achievement tests that demand strength in the English language.

Recent College Admissions Achievement Test Performance

Two out of three Asian American high school seniors took the SAT. A very high percentage of these SAT takers also took at least one Achievement Test, 39% compared to 21% for all students. Since 1980, the proportion of Achievement Test takers has risen from 33% to 39% among Asian Americans, and decreased from 22% to 21% among all students (Ramist & Arbeiter, 1986). The College Board Achievement Tests are intended to measure attainment in subject matter areas, in contrast to the SAT, which is designed to identify individuals who have the general academic skills needed to success in college. Various achievement tests are used in the college application process for making admission and placement decisions. For example, many applicants to highly selective colleges score in the upper ranges of the SAT score scale; institutions thus find it useful to examine the applicants' achievement test scores in order to distinguish among highly able candidates (Donlon, 1984).

Among Asian American applicants, high proportions taking Achievement Tests may be due to the fact that areas of Asian population concentration correspond roughly with locations of ATP institutional users. Also, the selective institutions that require Achievement Tests have become top-choice targets for growing numbers of Asian American applicants. In 1984–1985, Asian Americans were 4% of all students who took the SAT. The ratio of white to Asian American SAT takers was about 17:1. The ratio was lower for Achievement Tests because more Asian Americans took one or more Achievement Tests. For Literature and English Composition, the ratios were about 10:1. For chemistry, Mathematics Level 2, and Physics, the ratio was closer to 5:1. The population ratio is closer to 50:1. The relative proportions of test takers from each group should be taken into account when comparisons are made between group mean scores.

1984–1985 ATP Achievement Test Scores. Average Achievement Test scores of Asian American and white college-bound seniors are shown side by side in Table 4.5. The tests are grouped under three areas: English and history, modern and classical languages, and mathematics and sciences.

White students' average scores in English Composition and Literature were higher than Asian Americans' by about one half S.D. The differences between mean scores in American and European history were 27 and 13 points, respectively, in favor of white students. White students scored higher than Asian Americans in Spanish, French, and German; and Asians did better in Latin. In mathematics and sciences, Asian Americans obtained higher average scores in Mathematics Level 1 and 2 and Chemistry. The two groups scored about the same in Physics. White students' mean

TABLE 4.5
ATP Achievement Test Mean Scores of Asian American (AA) and White (W) College-Bound Seniors
Classified by Subject Areas 1984–1985[a]

English and History

	English Composition		Literature		American History		European History	
	AA	W	AA	W	AA	W	AA	W
N	14,856	128,767	1,547	16,039	3,403	29,887	194	2,200
Mean	480	535	489	533	504	531	531	544
S.D.	112	98	112	102	105	97	115	101

Languages

	Spanish		French		German		Latin	
	AA	W	AA	W	AA	W	AA	W
N	1,616	16,544	1,386	16,459	120	2,392	171	1,859
Mean	505	519	524	542	549	567	582	547
S.D.	104	103	116	106	106	115	104	110

Mathematics & Sciences

	Biology		Chemistry		Physics	
	AA	W	AA	W	AA	W
N	3,458	28,615	4,131	24,564	2,301	11,548
Mean	548	557	587	575	593	594
S.D.	123	103	109	98	104	95

	Mathematics Level 1		Mathematics Level 2		Average of Scores	
	AA	W	AA	W	AA	W
N	11,215	100,458	5,798	30,768	15,755	137,984
Mean	563	544	674	660	537	545
S.D.	98	89	92	87	97	86

[a]From Ramist and Arbeiter, 1986

Biology achievement test score was higher by 9 points. The greatest discrepancy in mean achievement scores were observed in English Composition and Literature achievement tests. In 1985, 27% of Asian American ATP candidates reported English was not their best language, compared to 1.7% of white candidates.

Although students who took the Achievement Tests were self-selected and not nationally representative samples, the 1984–1985 ATP Achievement Test performances of Asian American college-bound seniors corresponded to the achievement test patterns from the Equality of Educational Opportunity Survey of 1965, and the NCES longitudinal studies of high school students in 1972 and 1980.

1982–1983 ACT High School Profiles. The American College Testing program (ACT) assessment includes four tests in the areas of English, mathematics, social studies, and natural sciences. Standardized scores from 1 to 36 are reported to institutions and test takers. A composite score, also ranging from 1 to 36 in value, provides an estimate of the candidate's overall potential for college achievement across basic subject areas (American College Testing Program, 1983b).

Average ACT scores, based on a random national sampling of 10% of high school students who took the ACT assessment during the 1982–1983 school year, are available by ethnic groups. The ACT assessment was discussed in chapter 3 with summary statistics shown in Table 3.6.

The pattern of ACT test scores of Asian Americans in 1982–1983 was similar to 1983 ATP achievement profiles in that they manifested weakness in English and social sciences in comparison with their white peers but showed relative strength in mathematics.

The ATP and ACT programs are not mutually exclusive. In fact, some candidates take both batteries of tests. The consistent patterns of standardized achievement tests that were found among the representative samples of NCES's longitudinal studies, as well as among the college-bound students of the ACT and ATP programs, reinforce the reliability of the objectively scored, standardized achievement test results at different developmental levels as well as the stability of achievement patterns over time.

Thus far the yardsticks for academic achievement have included objective, verifiable criteria such as years of schooling, cross-sectional and longitudinal changes in achievement of students over time, measured by standardized, objectively scored assessment batteries, and typical performance on admissions tests by college-bound high school students. There are, however, a variety of other criteria for assessing academic achievement. Some are obtained via subjective judgments on the part of teachers or interviewers; others are self-reports. These are examined in turn, to see whether the criteria are in agreement with the achievement test profiles observed up to this point.

Grades Earned in School

Grade inflation occurred between 1972, the base year of the NLS longitudinal study of high school students, and 1980, when HS&B began. Analyses by Rock and associates (1984) showed that IRT-equated achievement test scores went down, whereas self-reported grades went up between 1972 and 1980. This phenomenon was observed across all ethnic groups. Asian American high school seniors reported higher grades than all their classmates in both years. Their typical high school grade point averages (HSA) were about one-fourth of a standard deviation above white classmates'. Forty-two percent of the Asian American seniors reported they received mostly "A"s or "A"s and "B"s, compared to 35% of their white classmates. Fewer than 1% of Asian American seniors had received mostly "C"s and "D"s or below, whereas 17% of white seniors did (National Center for Education Statistics, 1983a).

The same pattern prevailed among college-bound seniors. In 1983, ACT reported that among college freshmen who had taken the ACT assessment in 1982–1983, highest HSA (3.12) was reported by Asian American freshmen. White freshmen's HSA of 3.05 was next. The HSA was based on high school grades in English, mathematics, social sciences, and natural sciences, with a value of 4 being assigned to A, down to 0 for F. ACT college freshmen who were Asian American reported higher average grades than their white classmates did in English, mathematics, and natural sciences and the same average grade in social studies. Asian American college freshmen's mean high school grades did not correspond to typical ACT test scores. Asian Americans had lower scores than white classmates in English and social studies.

Also, in 1983, the 34,000 Asian American college-bound seniors who registered for the ATP program reported a weighted academic high school course grade point average of 3.17 and achieved a median class percentile rank of 81.5. The more than 700,000 white college-bound seniors had a weighted mean HSA of 3.09 and median class percentile rank of 76.0 (Arbeiter, 1984.) In 1985, Asian American college-bound seniors reported HSA of 3.18 and median class rank of 81.3, compared to white classmates' HSA of 3.06 and median percentile rank of 74.6 (Ramist & Arbeiter, 1986).

Data have been tabulated for first-time, full-time, college freshmen enrolled in 4-year colleges and universities in 1983 by the Higher Education Research Institute of the University of California at Los Angeles. Of Asian American freshmen, 46% had earned "A" average in high school, compared to 29.4% of white classmates and 27.6% of all classmates. The proportions of Asian American freshmen who had maintained "A" averages while in high school was higher than all other groups for all planned major fields of study. The planned major fields with the highest proportion of Asian American "A" students were in the sciences and engineering, with 52.7% and 56.1% respectively. The figures for probable business and education majors were 27.7% and 23.1% (National Science Foundation, 1986). These data confirm the reports of relatively high Asian American high school grade point averages of high school seniors and college-bound seniors.

Asian American students, college-bound or not, typically seem to have earned higher grades from their teachers and hence ranked relatively higher in their classes than all other classmates. High school grades did not fully correspond to the areas of relative strength and weaknesses demonstrated through their performance on standardized achievement tests. Their English grades would have been lower if grades and test scores related to each other perfectly. There could be a number of explanations for the discrepancy between grades and achievement test scores. One of them, often referred to as "the criterion problem" by researchers who conduct validity studies, is the subjectivity and consequent lack of reliability of grades as a criterion of achievement. Moreover, self-reported grades may not be as reliable as official transcript grades. Teachers at elementary as well as high schools, however, seemed to be quite consistent in assigning slightly higher grades to their Asian American students.

Is the phenomenon due to leniency on the part of teachers or based on academic performance of the students? No unequivocal answer is available, but a number of factors other than academic achievement could influence teacher grades. Regular attendance could improve grades earned, so can consistency and timeliness in completing homework assignments. Wong (1980) studied teachers' perception of 616 white and 546 Asian elementary and secondary students randomly selected from a stratified random sampling of San Francisco schools. Teachers were asked to evaluate social, emotional, and academic characteristics of their students, and to estimate the probable educational attainment of each student. White secondary school students scored slightly higher than Asian students in sociability, but the differences were not statistically significant. Asian secondary school students were perceived by their teachers as being significantly more emotionally stable and more academically competent than white students. Teachers' educational attainment expectations of their Asian students were slightly higher than of their white students. The differences increased when father's occupation was taken into account. Average father's occupational level was lower for Asian students. Teachers' perceived academic competence of their students could also be a factor in assigning grades.

Academic Credits and Enrollment in College Preparatory and Advanced Placement Programs

Other ways of examining achievement important for gaining access to college include the type of high school program in which students are enrolled, and years of study completed in academic subjects. Asian American students are more likely than other groups of students to enroll in college preparatory programs in high school, and consequently they are more likely to take academic subjects. Table 4.6 shows the proportions among all Asian American and white high school seniors and among college-bound seniors who enrolled in college preparatory and other types of programs

TABLE 4.6

Enrollment of Asian American and White High School Seniors and College-Bound Seniors by Types of High School Programs, 1980[a]

Source	High School Seniors (HS&B)		College-Bound Seniors (ATP Program)	
Ethnicity	Asian American	White	Asian American	White
Program	%	%	%	%
Academic/college preparatory	51.8	39.3	72.1	78.4
General	28.7	36.6	21.7	14.7
Vocational/technical	18.3	22.8	5.3	6.4
Other or NR	1.1	1.3	0.8+	0.4

[a]From National Center for Education Statistics, 1984a; College Entrance Examination Board, 1980

in 1980. More than half of the Asian American seniors in the HS&B sample were enrolled in college preparatory programs, compared to 39% of white seniors (Grant & Eiden, 1982). In the same year, among seniors who registered for the College Board's ATP program and responded to the Student Descriptive Questionnaire (SDQ), 72% of Asian American and 78% of the white college-bound seniors reported they had enrolled in college preparatory programs.

Asian American college-bound seniors took heavier academic course loads than their classmates. Their typical numbers of years of study in academic "new basics" exceeded the minimum 15.5 years requirement for college-bound students recommended by the National Commission of Excellence in Education (1983) in *A Nation at Risk*. Table 4.7 shows the average years of study in each subject obtained from transcripts of HS&B 1982 high school graduates, and self-reported by the College Board's 1982 college-bound seniors. Asian Americans had completed more "new basic" courses than all college-bound seniors. They had also completed more years of mathematics, foreign languages, and science than white classmates, but they recorded fewer years of social studies and English than whites and all college-bound seniors. By 1985, college-bound Asian American seniors had completed 17.13 years of academic subjects compared to 16.55 years for all college-bound seniors. The number of years completed was high for all subjects except for social studies and English (Ramist & Arbeiter, 1986). The pattern of fewer years of study in English and social studies could explain, in part, Asian American students' consistently lower average achievement test scores in these subjects. Conversely, more years in science and mathematics very likely increased achievement test scores in physical sciences and mathematics (National Center for Education Statistics, 1984b). Students with a balanced high school academic program, embracing the humanities as well

TABLE 4.7

Average Years of "New Basics" Completed by HS&B 1982 High School Graduates and by 1982 College-Bound Seniors

New Basics Subject	Recommended[a] Years of Study	High School Graduates	College-Bound Seniors		
			Asian Americans	Whites	All Students
Social Studies	3	3.1	3.19	3.26	3.23
English	4	3.8	3.92	4.01	3.98
Mathematics	3	2.6	3.77	3.61	3.57
Foreign Languges	2	1.1	2.39	2.25	2.21
Sciences	3	2.2	3.50	3.24	3.22
Computer Science	0.5	0.1	—	—	—
Total	15.5	12.9	16.7	16.4	16.2

Note: From National Commission on Excellence on Education, 1983; Ramist and Arbeiter, 1984a; Sweet, D. A., 1983

[a]Minimum recommended curriculum of the National Commission on Excellence in Education

as science and mathematics, are most likely to enter a 4-year college, earn a bachelor's degree, and continue in graduate or professional school (Hilton & Schrader, 1986).

Multiple regression analyses were used to study growth rates of HS&B 1980 high school sophomores during their senior years by Peng et al. (1984). Numbers of credits in high-level mathematics and science courses were the most important variables in predicting growth rates. An independent analysis of the HS&B 1982 follow-up data was undertaken by Rock et al. (1985). Academic emphasis of the school, the number of academic courses taken, the amount of homework, and enrollment in the academic curriculum were reported to be related to achievement gains.

The Advanced Placement Program

The Advanced Placement Program (AP) provides students with the opportunity to complete college-level studies in high school. They earn credits and placement in advanced courses in participating colleges by doing well on the AP examinations. About 15% of college-bound students participate in AP programs. Among more than a 250,000 AP examinations administered in 1984, about 7% were taken by students who indicated they were Asian Americans. The participation rate is more than 3 times higher than expected because Asian Americans were about 2% of the high school population. Advanced Placement grades range from 1 to 5, with 1 meaning no recommendation for college credit to 5, equivalent to extremely well qualified. In 24 subject examinations, average AP grades earned by Asian American candidates were higher than white and/or total means in 17 subjects and lower than white and/or total means in 7 subjects: computer science, English Language and Composition, French language, music listening and literature, music theory, Spanish language and Spanish literature, as shown in Table 4.8 (Advanced Placement Program, 1984). By 1986, 10% of AP examinations were being taken by Asian Americans—5 times their population proportion, and 3 times greater than expected in terms of the population of SAT-takers (Rothman, 1986).

DIFFERENTIAL ACHIEVEMENT IN ENGLISH AND MATHEMATICS

Although Asian American students earned higher grades than other students in many subjects, including English, their scores from ability and achievement tests provide unequivocal evidence that Asian Americans, particularly newcomers, do not do well on tests that measure English verbal abilities or achievement in vocabulary, reading, and writing. On the other hand, in tests of mathematical reasoning ability and achievement, Asian Americans, particularly first-generation immigrants, do better than all other groups, including native-born Asian Americans. There are some research studies that suggest that the observed differential performance in English and mathematical tests among Asian Americans may be a conservative estimate of real differences. That is, Asian Americans may be less capable of using English as

TABLE 4.8

Average Advanced Placement (AP) Grades of Asian American (AA), White (W), and All Candidates (T) 1984[a]

Ethnic Group	AA	W	T	AA	W	T
Subject	Total AP Exams			American History		
N	16,564	167,375	236,599	3,070	36,292	49,632
Mean Grade	3.25	3.11	3.12	3.12	3.11	3.10
	Art History			Art Studio Drawing		
N	71	870	1,242	16	187	281
Mean Grade	3.14	3.14	3.12	3.63	3.25	3.29
	Art Studio General			Biology		
N	59	664	967	1,560	12,887	19,118
Mean Grade	3.29	3.19	3.22	3.53	3.24	3.25
	Chemistry			Computer Science		
N	1,368	7,543	11,362	371	2,959	4,185
Mean Grade	3.22	3.01	3.02	2.99	3.12	3.08
	English Language & Composition			English Literature & Composition		
N	549	7,616	10,121	2,760	45,071	60,507
Mean Grade	3.02	3.06	3.02	3.07	3.07	3.05
	European History			French Language		
N	582	8,923	12,486	288	3,544	4,949
Mean Grade	3.20	3.14	3.13	2.94	2.94	2.96
	French Literature			German Language		
N	75	1,016	1,524	55	1,169	1,484
Mean Grade	3.28	3.15	3.22	3.22	3.17	3.19
	Latin, Vergil			Latin—Catullus, Horace		
N	93	912	1,285	23	280	418
Mean Grade	3.52	3.06	3.09	3.17	3.09	3.17
	Math-Calculus AB			Math-Calculus BC		
N	2,829	21,183	30,151	1,430	5,820	9,325
Mean Grade	3.39	3.12	3.13	3.55	3.36	3.38
	Music Listening Literature			Music Theory		
N	9	135	192	29	302	418
Mean Grade	3.00	3.10	3.05	2.97	3.00	3.02
	Physics B			Physics C Mechanics		
N	352	2,383	3,547	379	1,725	2,752
Mean Grade	3.03	2.93	2.93	3.54	3.41	3.44

TABLE 4.8
(*Continued*)

	Physics C Electricity & Magnetics			Spanish Language		
N	280	1,181	1,901	248	3,830	6,857
Mean Grade	3.40	3.31	3.36	3.23	3.01	3.47

	Spanish Literature		
N	68	883	1,895
Mean Grade	3.12	3.15	3.23

[a]From Advanced Placement Program, 1984

a medium for communicating with others than standardized test scores or grades would suggest. On the other hand, the typically high mathematics reasoning ability test scores of Asian Americans with limited English proficiency may still be underestimates of their true abilities in carrying out quantitative tasks because there is verbal content in some mathematical test items.

Direct and Indirect Measures of Writing

The Test of Standard Written English (TSWE). TSWE is administered at the same time as the SAT in the college application process. It is a multiple-choice format achievement test designed to assess a student's ability to deal with the conventions of standard written English and is a reliable, indirect measure of writing ability. TSWE scores are reported on a scale that ranges from 20 to 60 + . Validity studies have shown that TSWE scores generally correlate with essay ratings better than intercorrelations between essays (Donlon, 1984). Asian Americans typically score about one half of a standard deviation below white test takers in TSWE. Because more than a fourth of Asian American test takers report that English is not their best language, the lower mean score may be attributable in part to students not yet having mastered basic conventions of standard English.

In one of a series of continuing test fairness studies supported by the College Board, performance of Asian American TSWE test takers was compared with that of white and other groups of students who took the same form of TSWE in 1980 by the standardization method described in chapter 3 under Validity and Bias. Asian Americans found one item type to be unexpectedly difficult and another to be relatively easy. Asian American and white students with the same total TSWE scores did not have equal probabilities of successful performance on usage and sentence-correction types of items. Usage item types require the test taker to recognize writing that does not follow the conventions of standard written English, such as use of appropriate tense sequences, agreement of pronoun with its antecedent, and the use of appropriate idiom and diction. Asian Americans performed unexpectedly poorly on usage items. On the other hand, they did better than expected on sentence-correction items. These items require the students to identify unacceptable phrasing in a sentence and to choose from five possible alternatives the best way of rephrasing that sentence.

The TSWE results showed a greater overall level of unexpected differential item performance than any other test studied with the standardization approach to date; 19 of 50 items showed a questionable level of unexpected differential item performance among Asian American examinees. Because the study group included both English is best language (EBL) and English is not best language (ENBL) Asian Americans, the investigators postulated that items covering English language skills not mastered by ENBL group would be unduly difficult for them (Kulick & Dorans, 1983).

The hypothesis was tested by a further study of the November 1983 administration of SAT and TSWE (Bleistein & Wright, 1985). First, EBL white students were the base group, with EBL Asian Americans, ENBL Asian Americans, and ENBL white students as study groups. Only a handful of items were found to merit careful review for possible content bias for both Asian American and white EBL groups and for the white ENBL group. However, when Asian American ENBL group was the study group, and white EBL students were the base group, the standardization analysis identified 25 of 49 TSWE items as displaying a questionable level of unexpected differential item performance. Inspection of the 25 items suggested language content as a possible cause of differential performance. When the performances of EBL and ENBL Asian American test takers were compared, 22 of the 50 TSWE items analyzed displayed a questionable level of unexpected differential item performance. The investigators considered small sample size as a possible factor in their findings, but the ENBL white study group was about the same size. They concluded that for Asian American candidates, differential item performance was in large measure a function of language skills. Asian Americans whose first language is not English are at a decided disadvantage relative to all other groups. Summary statistics of the four groups studied are shown in Table 4.9.

English Placement Test-Essay Score. Not only do Asian Americans typically achieve substantially lower TSWE scores than other college-bound seniors, but there is

TABLE 4.9

Average TSWE Scores of Asian American and White Candidates Who Reported Whether English Was or Was Not Their Best Language November, 1983[a]

	AA/EBL	AA/ENBL	W/EBL	W/ENBL
	9,893	3,314	278,166	3,995
Mean	42.2	30.9	45.1	38.0
S.D.	10.8	10.2	10.0	10.2

[a]From Bleistein and Wright, 1985

reason to believe that TSWE scores overpredict the actual writing skills of Asian American students. Breland and Griswald (1981) evaluated the fairness of TSWE to sex and ethnic groups. The instruments they used in addition to TSWE included SAT-verbal and mathematical scores, and the four subtests of the California State Universities and Colleges' (CSUC) English Placement Test (EPT), based on data collected by CSUC for students entering in 1977. A principle objective was to use criteria other than grade point averages or course grades because these are subjective measures and could be biased. The criterion chosen for the study was the EPT-essay score based on a 45-minute writing sample. The scores range from 2 to 12, and were obtained by the sum of scores (awarded by two independent readers) on a 6-point scale. In cases of significant disagreement between readers, a third reader resolved the difference. Essays were read blind, without identification of the writers. The EPT essay scores were considered more objective than course grades, which could be influenced by factors other than the quality of the writing itself.

The investigators compared EPT-essay performance of different ethnic groups for four score intervals of TSWE. Proportionately fewer Asian Americans' TSWE scores fell in the 40 and above score intervals than white or all students'. Furthermore, top TSWE scoring (50+) Asian Americans wrote significantly fewer above-average essays than expected, compared to all other groups. The number of Asian Americans who were in the top score range of EPT-organization and logic subtest also wrote fewer above-average essays than expected. Breland and Griswald concluded that TSWE, an indirect measure of basic writing skills, overpredicted objective ratings of essays written by Asian American students.

1977 English Composition Achievement Test. The College Board Admissions Test Program began to publish summary data by ethnic groups in 1980. Since that time, the English Composition Test (ECT) has consistently shown large average-score differences between white and Asian American college-bound seniors. Average Asian American scores have been about a half standard deviation below white mean scores. A study of the ECT with Essay was undertaken to determine whether the relationship between the ECT essay and the multiple-choice portion of the ECT was the same for test takers from four demographic subgroups: black, Chicano, Asian American, and white. In addition, the study investigated the relationship between each section of the ECT and several other variables, including scores on SAT-Verbal, TSWE, high school class rank, and English grades (Petersen & Livingston, 1982).

ECT with Essay's two sections include a 20-minute essay section, consisting of a single question or topic, and a 40-minute objective section with 70 multiple-choice items. ECT with Essay is offered only at the December administration of the Achievement Tests. Subjects of the study included all students who took ECT with Essay in December, 1977. Among almost 56,000 test takers, 2,326 identified themselves as "Oriental." Among these Asian American test takers, 1,935 reported that English was their best language (EBL), whereas 391, or 17%, reported English was not their best language (ENBL). EBL Asian Americans had the highest average self-reported class rank and English grades.

Differences between groups in mean scores on the ECT were larger in relation to standard deviations (S.D.s) on the objective portion than on the essay. The mean ECT objective score of white test takers was about 0.3 S.D.s higher than the Asian American-EBL group, but their mean ECT Essay score was only about 0.1 S.D.s higher. Correlations between scores and the variable "English Best Language" were much higher (.36 to .55) for the Asian Americans than for the other three groups (.06 to .20). The investigators therefore continued all subsequent analyses with only the EBL Asian Americans. The information on ENBL Asian Americans was therefore limited.

It was possible to recalculate some descriptive information about the ENBL Asian Americans from aggregated figures in the tables. Their mean ECT objective and Essay scores were about 1.3 S.D.s below white means, about one S.D. below the mean scores of EBL Asian Americans. The typical ENBL Asian American ECT performance was also below the mean scores of all other groups studied. Their average grade in English was lower than grades of all other groups by .4 to .8 S.D.s. In contrast, ENBL Asian American high school class rank was higher than all other groups with the exception of Asian Americans whose best language was English. Asian American students whose best language was not English reported relatively high class ranking, in contrast to low ECT test scores and English grades.

One strategy that might have been used by these students to maintain high class ranking could be by taking relatively fewer courses requiring communicative skills in English, and more courses demanding quantitative skills. The strategy would maintain the high grade point average across most subjects needed for high class rank. However, the failure to take high-level English courses may mean opportunities foregone to master verbal reasoning abilities important to subsequent performance in higher education and on the job. For Asian Americans, there is an exceptionally strong relationship between the number of academic courses taken in all subjects and the SAT verbal score. Immigrant Asian students may be using a strategy that could enhance short-term rewards, high grades, but exact long-term costs in inability to communicate adequately for a fast-track career path.

For all students, the ECT objective scores were more highly correlated with class rank and English grades than were the Essay scores. EBL Asian American and White students showed higher correlations than did Black and Chicano candidates. This finding supports the validity of standardized tests for English-proficient Asian Americans reported in chapter 3. The relationship between the two portions of the ECT was .51 for EBL Asian American and .48 for white students.

Regression analysis of essay scores on objective scores of all groups showed statistically significant differences in intercepts but not in regression slope. Given a specific ECT objective test score, white candidates performed better on the essay than minority groups. Among minority groups, EBL Asian Americans obtained slightly higher mean essay scores than the others. However, Asian American candidates whose best language was not English performed at a lower level than all groups on both the objective and the essay portions of the ECT with Essay.

The students themselves are aware of their own deficiencies in communications skills. Typically, Asian American students rated themselves lower in spoken expression than their peers. In responding to the College Board's SDQ, more Asian American college-bound seniors asked for special assistance in reading and writing skills. Since 1975, requests for help in writing skills have increased (Ramist & Arbeiter, 1986). Yet, Asian American high school students, college-bound or not, took fewer courses in English and Literature than their white classmates.

Achievement in Mathematics and Sciences

The National Science Board Commission on Pre-college Education in Mathematics, Science and Technology reported in *Educating Americans for the 21st Century* (1983) that American students learn less mathematics, science, and technology than students in other developed countries. The Second International Mathematics Study summary report for the United States (Travers & McKnight, 1985) confirmed the Commission's disquiet by recording that in 1981–1982, United States Grade 12 mathematics classes ranked in the bottom third among 15 countries that participated in the study.

Asian American high school students, even when they were quite limited in their command of English, achieved better than their classmates. Asian American high school students were more likely than their classmates to enroll in the more challenging advanced science and mathematics courses, as shown in Table 4.10. These are the courses that generally result in lower average grades for all groups of students, but Asian American students achieved better than average grades in these subject areas. They also scored higher than other peer groups in a variety of mathematics achievement tests, even when they were newcomers who have resided in the United States for less than 5 years and have a limited command of English. For seniors who have lived in the United States for 6 years or more, science achievement test scores were also higher. Furthermore, they were more likely than other groups to judge mathematics to be both useful and interesting (Peng et al., 1984). Among college-bound high school seniors who took ATP Achievement Tests, a higher proportion of Asian American elected to take one or more science or mathematics achievement tests. Among 1985 college-bound, Asian American seniors who took ATP Achievement Tests, 54% took one or more tests in Science and/or Mathematics. Among all achievement test takers, 48% took one or more achievement tests in science and/or mathematics. Proportionately, more Asian American college-bound seniors also took more Advanced Placement Tests and generally earned higher grades in science and mathematics subjects than other college-bound seniors. They more frequently rated themselves high in mathematics, science, and mechanics (Ramist & Arbeiter, 1986).

TABLE 4.10

Percent of 1980 High Scool Sophomores Who Graduated in 1982 and Took Physical Sciences, Life Sciences, and Mathematics Courses[a]

	Asian American	White	Total
	%	%	%
Physical Sciences			
Chemistry I	58.1	39.3	35.5
Chemistry II	9.1	5.1	4.4
Physics I	35.6	19.8	16.9
Physics II	7.1	2.0	1.7
Life Sciences			
Biology	78.7	79.2	78.8
Advanced Biology	24.5	19.5	18.0
Mathematics			
Algebra II	38.7	38.1	34.3
Analysis	17.0	11.1	8.9
Geometry	68.4	60.4	54.2
Trigonometry	42.7	26.3	22.9
Calculus	19.4	8.3	6.9

[a]From National Center for Education Statistics, 1984b

It is clear that even before college, proportionately more Asian American students excel in mathematics and other quantitative subjects such as the physical sciences in terms of the numbers of advanced courses completed, grades earned, and average performance on standardized, objectively scored tests of developed abilities in quantitative reasoning as well as in achievement tests. Asian Americans' achievements in Science and Mathematics appear to personify the Matthew effect in education: those who begin well learn faster throughout school—there is cumulative advantage. Achievement in sciences has been shown to be significantly related to early educational experiences, current educational activities, and motivation to learn (Walberg & Tsai, 1983).

In contrast, even though their high school grades in English and other verbally loaded subjects were not lower than average, objective assessment of Asian American performance in reading, vocabulary, and writing consistently demonstrated levels of performance below their white peers'. They take fewer courses in English and social studies. Little information is available about college-bound seniors' speaking skills, except for Asian American students' own low self-assessment in their ATP Student Description Questionnaire profiles published annually since 1981. It is understandable that recently arrived Asian immigrants and refugees would be assigned to ESL rather than the regular curricular sequence in English and would be limited to mathematics and sciences in their pursuit of excellence. However, the preference for quantitative subjects does not seem to be limited to the newcomers.

EXTRACURRICULAR ACTIVITIES, HONORS, AND AWARDS

Academic interests also influence the extracurricular activities preferred by Asian American students.

Extracurricular Activities

Consistent with a commitment to academic coursework and time spent on homework, the 1980 High School and Beyond survey of high school seniors and college-bound seniors' annual profiles from the College Board's SDQ questionnaires reported that fewer of the responding Asian American seniors held part-time jobs in high school. Sixty-seven percent of white high school seniors and 57% of Asian or Pacific Islander Americans worked 15 or more hours per week in 1980. Among college-bound seniors in 1985, 48% of the Asian Americans and 61% of all students held part-time jobs.

In extracurricular activities, college-bound Asian American students reported that they were more likely to participate in social, ethnic, or community organization sponsored activities; but they participated less frequently in athletics or church groups (Ramist & Arbeiter, 1986). ACT high school students reported that their most frequent activity in high school, which they planned to continue in college, was special interest groups. They were less interested in athletics, the top choice of their white classmates (American College Testing Program, 1983a, 1983b).

Honors and Awards

Commitment to excellence in academic and extracurricular activities can have its rewards. There is evidence that Asian American students garnered more than their share of academic and artistic honors, considering their numbers in the total student population. Furthermore, it is apparently difficult but not impossible to win recognition even if the students were first-generation immigrants with less than perfect mastery of English. The differences in strategy pursued by young Asian Americans who are native-born or long-time residents and by Asian newcomers can be inferred from the types of honors for which they vie. Each group focused their energies upon pursuit of scholarships or awards in their own areas of strength. National recognition programs for excellence in academic and performing arts can serve as examples: the National Merit Scholarship Program, which uses as a qualifying test the Preliminary Scholastic Aptitude Test/National Merit Scholarship Qualifying Test (PSAT/NMSQT);

the United States Presidential Scholars Program; the Arts Recognition and Talent Search (ARTS); and the Westinghouse Science Talent Search (STS).

The National Merit Scholarship Program. The National Merit Scholarship Program, begun in 1956, is an annual competition in which scholastically talented United States high school students are identified and honored. In each year's Merit Program, the National Merit Scholarship Corporation announces the names of high performers publicly. The most distinguished competitors receive scholarships for college. Two groups are recognized for high performance on the PSAT/NMSQT, a qualifying test offered to eleventh graders who are United States citizens and meet participation requirements. Commended Students receive acknowledgement of their potential for academic success in college. Semifinalists are eligible to advance to the Finalist level and compete for Merit Scholarships (National Merit Scholarship Corporation, 1985).

The 1984 program began in the fall of 1982, when more than 1 million students entered by taking the PSAT/NMSQT. There were more than 37,000 Asian American eleventh graders among them, about 3.6% of the total. The proportion of Asian American Semifinalists was 6%. In addition, 4.7% of the students who received Letters of Commendation identified themselves as Asian Americans. In 1984, Asian Americans were about 2% of the United States population.

The recognized groups of the National Merit Scholarship Program, Semifinalists and Commended Students, together represent about 2% of the nation's high school graduating class. The proportion of recognized Asian Americans, more than 10%, was high in relation to their numbers in the graduating population. Two requirements of the Merit program limit the possibility for Asian newcomers to participate and be recognized. First, the competition is open to all high school students who are United States citizens. Recent immigrants who have not yet become naturalized citizens would not be eligible to compete. Second, and more important, the Selection Index used by the Merit program to identify Semifinalists and Commended Students is weighted in favor of the verbal portion of the qualifying test. Asian Americans who report English as not being their best language would have difficulty in attaining the minimal verbal scores necessary to be among the recognized groups in their states. Asian Americans who have been recognized by the Merit Program are therefore more likely to be either native-born or naturalized American citizens who have mastered English.

The U.S. Presidential Scholarship Program. Since 1964, the United States Presidential Scholars Program recognizes and honors each year the most distinguished graduating high school seniors. Presidential Scholars are chosen on the basis of excellence of their accomplishments in many areas: academic and artistic success, leadership, and active involvement in school and community. They are selected by members of the Commission on Presidential Scholars, who are appointed by the president. Each year, 141 students: one young man and a woman from each state, the District of Columbia, and the Commonwealth of Puerto Rico; and from several

other categories, including the performing arts, are honored for their accomplishments by being invited by the Commission to Washington, DC to participate in
Presidential Scholars National Recognition Week. The scholars' parents and teachers
are invited to accompany them to a ceremony sponsored by the White House (White
House Commission on Presidential Scholars, 1985).

In the past few years, the number of Asian Americans among Presidential Scholars
has increased. In 1980, there were 6 Asian Americans. In 1983, 1984 and 1985
there were 14, 13, and 16 Asian American Presidential scholars, respectively. The
proportion of Asian American Presidential Scholars had risen from 4% to 11%
between 1980 and 1985, whereas their proportion in the high school senior population hovered around 2%. The names of these students represented diverse Asian
ethnic backgrounds. Asian Indian, Chinese, Filipino, Japanese, Korean, and Vietnamese were among some of the clearly identifiable names. Some were from states
with high concentrations of Asian Americans, such as Hawaii and California. Others
were from areas sparsely populated by Asians (Presidential Scholars Program, 1980–
1985). The Scholars represent exceptional promise as well as excellence in educational
achievement. The relatively high proportions of Asian Americans among the Scholars, and their diversity, suggest a common commitment to and pursuit of excellence
across many Asian American groups.

The Arts Recognition and Talent Search. The Arts Recognition and Talent Search
(ARTS) program recognizes and rewards excellence in the performing arts among
high school seniors. The ARTS program conducts annual nationwide competitions
for documented and live performance in dance, music, theater, visual arts, and
writing. Judges are professional performers and teachers in each area. Unpublished
tabulations of applicants, semifinalists (SF) and finalists (F) are available by ethnic
groups from 1980–1981 through 1983–1984. Winners are awarded scholarships
and are eligible to be designated one of the Presidential Scholars in the Performing
Arts category. The number of ARTS applicants ranged from just under 3,000 to
about 3,500 each year. Asian American applicants fluctuated between 3.4% to 3.7%
of the total. Finalists and semifinalists ranged from 1 to 22 in each category over
the four competitions. Asian Americans have been semifinalists and finalists in each
category, and also have received a significant proportion of honorable mentions.

The percentages of Asian American finalists and semifinalists varied from year
to year. Consistent strength has been shown in music, with 10% to 38% of finalists
and 6% to 14% of semifinalists being Asian Americans. Visual Arts also had 9%
to 21% Asian American representation among semifinalists or finalists each year.
The dance category named Asian Americans as semifinalists or finalists in 3 of the
4 years. The theater, which usually requires verbal fluency among other talents, and
writing are two areas in which Asian American performance has not been as consistent, as shown in Table 4.11 by the percentages of applicants, semifinalists, and
finalists for each year:

TABLE 4.11
The Arts Recognition and Talent Search (ARTS)[a]

Year		1980–81 %	1981–82 %	1982–83 %	1983–84 %
Percent Asian American Applications		3.5	3.7	3.4	3.6
Percent recognized Asian Americans:					
Dance:	Finalist	5	5	33	—
	Semi-Finalist	8	—	—	—
Music:	Finalist	1	21	38	10
	Semi-Finalist	7	6	13	14
Theater:	Finalist	11	6	—	—
	Semi-Finalist	4	—	—	—
Visual Arts:	Finalist	—	15	—	—
	Semi-Finalist	11	—	21	9
Writing:	Finalist	—	—	25	—
	Semi-Finalist	—	6	—	—

[a]From ARTS program, 1980–1984

The Westinghouse Science Talent Search. The Westinghouse Science Talent Search (STS) for Westinghouse Science Scholarships and Awards has been administered by Science Service Inc. since 1942. Each year, 40 finalists win trips to Washington, DC to compete for scholarships and awards for college. Among earlier winners, there have been five Nobel laureates and two Field medalists for mathematics named in the past 12 years. More than 20 winners have been elected to the National Academy of Sciences. The number of Asian American finalists has increased in recent years.

Each year, about 1,000 high school students fulfill the rigorous requirements for participation in STS. Each participant must plan, design, carry out and report on an independent science, engineering, or mathematics project, in addition to fulfilling other conditions for participation. Their work is judged by panels of professionals in the discipline of each project. Between 1978 and 1985, 49 of the 280 STS Washington trip winner finalists have come from Asian backgrounds. Two-thirds of them were first-generation Americans, having been born in Hong Kong, India, Korea, Sri Lanka, Taiwan, Vietnam, and other Asian nations. The rest were mostly second-generation Americans, whose parents were born in Asia (Science Service, 1978–1985). The five top scholarships of 1986 were all awarded to Asian Americans, two were native born, three were immigrants, bearing out the proportions of native and foreign born in earlier years (Browne, 1986; Rokter, 1986).

Requirements and criteria for becoming an STS finalist are different from the other national academic honors programs. Competitors are judged primarily on the creativity, quality, and promise of their independent research projects. Academic ability is a necessary, but not sufficient, prerequisite for research careers in science, engineering, and mathematics. Creativity, drive, persistence, tolerance for ambiguities, and other personal characteristics are also important. Behaviors important to becoming research scientists are required of 15- to 18-year-old high school seniors who compete each year in the Science Talent Search. Verbal skills are required only in report writing; and during the finalist stage, when interviews and discussion of their projects with the judges take place. A few of the Asian American finalists have reported SAT verbal scores in the range of test takers who indicate that English is not their best language. These students were clearly talented and committed to excel in science, engineering, or mathematics, fields that would capitalize upon their strengths. At the same time, lack of English proficiency need not deter highly motivated and creative first-generation Americans from entering the competition. In fact, there have been first generation Americans from all parts of the world each year among recent finalists.

For the past decade, Campbell et al. (1984), Connolly and Primavera (1983), and a group of colleges in the New York metropolitan area, have followed the progress of ethnic Asians and their classmates in New York City programs for gifted students in science and mathematics. In 1980, Asian Americans were 2.5% of the New York State population. They concentrated in the New York metropolitan area, and made up more than a fifth of the students in the New York metropolitan area gifted programs. From 1975 to 1983, Asian Americans accounted for 18% of the New York region's Westinghouse STS winners. Almost half of them were young women, whereas only about a quarter of white winners were female.

Campbell et al. (1984) studied 78 Asian American and 209 white males and females enrolled in research oriented advanced science and mathematics courses in 27 New York City public and private high schools through questionnaires and interviews. They were all in the process of planning or carrying out independent research projects, many being monitored by scientists or mathematicians at nearby universities, research institutes, or hospitals. The Asians simply worked much harder than their Caucasian classmates. Typically, they reported spending twice as much time as their classmates studying and working on their research.

More than 3 out of 4 Asian students were born overseas and were quite group oriented. Their decisions to enroll in advanced science and mathematics courses were influenced by their peers and by their parents and extended families who had instilled high expectations of academic success and future economic achievement. Asian American females came from less affluent families than the other three groups studied. They read more technical literature and knew more computer languages than white females and both male comparison groups did. White females, on the other hand, read more fiction and knew the fewest computer languages. The two variables, reading materials and computer languages, were defined as technical literacy by the investigators. The choice of college majors, future academic and career achievement in science and mathematics could be influenced by technical literacy. While young ethnic Asian females were devoting the time to gaining technical literacy, their white female counterparts were spending much more time in socializing activities, which they considered to be more important than the other three groups did.

Male 16- to 18-year-olds' attitudes toward gifted girls in their classes differed. White males perceived females gifted in mathematics and sciences more negatively than Asian males. White parents were reported by their daughters as considering "being happy and well adjusted" the primary goal for their offspring. None of the white male students had sisters in advanced science and mathematics classes. Asian parents' expectations were the same for boys and girls—very high. The authors concluded that although the "differential coursework" hypothesis for achievement and interest in science majors and careers was upheld by their studies, time on task, high parental expectations, and absence of gender expectations on the part of Asian American parents, boys, and girls also contributed to the relative absence of gender differences in achievement among Asian American winners in the Westinghouse STS and other science achievement and independent research competitions.

CONCLUSIONS AND DISCUSSION

This chapter has presented data that show Asian American youth making plans for higher education early in their high school years. They chose college preparatory programs, took more academic courses, and earned more credits than their classmates, spent more time on homework and less time earning money by part-time jobs, earned better than average grades, and took more high-level courses in mathematics and sciences as well as Advanced Placement courses.

When they took objectively scored, standardized achievement tests and Advanced Placement tests, they earned better scores than average in quantitative subjects. However, in the humanities subjects, such as English Literature, modern foreign languages, and social studies, they typically fell below the average performance of their white classmates. With the increasing numbers of recent immigrants whose best language is not English, it is unlikely that Asian American students will be able to catch up easily with their classmates in these subject areas. Asians with 5 years or less of residence have not mastered enough English to keep up with their classmates in subjects requiring verbal skills.

The below-average test scores and other performance of Asian American students in language-related subjects may still fail to fully reflect their lack of communicative skills. More Asian American college-bound seniors rated themselves as below average in spoken expression, compared to all college-bound seniors. More Asian Americans also expressed the need for help in reading and writing skills. Their self-ratings were generally high in other subjects, particularly mathematics, art, science, and mechanics.

For the 27% of Asian American college-bound seniors whose best language is not English, problems with subjects that require mastery of English would be expected. However, even among Asian American students who have mastered most of the mechanics of standard written English and could organize information and master logical trains of thought, relatively few could write essays as well as their white and other minority peers. Yet, teachers perceived Asian American students as being academically competent and awarded them above-average grades in English, social studies, and other subjects that required well developed verbal skills.

The discrepancy between objectively scored indirect and direct tests of writing and teacher-assigned grades is disquieting. By perceiving their Asian students relatively favorably, and awarding them above-average grades in language-related subjects, teachers may unintentionally be doing them a disservice. If teachers fail to hold Asian American students to the same standards of achievement in language-related subjects as other students, Asian Americans will never master the fundamental communication skills necessary to participate broadly and effectively in all aspects of American society.

College-bound Asian American students, especially those from economically disadvantaged and non-English-speaking families, also find themselves in a dilemma. They are aware of inadequacies in their English language communication skills. On the other hand, they also know the importance of a college degree from the best institution possible, if they are to realize their parents' as well as their own dreams of an honorable profession and relative financial security. In order to optimize their chances for admission and financial aid, Asian American students concentrate on high-level courses in mathematics and sciences and take fewer courses than their classmates in English and social studies. This risk-adverse strategy is successful in keeping average rank in class high, at the cost of limiting opportunities to improve crucial reading, writing, and speaking abilities. This dilemma is one that needs to be confronted together by teachers, the Asian American students, and their parents. New curricula and innovative teaching and learning approaches need to be developed and tested to help "English not best language" Asian Americans master the multiple modes of communication skills necessary for life in the United States.

Despite the handicap of lower-than-average performance in subjects that require developed verbal abilities and mastery of English, first-generation Asian American youth clearly demonstrated commitment to academic excellence and determination to continue their education in college and beyond. The language/mathematics gap, and other cultural characteristics common to a number of Asian American ethnic groups, have far reaching influence upon a series of developmental events, including access to higher education, choice of major fields, career decisions, and later experiences in the labor market.

5

Asian Americans in Higher Education: Aspirations, Access, Enrollment, Major Fields, and Persistence

More than all other groups, Asian Americans aspire to go on with their education after high school. Most hope for 4 years of college. Many also plan to continue on to a graduate or professional degree. Demographic and educational data reviewed in earlier chapters support the conclusion that Asian American high school students avail themselves of existing educational opportunities to prepare for college. They choose academic rather than general programs; complete more academic and advanced-level courses, particularly in science and mathematics; maintain above-average grades and rank in class; and take required college admissions tests. Except for about a quarter of them, who are hampered by inadequate English, Asian Americans are as well prepared as or better prepared than their peers in the prerequisites for admission to a range of higher education institutions.

Many Asian American students who hope to attend selective colleges and universities have chosen to enroll in private college-preparatory schools or highly selective magnet public high schools. Since 1980, the proportion of Asian Americans in nonpublic schools has held steady at about 20%. However, because the total numbers of Asian American youth have increased, enrollment in private schools has also grown. Median SAT scores of Asian Americans in private schools have risen more rapidly than the scores of those in public schools. SAT-Verbal median scores of private school college-bound seniors rose 31 points between 1980 and 1985, from 391 to 422. Median SAT-Mathematics scores rose from 517 to 532, a 15-point gain. Public school students have only gained 1 point on the SAT-Verbal and 10 points on SAT-Mathematics median scores (Ramist & Arbeiter, 1986). There is also evidence that Asian American students from education-minded immigrant families are increasingly entering training programs that prepare them for selective independent schools. About 40% of enrolled minority students in more than 600 independent schools surveyed recently were from Asian backgrounds (Sherman, 1986).

Well-informed immigrant parents are keenly aware of the improved chances for graduates of elite preparatory schools to be admitted to the most selective Ivy League institutions (Cookson & Persell, 1985).

Magnet public schools with selective admissions policies offer rigorous college preparatory programs in big cities. Asian American students apply to and are enrolled in these high schools in substantial numbers. At Lowell High School in San Francisco, for example, more than 60% of the students are ethnic Asians. Twelve percent of the population of San Francisco was Chinese in 1980. Lowell's Chinese American students made up 44% of the student body. The school district has a policy of not admitting more than 45% of any ethnic group, which placed a ceiling on the number of Chinese Americans at Lowell. Competition was reported to be particularly keen in the sciences and mathematics, because many students were bilingual. Asian American students said they attended Lowell in order to maximize their chances of being admitted to the University of California at Berkeley and Stanford University (Rafferty, 1984). Other examples of selective public schools with significant numbers of Asian Americans include Benjamin N. Cardozo High School, Stuyvesant High School, and the Bronx High School of Science, all in New York (Berger, 1987; Butterfield, 1986; Gamarekian, 1986), and the Boston Latin School. Through strategies such as these, Asian American students, even the newcomers, attempt to improve their chances of being accepted by the college or university of their choice.

ASPIRATIONS AND REALITIES

Although not every hope becomes reality, Asian Americans do manage, by and large, to go on with their education. Sights may be lowered but are not given up. This section reviews evidence of Asian American aspirations, access, enrollment, and persistence in higher education.

High School Students' Aspirations

High School and Beyond (HS&B), the NCES-sponsored longitudinal study, has followed a national representative sample of subjects who were high school sophomores and seniors in 1980. In Spring 1980, about 16% of the seniors and 13% of the sophomores in the Asian American sample had no plans for further schooling beyond high school. Table 5.1 shows the percent of 1980 seniors, classified by ethnic group membership, who planned various types of postsecondary education the year following graduation. More than 84% of Asian Americans planned to go on. Sixty-one percent expected to attend a 4-year college. Among white classmates, the figures were 58% and 38%, respectively. The pattern of black seniors' choices for continuing in school was similar to that of the white students'. The proportion of Hispanic and American Indian seniors who made plans for postsecondary schooling was lower than the other groups' (National Center for Education Statistics, 1984a).

TABLE 5.1
Postsecondary Education Plans for the First Year After High School of 1980 High School Seniors
by Ethnic Groups

| | | Percentage Distribution | | | |
	4-Year College	Junior College Academic Program	Junior College Technical or Vocational Program	Trade or Business Business School	Total[a]
	%	%	%	%	%
Asian Americans	61.5	12.0	7.2	3.6	84.3
White	37.7	8.7	5.6	5.7	57.7
Black	37.6	5.9	5.2	7.2	55.9
Hispanic	27.4	9.3	6.8	6.6	50.1
American Indians	19.4	9.1	8.4	8.1	45.0
All students	37.5	8.5	5.7	5.9	57.6

Note: From National Center for Educational Statistics, 1984a
[a]The total is less than 100% because the remainder planned full- or part-time work, apprenticeship or on-the-job training, military service, homemaking, and other activities.

In Spring of 1982, almost all sophomores and a subsample of seniors who participated in the 1980 base-year survey were resurveyed. The same seniors and a subsample of sophomores were contacted again in Spring, 1984, to obtain information about their educational, occupational, and personal progress. Table 5.2 shows the proportion of the 1980 seniors who had actually entered some kind of postsecondary educational institution by February 1982. When all types of postsecondary educational programs were combined, every group enrolled in higher proportions than they had originally planned as seniors in 1980. Eighty-four percent of Asian American seniors planned postsecondary education in 1980. Two years later, 86% had entered a postsecondary institution.

TABLE 5.2
Percent of 1980 High School Seniors by Ethnic Groups Who Had Entered Postsecondary Institutions
by February, 1982

	4-Year College	2-Year College	Voc/Tech School	Total[a]
	%	%	%	%
Asian American	51	37	4	86
White	37	25	7	64
Black	33	20	11	60
Hispanic	20	28	9	52
American Indians	20	22	14	53
All Students	35	25	8	63

Note: From Peng, 1985
[a]Sum of cells can exceed totals because some respondents entered more than one type of institution.

The distribution of students among different types of programs changed, particularly for Asian Americans. Although 61.5% planned 4-year colleges in 1980, 51% had actually entered a 4-year college by Spring of 1982. About 1 out of 10 Asian Americans had not yet reached their objective of attending a 4-year college. However, they entered 2-year colleges at much higher rates than planned. As seniors, 12% planned to enroll in an academic program at a junior college; and 7%, in a technical or vocational program. Two years later, 37% of the Asian Americans had entered a 2-year program. The proportion that had planned a trade or business school remained the same. The figures for the 2 years were not comparable, because students had entered more than one type of program during the interval. Nevertheless, it appears that the 10% decrease in students who expected to enter 4-year programs and the 20% increase in 2-year program enrollment represented proportionately greater changes among Asian Americans, in terms of institution planned and entered, than was found among all other groups. Asian Americans entered both 2- and 4-year colleges at higher rates than all other groups. The high college entrance rate held for the 1980 sophomores as well. Overall postsecondary entry rate by February 1984 was 80% among Asian Americans. For white, black, Hispanic, and American Indian classmates, the rates were 63%, 55%, 51%, and 41%, respectively (Peng, 1985).

College-Bound Students' Aspirations

ATP Profiles

Aspirations among college-bound seniors also showed differences among groups. Proportionately more Asian Americans reported plans to pursue advanced and professional degrees than white and other minority peers. Between 1980 and 1985, the proportions who planned to complete various levels of postsecondary education have been changing among Asian American college-bound seniors. Fewer remained undecided at the time they responded to the SDQ. In 1980, more than 16% of the Asian American seniors were undecided. By 1985, the undecided were down to 14%, during a period when the number of ethnic Asian college-bound seniors had grown from under 25,000 to over 42,000.

Students Who Planned 2-Year Programs. The median SAT scores rose for each higher degree goal level among all groups. In 1985, the 1,200 Asian American college-bound seniors who took the SAT and planned a 2-year program had an unexpectedly low median SAT-Verbal score of 262. Their median SAT-Mathematical score was 367. The median SAT-Verbal and Mathematical scores were 272 and 522, respectively for Asian Americans who reported English was not their best language (Ramist & Arbeiter, 1986). These unexpectedly low SAT scores of 2-year program aspirants suggested that not only was the self-selected group limited in English proficiency, but these Asian Americans may not have had the opportunity to acquire developed mathematical reasoning abilities typical of immigrant Asian students who have had access to regular schooling. It is possible that this group included substantial numbers of recent Southeast Asian refugees whose opportunities for education have been extremely limited.

ACT Profiles

High school students who take the ACT assessment for college admissions are also asked to respond to questions about educational degree aspirations and other college and career plans. More than 11,000 of the high school students who took the ACT assessment in 1982–1983 identified themselves as Asian Americans. Profiles by ethnic groups were based on a 10% random sample of the test-taking population. Among Asian Americans, 7% planned 2 years or less of postsecondary education. Terminal bachelor's degrees were planned by 27%, 1 or 2 years of graduate study by 18%, and doctoral or professional level degrees by 46%. The last figure was higher than the 30% of SDQ respondents of the same year who aspired to M.D., Ph.D., or other professional degree, but wording of the two surveys items was different. The plurality of Asian Americans who aspired to a doctoral- or professional-level degree was confirmed by the ACT figures. In comparison with their white peers, fewer Asian Americans planned terminal bachelor's degrees. They were twice as likely as their classmates to aspire to a doctoral or professional degree (American College Testing Program, 1983b).

Compared to white and other minority peers, Asian Americans were as well qualified for postsecondary education as their classmates and expected to obtain higher level degrees. More than 8 out of 10 Asian American high school graduates did go on to some type of higher education. However, there is a growing gap between the developed abilities of educationally and economically advantaged college-bound students and the least advantaged newcomers. The latter were still far from comfortable with the English language, and may have had limited prior access to formal education. They were more likely to plan a 2-year postsecondary program. Given their limited proficiency in English, the newcomers may encounter academic difficulties without remedial and support programs. Even the most academically capable and prepared Asian Americans may experience difficulties in access to quality higher education, as greater numbers press for admission to top colleges and universities each year.

ACCESS TO SELECTIVE INSTITUTIONS

Well-qualified Asian American students have been applying to the most selective and prestigious institutions, public and private, on both coasts in record numbers. They and their parents have demonstrated keen awareness of value-added credentials of a degree from a top college. They have "an unsentimental view of its key to career doors" (Foell, 1984, p. 3).

Which institutions are the "most selective" or "highly selective"? The list is slightly different from one authority to another. If the service academies are not counted, about 30 institutions have appeared repeatedly on almost all lists of the most selective institutions, and perhaps another 50 are considered highly selective. The definition of selectivity changes from one source to another. The authors of *Comparative Guide to American Colleges* described selectivity as "a comparative measure of the scholastic potential of the student body, an indication of the hurdles a student will face in applying for admission and the level of intellectual competition he will meet after matriculation. It must be remembered that the scholastic quality of the student body is the single most important factor in determining the nature and quality of the academic experience" (Cass & Birnbaum, 1983, p. xxxix). Another source grouped institutions by the following factors: entrance examination, ACT or SAT scores, high school rank, grade average, and prerogative institutional require-ments. Examples of prerogative requirements included: social prestige of the appli-cants' family, letters of recommendation from distinguished individuals, family ties to the institution, religious affiliation when the school is affiliated with a religious organization, admissions priority for a particular student body composition, and extracurricular activities (de la Croix de Lafayette, 1984).

Breland, Wilder, and Robertson (1986) defined institutional selectivity in two ways for reporting a 1985 national survey of undergraduate admissions policies, practices, and procedures. The first definition of selectivity classified the admissions practices of 2,203 responding institutions into three categories: open-door, selective, and competitive. The second operational definition was based on acceptance rates computed from numbers of applicants and accepted students supplied by the insti-tutions. The most selective institutions were those that accepted 50% or less of their applicants. More selective institutions accepted 51% to 80%, less selective, 81% to 95%, and least selective accepted more than 95% of their applicants. Survey response rates differed according to institutional types: 65% from private 2-year, 69% from private 4-year, 78% of 4-year public, and 80% of 2-year public insti-tutions. The responding institutions enrolled about 2 million freshmen for 1985, approximately 80% of all first-time freshmen.

There were public as well as private institutions among the 98 most selective 4-year institutions that responded to the survey conducted by Breland and his collab-orators. When 1985 acceptance rates of Asian Americans to the most selective public and private institutions are compared to the acceptance rates of all applicants, Asian Americans were more likely to be accepted to the most selective public institutions, and less likely to be accepted by the most selective private institutions. Across all types of institutions, Asian Americans were less likely than average to be accepted by both private and public institutions, by about 6% in the case of public, and 14% in private institutions. Ethnic Asian students tended to apply to the most selective institutions, so that the proportion of accepted students among all appli-cations filed by Asian Americans was lower than those for all 1985 applicants, who did not tend to apply to the most select colleges and universities, as shown in Table 5.3.

The student acceptance rates in Table 5.3 show an advantage for Asian Americans in gaining acceptances to the most selective public institutions, and a disadvantage to the most selective private institutions that responded to the 1985 national survey. The difference in overall acceptance rates were probably associated with differences in admissions policies, practices, and procedures between public and private institutions. Selection and admission practices can be classified as flexible or inflexible (Sjogren, 1986).

Public undergraduate admissions practices have been generally inflexible or unambiguous. These institutions follow standard, formula-driven requirements, usually based on legislatively mandated standards. The 1985 survey reported that criteria for admission to 4-year public institutions had risen since the first national survey in 1979. Standards had increased in terms of high school academic course requirements, average high school GPAs, and in some cases, minimum test scores that are entered into the standard admission formulas. Inflexible admissions practices are easily understood by the general public, and can be used to process large volumes of applicants by computers efficiently and economically. The formulas can also be adjusted readily to accommodate changing college-age populations and enrollment goals.

Admission officers of private, 4-year institutions did not report higher admission standards in their schools between 1980 and 1985. Admissions practices at selective private, 4-year institutions have historically been flexible or personalized. The admissions committees can take into consideration a broad array of academic and personal factors. In addition to academic criteria, extracurricular interests and participation, quality and origin of recommendations, ratings of personal essays or interviews, and

TABLE 5.3

1985 Overall Acceptance Rates[a] of Asian American and Total Applicants to Public and Private 4-Year Institutions Classified by Selectivity[b]

	Public		Private	
Selectivity/Group	Asian	Total	Asian	Total
Most selective	47%	38%	30%	34%
More selective	67%	68%	69%	68%
Less selective	81%	87%	82%	84%
Least selective	98%	97%	88%	93%
All responding institutions	66%	72%	48%	62%
N responding institutions	167	328	338	689

[a]Overall acceptance rate is the ratio of all acceptance for all institutions to all applications for all institutions.

[b]Most selective = 50% or less, more selective = 51–81%, less selective = 81–95%, and least selective = 95%.

other personal qualities and ascribed characteristics can influence admissions decisions. Institutional priorities and societal interests can also play a role.

The 1985 survey also reported that the proportion of 4-year institutions offering exceptions to admissions standards, and the number of exceptions made to formal admissions policies had both decreased between 1979 and 1985. Exceptions include waiving of formal academic requirements for special groups such as athletes, underrepresented racial/ethnic minorities, alumni or faculty offspring, disadvantaged students and those with special talents or handicaps.

Klitgaard (1985) has described how difficult it is for the most selective universities to decide on the few to be accepted from too many outstanding applicants, all from the "right tail" of the distribution of talent. At Harvard College, according to Klitgaard (1985), a balanced class is considered most important: "All students must have academic talent, and some students are admitted almost exclusively on that basis, but the college values a diverse set of attributes and factors, such as athletic ability, artistic talent, leadership, demographics, and whether one's parents attended or teach at Harvard" (p. 6).

It is the most selective institutions that are currently the top choices of well-qualified and highly motivated Asian American youth, many from immigrant families. By their own account, the determination to achieve by their own as well as American standards has been instilled from early childhood. They are encouraged by tightly knit families that believe in hard work as being the only route to success (Stevenson et al., 1986). They felt an obligation to do well not only for the sake of their families but for their communities as well. An article on Washington DC area Asian American valedictorians and other top-ranking students quoted the same theme repeatedly: "We know we are a minority in this country, and we have to do better than other Americans. . . . That's the only way we'll get ahead," explained a Korean American from an educationally and economically advantaged family. "They felt I should do well in school. . . . They see me as their future. They want me to get ahead," said a Chinese American whose parents were restaurant workers (Feinberg, 1984). For newcomers who identified closely with their own ethnic communities, more than family honor can be at stake. "If I don't go to an Ivy League school, I feel I would let my ethnic group down," said a member of a Korean church youth group (Williams, McDonald, Howard, Mittlebach, & Kyle, 1984). On the West Coast, a similar pattern of striving for excellence prevailed in Southeast Asian refugee communities. The superintendent of Orange County's Garden Grove Unified School District reported that 85% of 1985 valedictorians were Asian, most of them recent immigrants (Smith & Billiter, 1985).

College-bound Asian Americans, their families, and their ethnic communities may have been overestimating the importance of test scores, grades, and class rank, and underestimating institutional prerogative factors with respect to the manner in which the most selective institutions are applying broad admissions policies to Asian American applicants. Asian American access may be restricted by unspecified ceilings or quotas (Butterfield, 1986; Hechinger, 1987).

Limited Access to the Most Selective Institutions

"In the free-market economy of college admissions, Columbia University is a hot seller" reported one Ivy League institution to its alumni (Givens, 1985). The same theme of the admissions process of selective colleges and universities behaving in accordance with economic laws of supply and demand is assumed in educational literature. The Ivy League colleges, the University of California system, and other highly selective institutions receive many more applications than they have places in an entering class. This demand is seen as a result of institutional excellence "in faculty, library, physical plant and a selective, enduring notion of education" (Givens, 1985, p. 21). Admission criteria are assumed to be merit based, and complex but essentially fair.

Yet, in this presumably free market, Asian Americans have noticed signs of barriers that specifically restrict their group's access to the most selective institutions. For the past decade, increasing numbers of qualified Asian Americans are making applications for admissions. Substantial numbers are being accepted. However, their admittance rate is declining each year, and is now the lowest among all groups of applicants. Informed Asian Americans are wondering out loud if different standards have been applied to ethnic Asian youth in defining excellence, with more being demanded from them than from all others (Sue, 1985).

Selective East and West Coast Private Institutions

Students on campus are acute observers of changing trends in class composition. Early warning of difficulties ahead for Asian American applicants to the most selective East Coast universities was sounded in 1983 by students of the East Coast Asian Student Union (ECASU). A survey of 25 universities by Asian American members of the Joint Admissions Task Force of ECASU was reported by David Ho, Princeton 1983 and Margaret Chin, Harvard 1984. In most schools surveyed, Asian American applicants had skyrocketed during the late 1970s and early 1980s, but the actual number of Asian Americans admitted increased slightly if at all. The percentages of Asian Americans accepted lagged behind admittance rates for all other ethnic groups, including whites. Furthermore, the admitted Asian Americans seemed homogeneous socioeconomically, although they may have come from different ethnolinguistic backgrounds. Almost all were from middle- and upper class suburbia. The investigators concluded:

> Those from inner cities and from economically disadvantaged backgrounds are being left outside the entrance gates . . . the average college-bound Asian American high school student has an extremely low chance of being admitted to the colleges we surveyed. And applicants who are poor and/or from inner cities have the lowest chances of being admitted. These facts point to an alarming barrier to those of (us) who are seeking higher education and better lives, both for ourselves and for our families. The answer lies behind the closed doors of the college admissions process . . . and in the psychologies of those who do the picking and choosing. (Ho & Chin, 1983, p. 7)

They concluded that personal ratings by admissions officers, with little understanding of the Asian American experience but many preconceived notions about over-representation, narrow career interests and passive personalities, and the "model minority" myth have led to the turning away of qualified Asian American applicants.

Within the past year, deans of Harvard, Yale, and Princeton Colleges have issued public statements about admissions policies regarding Asian Americans. Not only have Asian American students and faculty raised questions about decelerating admittance rates, but the media have also focused on the admissions policies of these most selective institutions (Lindsey, 1987; Winerip, 1985). Each institution has denied inequity in admissions policies, and cited the increasingly visible presence of Asian Americans on campus as proof of fair admissions processes. To explain the lower admittance rates of Asian Americans, institutional spokespersons explained the need to build each class according to an overall framework in order to ensure balance and appease diverse interest groups.

Dean of Harvard's Faculty of Arts and Sciences until 1984, Henry Rosovsky, referred to Asian American students as "no doubt the most over-represented group in the university" (Butterfield, 1984, p. 8). He also worried that "other ethnic groups on campus, particularly blacks, feel they have been leapfrogged by yet another group of later arrivals when it comes to scholarships, class rank, and jobs" (Foell, 1984, p. 3). The admit rates of Asian Americans have been up to 30% lower than average at Harvard for the past several years (Butterfield, 1986). Another explanation was cited by Anthony Cummings, Dean of Admissions at Princeton who suggested that one of the things that works against Asian Americans was that they are "under-represented among groups given preference for general undergraduate admissions—such as athletes, Blacks and the children of alumni" (Winerip, 1985, p. 134). Narrowness of subject field and career interests was a third reason cited to account for lower admission rates of Asian Americans. "It is the diversity element that hurts most of the Asian applicants because many who apply are pre-medical, science, technical types" explained a Harvard Admissions Officer to the Joint Admissions Task Force of the East Coast Asian Student Union (Ho & Chin, 1983, p. 8).

Diversity was also cited as a goal of the Yale Admissions Office. At Yale, 1,018 Asian Americans applied for admission to the class of 1988, and 201 were accepted. For the class of 1989, there were 1,206 applicants and 202 acceptances. This is the first time Asian Americans have been admitted at a lower rate than average to Yale. Dean of Undergraduate Admissions, Warren David, described Yale's "target" system. Although Yale does not set "quotas" or "ceilings" on the number of students from an ethnic or athletic pool, the university does have a "target" or expected notion of distribution within each class. Statistics for admittance rates have been relatively constant for most groups. Between 1978 and 1985, Asian American admittance rate at Yale fell from one acceptance for two applicants to one in six (Chang, 1985).

A carefully formulated and documented statement by the Faculty and Student Committees on Undergraduate Admission and Financial Aid of Princeton (1985) provided applicant, admission, and matriculant figures for the classes of 1980 to 1989. In 1976, when the class of 1980 was admitted, Asian Americans constituted 2.5% of all Princeton applicants, 2.6% of the admitted students, and 2.2% (25 Asian Americans) of the matriculants. The admission rate for Asian Americans (23.2%) was higher than total admission rate (22.6%). The numbers of Asian American applicants has increased each year at a higher rate than all applicants. By 1978, the admission rate for Asian Americans (18.4%) was lower than the total admission rate (20.9%). That trend has held for each class except the class of 1983. For the class of 1988, the Asian American admission rate was 14.5% compared to a total admission rate of 16.8%. The "yield" or percent of admitted students who decide to matriculate, of Asian Americans has consistantly been lower than the total yield during the past 5 years. The yield of Asian Americans was, for example, 6.7% of the class of 1986 compared to a total yield of 9.5%. The faculty and student committees argued, as did the Dean of Admissions, that the admission rates of Asian Americans was therefore comparable to other groups' admission rates, excluding alumni children, athletes and members of minority groups with small numbers of applicants.

Asian Americans were also more likely to apply to the School of Engineering, which has a lower admission rate than average. Although the committees provided a rationale for excluding preferential groups from the non-Asian American applicant pool, academic data of from 33% to 42% of the non-Asian American applicants was removed for the 5 years of data provided for the classes of 1985 through 1989. The figures would have been more interpretable if the mean academic and nonacademic ratings of applicants in the protected groups were included as a separate category. One observation based on the data provided by Princeton's committees for the classes of 1980–1989 can be that the chief competition for admissions now appears to be among Asian Americans themselves and with white, non-alumni, non-athletic applicants. The 1,152 members of the class of 1988 had 77 ethnic Asian matriculants, including 15 Asian Nationals who were permanent United States residents.

On the West Coast, essentially the same pattern prevailed at Stanford University, one of the nation's most popular and prestigious private institutions. Although the numbers of Asian American students at Stanford were proportionately much greater than their population representation in California and the United States, their admit rates were consistantly lower than white applicants'. In 1985, Asian Americans were 11% of all students admitted to Stanford's freshmen class and 8% of matriculating freshmen. Between 1982 and 1985, Asian American acceptance rates ranged between 66% to 70% of white acceptance rates. Following work done by a subcommittee on Asian American admissions, the Committee on Undergraduate Admissions and Financial Aids issued policy statements relating to Asian American admissions in the context of overall undergraduate admissions in the 1985–1986 annual report. The report clarified the "academic plus" criteria that govern undergraduate admissions, and affirmed Stanford University's policy not to discriminate against applicants of Asian American or any other ethnic group. Asian American admit rates for the 1986 freshmen class was 89% of white applicants. Sixteen percent of the autumn freshmen class were Asian American citizens (14%) or permanent residents (2%).

The six-member subcommittee on Asian American Admissions, that examined the processing of Asian American applications through Spring of 1985, included a Chinese American Student and a Japanese American faculty member. The subcommittee found no evidence of conscious discrimination or quotas, or any objective factors that could explain completely the difference in admission rates between white and Asian American applicants. Separately or together, neither academic/non-academic ratings, nor interactions of ethnicity with gender or geographic origin, nor relative choice of majors in terms of science and engineering versus humanities or social sciences, nor overrepresentation of whites in special action groups such as faculty or alumni offspring could fully explain the differential rates of admissions. However, the possibility of real differences between Asian Americans and whites in subjective credentials, or unconscious bias in selection procedures could not be ruled out.

After extensive discussion of the subcommittee's findings, the Committee on Undergraduate Admissions and Financial Aids unanimously passed a resolution that conformed in substance with the subcommittee's recommendations. Stanford announced plans to revise its procedures for evaluating applications to ensure fairness in treatment of Asian Americans in a broad context of clearly articulated admissions criteria for all applicants (Lindsey, 1987). Asian freshman doubled for 1986.

There is no question that these selective institutions took seriously the concerns of inequities in the admissions process raised by Asian American students and faculty. Asian Americans have been, in fact, attending the most selective institutions in numbers far exceeding their proportion in the relevant age population. But there is also no question that, increasingly, admittance rates of Asian Americans are falling below overall admittance rates. Were there quotas? The numbers have remained relatively constant. Wesleyan, for example, has kept close track of specific groups and claimed to maintain target proportions by lowering score standards in order to achieve a class of about "10% blacks, 5% Asians, 3% Hispanic students, and 7% relatives of alumni" (Dowd, 1986, p. 138). Unless Wesleyan applicants were quite different from other Asian American applicants to selective East Coast colleges, not lower scores but perhaps higher standards would be likely to yield just 5% Asian Americans.

There is general agreement among admissions officers and informed observers that much of the selection has been done by the students themselves through their choice of schools. The individuals within the applicant pools to any school are generally quite similar to each other, to admitted students, and to entering freshmen (Astin, 1985). Asian American faculty and students believe, as do higher education experts, that applicants do apply to schools where they can be admitted and do the required work (Willingham & Breland, 1982). The colleges emphasize the admissions process as one of building a class according to an overall admissions policy framework as much as selecting individual students (Faculty and Student Committees on Undergraduate Admissions and Financial Aid, 1985; Klitgaard, 1985). Some Asian Americans see themselves as having been denied access solely on the basis of ethnicity. With increasing numbers of college age youth, Asian Americans will increasingly become less likely to be admitted than white applicants with the same qualifications.

Colleges have pointed to the significant proportions of Asian American students in their entering classes as evidence of fairness, diversity, and balance. Asian American students, faculty, and alumni have been more concerned with the issue of equal treatment in the admissions process, and examined admittance rates of Asian Americans in relation to the majority or total applicant pools. The importance of recruitment, admissions, and enrollment of underrepresented minority students has never been questioned by Asian Americans. And other minority groups have generally supported Asian Americans on equity issues at selective institutions.

Recent events at Brown University provided an illuminating case study of Asian American students, with the support of Puerto Rican, Latin American, and United African student groups, questioning Brown's admissions policies concerning ethnic Asian applicants. The Asian American Student Association Committee (AASA, 1983) of Brown University carried out some statistical analyses of Asian American applications, admissions, and matriculation rates based on data provided by the Admissions Office. The class of 1985, admitted in the fall of 1981 was the first group whose admission rate was lower than the overall admission rate at Brown University. The pattern paralleled those of Harvard, Yale, and Princeton; with rapid increases in applicants, followed by an increase in admission rates and increasing percentage of Asian Americans in the entering classes from about 1980 to 1984. Thereafter, admission rates of Asian Americans fell, although applicants continued to increase, as shown in Table 5.4. Between the classes of 1980 and 1987 Asian American applicants to Brown increased more than five fold. But the percentage of Asian Americans admitted to each class did not keep pace. The percentage of Asian American matriculants continued to increase, but at a slower rate, because the yield rates of Asian Americans was lower than the overall yield rates at Brown, as was the case at Princeton. The lower yield rates were an indication that the most desirable Asian American applicants were applying to and being admitted by more than one top choice institution, which essentially competed for the same few top applicants from the right tail of the Asian American distribution.

One reasonable explanation for the differential admission rates would be that the increased pool of Asian Americans was not as able as the general applicant pool. This plausible hypothesis was advanced by Dean L. Fred Jewett of Harvard, who suggested "family pressure makes more marginal students apply" (Bell, 1985). The data from Brown University's AASA report did not support the notion. Table 5.5 shows the average academic predictors of Asian American and non-minority applicants, and admitted students, to the class of 1983–1987 at Brown. Each year, the academic quality in terms of test scores of Asian American applicants became higher. Each year the SAT-Mathematics scores and rank in class of Asian American applicants

TABLE 5.4

Asian American and Total Applicants, Admission Rates, Matriculants, and Yield Rates for Princeton, Classes of 1980–1989, and for Brown University Classes of 1980–1987

Class of:	1980	1981	1982	1983	1984	1985	1986	1987	1988	1989
Princeton University										
Asian American:										
Applicants	259	309	403	424	508	901[a]	949[a]	1,028[a]	1,266[a]	1,366[a]
Admitted	60	71	74	99	105	114	152	159	183	193
Admission Rate	23.2%	23.0%	18.4%	23.3%	18.1%	12.7%	16.0%	15.5%	14.5%	14.1%
Matriculants	25	27	28	41	31	44	71	72	77	NA
Yield	41.7%	38.0%	37.8%	41.4%	29.5%	38.6%	46.7%	45.3%	42.1%	NA%
Total:										
Applicants	10,305	10,449	10,637	11,106	10,950	11,602	11,804	11,007	12,718	12,216
Admitted	2,332	2,291	2,225	2,226	2,161	2,016	2,069	2,125	2,142	2,128
Admission Rate	22.6%	21.9%	20.9%	20.0%	19.7%	17.4%	17.5%	19.3%	16.8%	17.4%
Matriculants	1,121	1,163	1,163	1,148	1,210	1,141	1,154	1,168	1,152	NA
Yield	48.1%	50.8%	52.3%	51.6%	56.0%	56.6%	55.8%	55.0%	53.8%	NA%
Percent Asian Americans in Entering Class	2.2%	2.3%	2.4%	3.6%	2.6%	3.9%	6.2%	6.2%	6.7%	NA

Brown University

Asian Americans:								
Applicants	265	224	307	542	679	868	1,006	1,425
Admitted	101	106	141	140	153	156	188	204
Admission Rate	38.1%	47.3%	45.9%	25.8%	22.5%	18.0%	18.7%	14.3%
Matriculants	39	34	61	59	70	72	79	84
Yield	38.6%	32.1%	43.3%	42.1%	45.8%	46.2%	42.0%	41.2%
Total:								
Applicants	9,125	9,156	10,565	11,298	11,901	11,817	11,746	13,278
Admitted	2,830	3,016	2,846	2,673	2,559	2,593	2,604	2,624
Admission Rate	31.0%	32.9%	26.9%	23.7%	21.5%	21.9%	22.2%	19.8%
Matriculants	1,256	1,447	1,372	1,302	1,291	1,304	1,434	1,328
Yield	44.4%	48.0%	48.2%	48.7%	50.4%	50.3%	55.1%	50.6%
Percent Asian Americans in Entering Class	3.1%	2.3%	4.4%	4.5%	5.4%	5.5%	5.5%	6.3%

Note: From Faculty and Student Committee on Undergraduate Admissions and Financial Aid, Princeton University, 1985; Asian American Student Association, Brown University, 1983.

[a]U.S. citizens and permanent residents

TABLE 5.5

Average Academic Predictor Scores of Asian American and Non-Minority Applicants from Brown University's Classes of 1983–1987[a]

	Applicants		Admits	
Class	Asian Americans	Non-Minority	Asian Americans	Non-Minority
	Mean Sat Verbal Scores			
1983	566	601	624	643
1984	571	596	619	637
1985	580	597	640	635
1986	589	600	642	637
1987	596	603	651	637
	Mean SAT Mathematics Scores			
1983	658	638	693	671
1984	660	637	693	672
1985	657	638	682	665
1986	660	641	687	668
1987	665	651	690	667
	Mean Achievement Test Scores			
1983	605	613	651	651
1984	606	611	648	650
1985	607	611	650	644
1986	615	616	652	647
1987	615	617	657	649
	Mean Percentile Rank in Class			
1983	91.2	87.7	95.5	93.7
1984	91.3	88.1	95.3	92.6
1985	90.8	88.2	93.6	92.7
1986	91.1	89.2	94.2	92.8
1987	91.5	89.5	95.4	93.9

[a]From Asian Student Association, Brown University, 1983

were higher. SAT-Verbal and Achievement Test averages came very close to those of nonminority (white) applicants as shown in Table 5.5. Yet the admission rates for Asian Americans fell each year. Particularly notable was the trend, since the class of 1985, of admitting Asian American students, who on the average, scored higher than admitted white students on SAT-Verbal scores, as well as the expected higher SAT-Mathematics scores, many Achievement Test scores, and rank in class. This policy selected not only atypical Asian Americans in terms of academic credentials but also would bar virtually all recent immigrants. The Asian American high school students, who had dinned into them from childhood that they must be better than other Americans, were apparently being told no more than the truth. Figure 5.1 summarizes the combined admission rate of various groups of applicants to Brown for the classes of 1984 to 1987. Asian Americans had the lowest admission

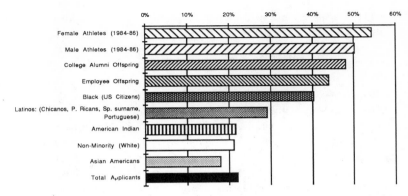

FIG. 5.1. Admission rates of applicants to Brown University classes of 1984 to 1987 by subgroups (from Asian American Student Association, Brown University, 1983).

rate in each class. A representative from the AASA was invited to address the university Committee on Admissions and Financial Aid (CAFA) and noted that AASA was not accusing Brown of a "grand conspiracy," but a serious problem did exist.

Brown responded to the challenge posed by its Asian American Student Association by appointing a subcommittee on Asian American admission with a member from AASA to CAFA, and to the Corporation Committee on Minority Affairs. The subcommittee reported to Brown's Committee on Minority Affairs and Committee on Admissions and Financial Aid with a recommendation to reaffirm the university's commitment to affirmative action in recruitment and admissions of disadvantaged minorities and to provide actions for implementing the goal. The Asian American enrollment figures for subsequent classes would be indicators of progress towards its goal. The minority affairs coordinator for Brown's undergraduate admissions office provided the following figures: in the classes of 1988 and 1989, Asian American matriculants were 7.4% and 8.4% of their classes respectively, compared to 6% in the class of 1987 (Brown University, 1986). Historic benchmarks of former years that closely guided the composition of each subsequent class were no longer held to be inviolable. However, Asian American acceptance rates for the class of 1989 is still the lowest among all groups. Asian Americans were 13% of Brown's class of 1989 applicants, 10% of acceptances, and 8.4% of matriculants. The Asian American admit rate for the class of 1990 was 15.5%, about 20% lower than the total admit rate.

As in the case of Princeton, Asian American applicants to Brown were clearly not being admitted at the expense of minority groups with small numbers of applicants, as shown in Fig. 5.1. Their competition was with white, nonathletic, nonalumni/employee offspring, and other Asian American applicants. Brown's subcommittee on Asian American Admissions agreed with the Asian American Student

Association that three factors in Brown's admissions policies accounted for Asian Americans being unfairly treated in the admissions process:

1. The "mirror" or "historic benchmark" phenomenon, the use of prior years' student body profiles as the appropriate standard for achieving balance in the entering class, which would not allow flexibility in dealing with a suddenly enlarged pool of qualified Asian American applicants.
2. The "pre-med" factor, similar to the "engineer" factor at Princeton. Admissions officers at Brown inferred that Asian American applicants were disproportionately interested in pre-med programs. However, the actual admissions process did not look at the number of admitted pre-med applicants when shaping the class, but at the number of Asian Americans per se as being "over." Several admissions officers confirmed that the "pre-med" stereotype worked against Asian Americans in the admissions process. The Director of Admissions estimated 70% to 75% of Asian American applicants were pre-meds (Winerip, 1985).
3. The personal factor, usually evaluated through interviews and/or essays. These are considered by admissions officers to be valid and reliable nonacademic criteria for judging applicants. In contrast to their academic credentials, Asian American applicants received comparatively lower ratings for the personal factor.

Administrators of Princeton and Brown have been candid and responsive to the concerns raised by Asian American faculty and students about the possibility of excluding inner city, immigrant Asian applicants. Both universities have Asians in high level administrative posts as well as members of faculty. Other Ivy League and "most selective" institutions have also responded to the issues raised by Asian Americans, but detailed statistics by socioeconomic status and ethnic groups are not available. Yale's Dean of Undergraduate Admissions, Warren David, acknowledged a "target" or expected idea of class distribution, similar to that "building a class" of Princeton, and the "historic benchmark" factor at Brown. Harvard College Dean L. Fred Jewett stated: "categorically we have no quotas or limitations at Harvard" (Smith & Billiter, 1985, p. 33). Of Harvard's class of 1989, 11% is Asian American. Roughly one third are from economically disadvantaged inner-city backgrounds and/ or are immigrants as a result of vigorous recruitment campaigns begun in the late 1970s (Bell, 1985). The proportion of Asians and Asian Americans are as high or higher in top engineering institutions such as MIT (Hu, 1986) and California Institute of Technology, in conservatories such as Julliard, and in strong premedical programs such as Johns Hopkins, and honors medical programs that confer the B.S. and M.D. degrees in 6 years.

A few highly selective institutions have continued to accept Asian Americans at about the same or slightly higher rates as all applicants. Admissions officers at MIT recently declared that, unlike other schools, MIT is proud of its diversity and does not consider any group as being unfairly overrepresented on campus. MIT is known worldwide for strength in the sciences and engineering, and has been a top target institution for Asians and Asian Americans. Between 1976 and 1986, Asian American freshmen rose from 5% to 17% of the entering class. Asian Americans, particularly the women, have benefitted significantly from MIT's affirmative action program. Twenty-four percent of MIT women were Asian Americans in 1986 (Hu, 1986). Strong quantitative skills are required for succeeding academically in science and engineering programs such as those found at MIT (Zak, Benbow, & Stanley, 1983). Fourteen percent of all female SAT-takers in 1985 who scored between 750 and 800 in SAT-mathematics were Asian American. The proportion of Asian American females who plan to major in mathematics, physical sciences, or engineering is about the same as all other males' (Ramist & Arbeiter, 1986).

Wellesley College, a liberal arts college for women, has had a tradition of Asian students on campus for almost a century. Asian and Asian American students together made up almost 16% of the entering freshmen in Fall, 1986. The combined Asian and Asian American acceptance rate is slightly higher than average. Average Asian American SAT-verbal scores is lower, and mathematical scores, higher, than white students'. Contrary to popular stereotypes, two-thirds of the declared majors of Asian American students were in the humanities. Since 1980, the number of Asian/ Asian American freshmen has risen almost four-fold. The growth has been largely attributed to unprecedented growth in the applicant pool. With more than 25 nationalities and ethnic groups represented among them, Asian Americans are considered not only the largest and fastest growing, but also the most diverse minority group on the Wellesley campus (Chu, 1986).

Ivy League and other selective East and West Coast colleges will continue to experience an inundation of Asian American applicants. Demographics and academic indicators all point in the same direction. There have been meetings of admissions officers on both coasts to begin to deal with the Asian American admissions issue. Cogent if incomplete explanations of admissions policies and practices have been proffered by the most selective private universities. These institutions want a student body with ethnic and socioeconomic diversity, geographic distribution, and other desiderata: athletes, musicians, artists, and alumni legacies.

Admissions practices adopted by any individual institution to balance its student body may well seem reasonable and desirable within the single college where the selection decisions are made. When the results are aggregated across institutions, however, a pattern emerges that suggests a pervasive, if not systematic exclusionary policy. The possibility of Asian American quotas at prestigious colleges has been newsworthy. During the first quarter of 1987, a segment on Southeast Asian students and possible adverse impact of restrictive quotas was aired on *60 Minutes*. *The New York Times*, *The Washington Post*, and other influential newspapers have published articles or opinion/editorial essays on the issue (Gilliam, 1987; Hechinger, 1987). In a *College Board Review* article, Harvard College Assistant Dean of Freshmen, Thomas E. Hassan (1986–1987), warned admissions deans and directors of the potential problems with caps or ceilings for Asian Americans. Dean Hassan stressed the need for rational institutional policies for dealing with increasing numbers of qualified Asian American applicants. Dialectic tension between institutional goals of proportional representation and equal educational opportunity will grow along with projected changes in the population of college-age youth, who show different propensities for pursuit of excellence in higher education.

Controlled, if not limited, access to the most selective colleges and universities is only the tip of the iceberg for Asian Americans who desire quality higher education. The most selective East Coast private institutions are small in number as well as in size. If we assume there are 50 such institutions in all, and suppose further that each of these institutions has places for 1,200 students in every freshman class; then, if every institution were to matriculate 120, or 10% Asian Americans in each freshman class, the number of Asian American freshmen would total 6,000 altogether. In Fall, 1984, there were more than 360,000 Asian/Pacific Islander Americans enrolled in United States institutions of higher education (U.S. Department of Commerce, Bureau of the Census, 1986a). Asian American freshmen in the most selective colleges and universities might represent about 1% to 2% of the population. In fact, fewer than 1 in 7 Asian Americans attends private, 4-year institutions. Eight out of 10 are enrolled in public institutions, 3 in 10 in public, 4-year institutions. The issue of Asian Americans' access to higher education is a far greater challenge to public institutions.

Access to Public Institutions

The admissions policies of public higher education institutions are clearly articulated. State laws govern who can become eligible for admission, if he or she meets the necessary academic criteria. University administrators and admissions officers, however, can and do exercise considerable flexibility in their interpretation and application of state system guidelines in the selection and placement of individual applicants. The most selective public institutions are increasingly using a "subjective" review process like that of selective private colleges (Roark, 1986).

Applicants to public universities have been rising steadily for several years. The academic qualifications of the applicants have also risen, according to representatives of public member institutions at the College Board's 1985 annual meeting. Indiana University, Bloomington's director of admissions, Robert McGee, reported that Indiana University's applications rose by 44% for a period in which demographic trends would have predicted a drop of 15%. The mean combined SAT scores of applicants have also risen by 35 points. McGee attributed the bigger and better applicant pools to high costs of private education, a decline in funding available from federal student aid programs, and improved recruiting by state institutions. Furthermore, there has been growing respect for academic excellence of the public universities, reflected in more favorable ratings in college guidebooks (Biemiller, 1985a).

Although the higher average SAT scores of recent applicant pools were cited as an indicator of a public system's academic standing, the use of SAT scores in addition to high school records for admissions decisions is still being called into question by providers and consumers of public higher education. Professor James Crouse (1986) of the University of Delaware argued that even though SAT scores and high school grades or rank in class provided the best combination for predicting freshman grade point averages, the additional information may not be worth the cost of the tests. Asian American educators (Sue, 1983) and community leaders (Asian American Task Force on University Admissions, 1985) also remained skeptical about the validity and reliability of SAT scores for predicting academic performance of Asian American applicants, particularly recent immigrants. Still, test scores and grades remain the criteria most likely to gain Asian American applicants acceptance to selective public institutions.

Growing numbers of state governing agencies are requiring more stringent minimum statewide admissions standards for all public institutions. The possibility of negative impact of higher admissions requirements on minority applicants has been widely discussed (Anrig, 1985; Jennifer, 1984). Would access to selective state universities become more difficult for Asian Americans? Do the SAT and other prerequisites for admission to public institutions act as a barrier to quality, affordable public higher education? Some research studies and institutional data are now available to elucidate this complex educational and political question.

Gregory R. Anrig (1985), President of Educational Testing Service, acknowledged the political, educational, and financial pressures that have acted to push up admissions standards. Such pressures could also result in policy decisions that erode the commitment to educational opportunity codified in many state consititutions and laws. For some minority students, policies that stipulate minimum high school GPAs or rank in class, in addition to minimum test scores, may present difficult hurdles. Compensating policies and remedial programs can mitigate adverse impact. However, such compensatory policies have not curbed the decline in minority enrollment observed in the 1980s (American Council on Education, 1985). An investigation by Breland (1985) used data from the College Board's public use tapes to study the impact on black, Hispanic, and white applicants of state university and college admissions policies for higher admission standards. Breland examined differential effects of five models for undergraduate admissions used by state higher education systems. He concluded that the predicted performance model was preferable because it was the only selection mode that could take into account institutional differences. The predicted performance model uses regression equations, based on past performance of students in specific institutions, to predict the freshman-year performance of applicants. Recommendations to state and institutional admissions policy makers included these:

1. Careful examination of the rationale for current admissions policies. The rationale leading to specific cut-off scores or other indexes, in particular, should be examined.
2. The monitoring of the impact of admissions policies on major subgroups. How does that impact differ for different state populations?

3. The examination of data on the performance of students in specific institutions and the relation of admissions policies to those data.
4. The use of two-stage policies in which only the first stage (eligibility) is based on purely academic qualifications. The second stage (selection) can be based on a consideration of other applicant characteristics and on institutional goals (Breland, 1985).

Because Asian Americans generally present strong academic credentials, personal characteristics play a pivotal role in admissions decisions. Willingham (1985) has described the added predictive value of four personal factors for overall college success: productive follow through, defind as persistent and successful extracurricular accomplishments; high school honors; written personal statement from the student; and school reference in addition to the traditional academic predictors. Asian Americans, particularly new immigrants, are apt to encounter difficulties with extracurricular accomplishments and the written personal statement. School references may be bland from schools with large immigrant Asian enrollment because communication limitations and cultural differences prevent teachers and counsellors from getting to know these students. Asian American applicants to selective public institutions will need to consider their personal nonacademic track records, in addition to their pursuit of academic excellence. The California higher education system is most important to Asian Americans.

Universities of California. California has the largest Asian American population among the 50 states. In 1980 there were 1.3 million Asian and Pacific Islander Americans in California, 5.5% of the state's population. Asians constituted 8% of high school graduates in 1986. That proportion is now higher. Californians take pride in their strong, three-tier, public higher education system: community colleges, California State Universities (CSU), and the University of California system (UC). Each level has Asian American enrollment that exceeds the 5.5% that would be expected from census figures. The community colleges are open door institutions, whereas the University of California is selective. Only the top 12.5% of California's high school graduates are UC eligible. UC Berkeley is frequently listed among the most selective, and UC Santa Cruz and UC San Diego, among highly selective institutions in the nation.

The University of California receives more applications from Asian Americans than any other state higher education system. In a study of the high school graduating class of 1975, conducted at the beginning of the influx of Asian immigrants and refugees, 39% of Asian American high school graduates, exclusive of Filipinos, were UC eligible. The eligibility rate for white students was 16.5%. It was lower for other minority groups: 5% for black, 4.7% for Chicano, and 6.6% for Filipino high school graduates. By 1983, 26% of Asian American high school graduates were UC eligible, compared to 15.5% of white graduates, as shown in Fig. 5.2. The influx of Asian newcomers, most of whom were limited in English proficiency, had lowered

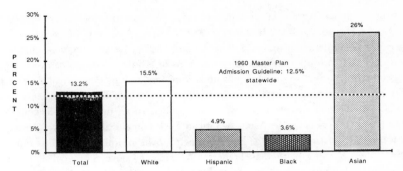

FIG. 5.2. Estimated eligibility rates for freshman admission to the University of California of 1983 California public high school graduates by ethnic groups (from Asian American Task Force on University Admissions, 1985).

the eligibility rate among Asian American high school graduates by about one third over the 8-year interval.

Most Asian Americans live in metropolitan areas. Immigrants concentrate in inner city ethnic enclaves. According to the 1980 census, within the city and in the county of San Francisco, 21.7% of the population was Asian, with Chinese being the largest ethnic group. In the Los Angeles/Long Beach metropolitan area, more than half a million Asians constituted 7.2% of the population (U.S. Department of Commerce, 1983c). Japanese and Filipino Americans were the largest ethnic groups. To be sure, Asian American students have been a visible presence for decades on UC campuses. But in 1966, when the first survey of ethnic Asian students was conducted at Berkeley, Asian Americans made up less than 6% of the study body. With new immigrants and refugees added to native-born Asian Americans, ethnic Asian applications have grown at a rate unexpected by university administrators, particularly to UC Berkeley and UCLA (Chan, 1985b, 1985c, 1985d). *The University of California, Berkeley, Long-range Academic Plan Statement, 1980–1985* had assumed that immigrant Asian college participation rate would be lower than that of the predominantly native Asian Californians on campus up to that time. Sucheng Chang, then on the faculty of UC Berkeley, later provost and professor of History at UC Santa Cruz, believed the assumption was unwarranted. She argued that "the propensity to seek higher education among Asian immigrants is not only as high, but may be higher, than the American-born Asians" (Chan, 1981). Chan projected that ethnic Asians would increase to about 7,000 or 30% of the undergraduate population by 1985. Actually, in 1985, about 5,500, or 24.7% of Berkeley's undergraduates were ethnic Asians (Mathews, 1985).

The Asian American community in the Bay Area has charged that university admissions policies have limited the numbers of Asian Americans admitted, and that the burden was borne unfairly by economically disadvantaged, limited English proficient newcomers.

Why did Asian American students, faculty, and community leaders voice profound dissatisfaction with UC Berkeley's 1983–1984 admissions policies, when Asian Americans were already almost 25% of the student body? At issue was equality of access, not the absolute numbers or proportions of ethnic Asians on campus. There has been a sharp decline in both absolute numbers and proportion of new Asian American undergraduate enrollment in the Fall of 1984. The public became aware of the decline when Chancellor Heyman responded to an inquiry by Regent Yori Wada. As a consequence, an Asian American Task Force on University Admissions was formed, co-chaired by Judge Ken Kawaichi of the Alemeda Superior Court and Judge Lillian K. Sing of the San Francisco Municipal Court. The goal of the Task Force was to determine causes of the sudden decline of new Asian American undergraduates at UC Berkeley and to study the impact of a set of new admissions criteria for Fall, 1985, on Asian American applicants.

The Task Force concluded that while the Asian American enrollment decline was precipitous from 1983 to 1984, key enrollment trend indicators such as demographics, college-going rate, UC eligibility pool, application rate, and general admission rates all pointed toward an accelerated growth in Asian American admissions. The unexpected decline was attributed to a series of deliberate, unannounced admissions policy changes, including:

1. A decision, later withdrawn, to use a minimum SAT verbal score cut-off for unprotected categories to disqualify applicants;
2. Redirecting Equal Education Opportunity Program (EOP) students who were not "underrepresented minorities," (i.e., Asian Americans and some white students) to other UC campuses; and
3. Reducing disproportionately the number of Asian Americans admitted by Special Action.

The Task force charged that these exclusionary policy decisions were inconsistent with publicly announced policies of the University, that they were made unilaterally without participation by the affected groups, and implemented without public knowledge. The Task Force considered the policy decisions irregular and irresponsible, and the consequences disproportionately unfair to Asian applicants "who were singled out to bear the brunt of what could only be characterized as an anti-Asian sentiment found among administrators, faculty, staff and students on the Berkeley campus" that was reported in an earlier University-sponsored study (Tang, 1983). "Therefore the University Actions in 1983–84 reflected political expediency rather than preservation of fairness and public trust" (Asian American Task Force on University Admissions, 1985, pp. 9–10). Applications, admissions, and enrollment figures provided by the Chancellor's Office and cited by the Task Force are shown in Table 5.6.

Berkeley's applicant/enrollment ratios of major ethnic groups for the Fall term from 1980 through 1984 are shown in Fig. 5.3. There has clearly been a continuous

TABLE 5.6

New Undergraduate Applicants, Admissions and Enrollment of University of California, Berkeley by Ethnic Groups, 1979–1984

	1979	1980	1981	1982	1983	1984
Asian/Pacific Americans:[a]						
Applicants N (% of all applicants)	1,652 (11.9)	1,871 (14.2)	2,471 (17.8)	3,328 (22.4)	3,671 (23.1)	4,314 (23.7)
Admissions fall term N (% admitted)	1,268 (76.7)	1,080 (57.7)	1,175 (47.6)	1,444 (43.4)	1,751 (47.7)	1,478 (34.3)
Enrolled N (% yield)		940 (87.2)	933 (78.4)	1,119 (77.6)	1,303 (74.7)	1,031 (70.7)
Applicant/enrollment ratio (%)		(50.0)	(37.7)	(33.6)	(40.7)	(23.9)
% of new undergraduates		(17.6)	(19.7)	(20.9)	(23.5)	(18.4)
Black:						
Applicants N (%)	649 (4.7)	690 (5.2)	638 (4.6)	625 (4.2)	691 (4.4)	873 (4.8)
Admissions N (%)	375 (57.8)	391 (56.7)	352 (55.2)	409 (65.4)	468 (67.7)	594 (68.0)
Enrolled N (%)		232 (59.3)	213 (60.5)	269 (65.8)	322 (68.8)	355 (59.8)
Applicant/enrollment Ratio (%)		(33.6)	(33.4)	(43.0)	(46.6)	(40.7)
% of new undergraduates		(4.4)	(4.5)	(5.0)	(5.1)	(6.3)
Hispanic:						
Applicants N (%)	587 (4.2)	618 (4.7)	607 (4.4)	806 (5.4)	793 (5.0)	974 (5.3)
Admissions N (%)	405 (69.0)	433 (70.1)	409 (67.4)	450 (55.8)	572 (74.0)	713 (73.2)
Enrolled N (%)		260 (60.0)	270 (66.0)	279 (62.0)	376 (65.7)	466 (65.4)
Applicant/enrollment ratio (%)		(42.1)	(44.5)	(34.6)	(48.6)	(47.8)
% of new undergraduates		(4.9)	(5.7)	(5.2)	(5.9)	(8.3)

(continued)

TABLE 5.6
Continued

	1979	1980	1981	1982	1983	1984
Filipino						
Applicants N (%)	154 (1.1)	198 (1.5)	237 (1.7)	272 (1.8)	395 (2.5)	397 (2.2)
Admissions N (%)	122 (79.2)	147 (74.2)	168 (70.9)	171 (62.9)	250 (63.3)	282 (71.0)
Enrolled N (%)		130 (88.4)	120 (71.4)	134 (78.4)	192 (76.8)	213 (75.5)
Applicant/enrollment ratio (%)		(65.7)	(50.6)	(49.3)	(48.6)	(53.7)
% of new undergraduates		(2.4)	(2.5)	(2.5)	(3.0)	(3.8)
White:						
Applicants N (%)	9,111 (65.5)	9,373 (71.2)	8,674 (62.4)	8,816 (59.4)	9,224 (58.1)	10,439 (57.2)
Admissions N (%)	6,624 (72.7)	5,327 (56.8)	4,254 (49.0)	5,020 (56.9)	5,639 (61.1)	5,017 (48.1)
Enrolled N (%)		3,386 (63.6)	2,915 (68.5)	3,307 (65.9)	3,710 (65.8)	3,280 (65.4)
Applicant/enrollment ratio (%)		(36.1)	(33.6)	(37.5)	(40.2)	(31.4)
% of new undergraduates		(63.4)	(61.5)	(61.7)	(58.4)	(58.5)

Note: From Asian American Task Force on University Admissions

[a]The number of Pacific Americans enrolled ranged from 3 to 10; the category is virtually all Asian Americans exclusive of Filipinos, who counted as a protected group until 1987.

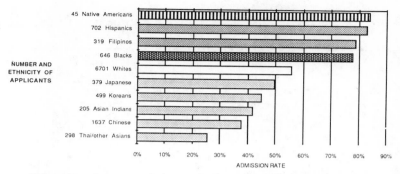

FIG. 5.3 New freshman admission rates of University of California eligible applicants to U.C. Berkeley by ethnic group for Fall 1984 (from Asian American Task Force on University Admissions, 1985).

downward trend for Asian Americans, not counting Filipinos, who were included among protected categories for affirmative action programs. This trend is very similar to the declining admission and yield rates reported during the same period for several Ivy League schools.

The Asian American Task Force on University Admissions attributed the 1984 drop in Asian American enrollment to sudden and unannounced changes in admissions policies. Admissions policies were recommended by a subcommittee of the Academic Senate, which consisted in 1983–1984 of six faculty members and two students, and the Director of Admissions and Records, ex officio. Recommendations for policy changes were reviewed and approved by the Chancellor. For 1984, a change was made in policy to redirect to other campuses, applications of "Some noncompetitive EOP students" who were not among the "underrepresented minorities."

Implementation of the policy for redirection "precipitated an unfair and devastating impact on many unsuspecting victims, those Asian applicants who were poor and disadvantaged" (Asian American Task Force on University Admissions, 1985, p. 8). Furthermore, the Assistant Vice Chancellor acknowledged that during the year, a written directive for an SAT-Verbal cut-off score of 400 for applicants not in protected groups was issued and later withdrawn. During the interim, the Task Force inferred, an unknown number of Asian applications were redirected to other institutions. The victims, again, were overwhelmingly from the ranks of recent immigrants. Their SAT-Verbal scores were indeed low, but they were UC eligible by virtue of their high grades, rank in class, and SAT-Mathematical scores.

Chancellor Heyman had responded to Regent Yori Wada's inquiry by indicating that if the revised 1985 policy for redirection of freshmen applicants had been implemented in 1984, 291 applicants with exceptionally high SAT-Verbal and English Achievment Test scores and 349 applicants with high SAT-Mathematics and Mathematics Achievement Test scores would have been automatically admitted

TABLE 5.7

UC Berkeley Freshment Redirected and Retained Applications and Admissions by Major Ethnic Groups, 1984[a]

	Applications	Redirected Applications		Retained Applications		Application/ Admission Rate	
	N	N (%)		N (%)		N (%)	
Asian/Pacific Americans	3,028	1,558	(51.4)	1,470	(48.6)	1,199	(39.6)
Black	646	60	(9.3)	586	(90.7)	505	(78.2)
Hispanic	702	73	(10.4)	629	(89.6)	582	(82.9)
Filipino	319	142	(44.5)	177	(55.5)	253	(79.3)
White	6,701	2,484	(37.1)	4,217	(62.9)	3,762	(56.1)
Total	15,229					7,934	(52.1)

[a]From Asian American Task Force on University Admissions, 1985

to Berkeley. Among the automatic admissions would have been 16% ethnic Asians who met the verbal criterion, and 36% of applicants who met the mathematics criterion, for a total of 173 automatically admitted Asian American freshmen. It can be inferred from Asian American test score distributions that virtually all of the high verbal students would have been native-born or long-term residents, whereas a high proportion of the high mathematics score students could have been recent immigrants. However, these hypothetically automatic admits could not have increased the absolute numbers of Asian Americans admitted. According to the revised 1985 admission and redirection policies, only the top half of the entering freshmen class could be admitted strictly on the basis of academic merit. Table 5.7 shows the proportions of redirected 1984 applications by major ethnic groups. Table 5.8 compares the direction and magnitude of changes in Special Action Admissions decisions among EOP applications by major ethnic groups. Asian Americans were disproportionately eliminated by redirection and reduced special action admissions.

TABLE 5.8

UC Berkeley EOP Applications, Admissions and Enrollment Changes by Major Ethnic Groups Between 1983 and 1984[a]

	Applications			Admissions			Enrollments		
	1983	1984	Change	1983	1984	Change	1983	1984	Change
	N	N	%	N	N	%	N	N	%
Asian American	404	460	+ 13.6	277	146	− 47.3	269	147	− 45.4
Black	256	292	+ 14.1	153	164	+ 7.2	124	114	− 8.1
Hispanic	284	330	+ 16.2	215	211	− 1.9	165	159	− 3.6
Filipino	27	37	+ 37.0	20	29	+ 45.0	19	22	+ 15.8
White	141	148	+ 5.0	90	75	− 16.7	69	57	− 17.4

[a]From Asian American Task Force on University Admissions, 1985

Chinese Americans constituted the largest Asian ethnic group on the Berkeley campus. Chancellor Heyman's response to Regent Wada postulated the recent decline in Chinese enrollment may have been "due to increased competition from other universities for these students." Table 5.9 of the applicant, admission, and enrollment rates of Asian American freshmen by ethnic groups in 1983 and 1984, shows that admission rates of all groups declined, with the exception of Asian Indians.

TABLE 5.9

UC Berkeley Asian American (Citizen and Immigrant) Freshmen Application, Admitted and Enrolled for Fall 1983 and 1984 by Ethnic Groups

Applications	1983 N	% of A/PAs	1984 N	% of A/PAs
Chinese	1,355	48.2	1,637	48.9
East Indian/Pakistan (Asian Indians)[a]	143	5.1	205	6.1
Filipino[b]	262	9.3	319	9.5
Japanese	368	13.1	379	11.3
Korean	392	14.0	499	14.9
Polynesian (Pacific Islander)[a]	17	0.6	10	0.3
Thai/Other Asian	272	9.7	298	8.9
Total	2,809	100	3,347	100

Admitted Freshmen	N	% Admittance Rate	N	% Admittance Rate
Chinese	764	56.4	617	37.7
Asian Indian	53	37.1	87	42.4
Filipino	216	82.4	253	79.3
Japanese	248	67.4	189	49.9
Korean	229	58.4	224	44.9
Pacific Islander	13	76.5	5	50.0
Thai/Other Asian	91	33.5	77	25.8
Total	1,614	57.5	1,372	41.0

Enrolled Freshmen	N	% Yield	% Applicant/ Enrollment	N	% Yield	% Applicant/ Enrollment
Chinese	589	77.1	43.5	418	67.8	25.5
Asian Indian	37	64.9	25.9	62	71.3	30.2
Filipino	166	76.9	63.4	195	77.1	61.1
Japanese	116	46.8	31.5	129	68.3	34.0
Korean	153	66.8	38.6	143	63.8	28.7
Pacific Islander	9	69.2	52.9	1	20.0	10.0
Thai/Other Asian	76	83.5	27.9	60	77.9	20.1
Total	1,146	71.0	40.8	1,008	73.5	30.1

Note: From Asian American Task Force on University Admissions, 1985
[a]UC Berkeley label (Census label)
[b]Filipino is a protected category in UC system

The admission rate of white applicants also declined, but not as precipitously. In addition to the Chinese, the applicant enrollment ratios of Koreans and Thais/other Asians also declined. If there was increased competition from other universities for these students, it should be possible to determine whether these students, and all admitted Asian Americans including the students who did not matriculate, were in fact better qualified academically than other students and therefore more sought after. The academic quality of the applicant pools can also be determined, if data were available for the redirected students. These data were not available, according to Assistant Vice Chancellor B. Thomas Travers in a letter to the Co-chairs of the Task Force. However, he pointed out that the UC system's decision for multiple filing of applications to all colleges and campuses for Fall 1986, should facilitate understanding of the qualifications and nature of the applicant pool (Asian American Task Force on University Admissions, 1985).

In addition to studying the impact of changes in 1984 admissions policies upon the enrollment of Asian Americans at UC Berkeley, the Task force also assessed the potential impact of new admission and redirection criteria adopted for screening and admitting freshmen for Fall 1985. The new set of recommendations were reviewed by the Admissions and Enrollment Committee of the Academic Senate and by a special task force convened by the Chancellor and chaired by the Provost of the College of Letters and Science (L&S).

A two-tier system was adopted. "Quotas" for the two tiers was described by the Office of Relations with Schools as follows: The top 50% of students admitted to Berkeley would be chosen according to rank order by an Academic Index which include self-reported GPAs for the first time:

$$\text{GPA (capped at } 4.0 \text{ for L\&S only)} \times 1{,}000 = \text{max. } 4{,}000$$
$$+ \text{SAT scores} + 3 \text{ Achievement test scores} = \text{max. } 4{,}000$$
$$\text{Total} = \text{max. } 8{,}000$$

For fall 1985, the College of Letters and Science selected as freshmen the following students:

	Academic Index
First 50% - Based on Academic Index alone	6,580–8,000
Next 45% - 2,100 from categories protected from redirection:	± 5,800–6,580
affirmative action	
athletes	
other groups	
660 based on Academic Index plus additional academic criteria and personal factors described by the applicant in an essay.	Asian Americans applicants can be considered for these places
Last 5% - Appeals from redirected students.	

Six percent of all freshmen spaces at Berkeley are reserved for Special Action admissions:

> 10% Chancellor
> 15% Athletic Department
> 65% Student Affirmative Action

The Asian American Task Force on University Admissions concluded 1985 revised criteria would result in adverse impact on Asian American applicants for the following reasons:

1. Asian American faculty did not participate in the formulation of the new policy.
2. The 1985 criteria were detrimental to Asian American immigrant applicants:
   a. The two-tiered system for screening would have adverse impact, particularly in the second tier, on Asian applicants.
   b. In the top tier, The Academic Index will select many Asians with high grades and test scores. Strict adherence to the a–f subject requirements will exclude recent immigrants who may not have had four years of English, 2 years of foreign language or American history.
   c. Asian applicants who just miss the first tier can only be eligible to compete for 660 slots in the second tier, left after the 2,100 set aside places for protected groups.
   d. The "additional academic criteria" for the unprotected slots in the second tier are even more rigorous than the a–f subject requirements. The essay for demonstrating leadership, character, motivation, and accomplishment in extracurricular activities is also unfair to most recent immigrants, whose ability to communicate personal qualities through English would be limited, and who are usually too preoccupied with keeping up with their studies to participate extensively in extracurricular activities.

The Task Force on University Admissions concluded:

> If the University as a public institution is to fulfill its long-held commitment to competitive academic excellence and equal opportunity for qualified applicants, it cannot erect artificial barriers, which on the surface appear to be neutral and color-blind, but which in effect cause an adverse impact on otherwise highly qualified and motivated Asian American students. Neither can the Univeristy continue to make admission policy decisions behind closed doors without adequate imput and participation of Asian faculty, staff, students and community, who after all, constitute collectively the largest single minority group on campus. (Asian American Task Force on University Admissions, 1985, pp. 13–14)

In November 1985, Berkeley announced that 27 percent of the freshmen class was Asian American. For the first time, non-Hispanic white students became a minority in the class of 1989 at 47.9%. Among 22,321 undergraduates, 24.7% were ethnic Asian citizens or immigrants. While the administration described the change as a part of natural year-to-year fluctuation, unrelated to university policy, Asian American faculty and Task Force members attributed the reversal of a 5-year downward trend in admissions to their protests (Mathews, 1985).

Asian American faculty at UCLA had observed a similar trend and raised essentially the same questions asked by the Bay Area task force. UCLA has the second largest number of Asian American students in the UC system with about 4,000 to the 5,000 at Berkeley. The ethnic mix was different at UCLA, with Chinese and Japanese Americans each being about one third of the total. There were also greater numbers of Korean and Vietnamese students at UCLA. The most popular major for Asians at Berkeley was engineering. Premedical; other allied health sciences; and physical science majors were proportionately higher among Asian American undergraduates at UCLA (Chan, 1981).

In 1985, 16.3% of UCLA undergraduates were Asian Americans. New enrollment of Asian American students had been declining at UCLA for several years during a period when Asian population in Los Angeles was growing rapidly. Ethnic survey data provided by the Asian American Studies Center of UCLA showed that new Asian freshmen, including citizens, immigrants, and permanent residents, decreased from 855 to 630 between Fall 1981 and 1984. In 1984, 40.7% of Asian applicants were accepted, compared to 50% of white, 77.6% of native American, 64.4% of black, 82% of Chicano and 87.3% of Filipino applicants. The proportion of redirected Asian American applicants for UCLA College of Letters and Science (L&S) for fall 1984 was particularly high for Koreans, Polynesians, East Indian/Pakistanis, and Thai/other Asians, whereas that of white, Chinese, and Japanese American applicants was about the same. UCLA staff of the Asian American Studies Center expressed the concern of the Asian American community and students, faculty, and staff on campus about changes in admissions criteria and processes that appeared to work against the interests of ethnic Asian, immigrant applicants. On December 10, 1984, the Undergraduate Enrollment Committee met to discuss redirection criteria for Fall 1985 without Asian American participation. An Index system similar to Berkeley's was adopted for acceptance of most of the 50% of students to be selected on academic criteria. A decision was made not to publish the new redirection criteria. However, members of the committee agreed to meet with Asian faculty about the revised redirection process (UCLA Asian American Studies Center, 1984).

Two days later a memo from Vice Provost Gerald Kissler to Provost Raymond Orbach and deans of L&S included a paper from Director of Undergraduate Admissions Rae Lee Siporin that assumed "the campus will endeavor to curb the decline of Caucasian students" and predicted "a rising concern will come from Asian students and Asians in general as the numbers and proportion of Asian students entering at the freshman level decline" (*East/West*, June 12, 1985, p. 1). Although the administration has denied a policy to curb the decline of white students, administrators admitted that the decline occurred because low-income Asians and whites had been excluded from the protected pool of Student Affirmative Action (SAA) applicants since 1982. About 85% of the decline in Asian enrollment was attributed to low-income Asians' being taken out of the protected pool of underrepresented minorities. The decline in Asian enrollment was considered inevitable because the university must simultaneously prevent enrollment increases and raise the number of SAA students. Under the SAA plan, all ethnic groups, income levels, and both sexes would be represented in all segments of higher education in the same proportion as California's population. UCLA determined its ethnic parity in accordance with the ethnic composition of California's high school graduating class each year. Asians were 6.1% of the high school graduates in 1984. Thomas Lifka, Registrar and Assistant Vice Chancellor of Student Academic Services, explained: "Something has to give . . . but we hope the decrease will not fall disproportionately on any one group" (*East/West*, June 12, 1985, p. 1).

Redirection and enrollment data showed that it was low-income, recent immigrants who were being denied access to UCLA. National surveys such as High School and Beyond, and California studies such as Chan's study of immigrant Asian applicants to UC Berkeley and UCLA have demonstrated marked differences among ethnic groups in the proportions of high school graduates who plan for higher education. UC eligibility also differed marked across ethnic groups. Additionally, studies cited in chapter 3 showed that Asian Americans generally received better grades in college than would have been predicted from their academic aptitude test scores and that SAT-M is the best predictor for recent immigrants. A study by UCLA professor Stanley Sue on the academic performance of Chinese American students on campus classified the students into three groups: American born (AB), early immigrants with more than 6 years in the United States (EI), and recent immigrants with 6 years or fewer in the United States (RI). Mean SAT percentile scores and grades for the three groups are shown in Table 5.10.

Recent Chinese immigrant students, despite extremely low SAT-Verbal scores, were typically able to earn grades higher than the university mean GPA of 2.87. Redirecting Chinese immigrants, who came from all parts of the world, because of their limited English could not be justified on the basis of their not being able to perform academically at UCLA (Sue, 1985; Sue & Zane, 1985).

TABLE 5.10
Mean SAT Percentile Scores and Grades for AB, EI, and RI Groups[a]

	N	SAT percentiles		GPA
		Verbal (%)	Mathematics (%)	
AB	83	68.7	77.7	3.02
EI	43	47.1	72.0	2.94
RI	43	18.0	81.2	2.96

[a]From Sue, 1985

Staff of the UCLA Asian American Studies Center and Professor Morton Friedman, chair of the Academic Senate Committee on Undergraduate Enrollment, have predicted that the courts might be the appeal of last resort for students who believe they were unjustly redirected. Professor Friedman expressed surprise that "we haven't been sued yet, because it's something someone would be concerned about" (*East/ West*, June 12, 1985, p. 1).

UC eligible, recent immigrants will be further affected by new admissions policies and standards announced by UCLA in November 1986. Even without the new admissions criteria, Asian American freshmen enrollment had declined from a high of almost 20% in 1981 and 1982 to about 16%. UCLA eliminated altogether, for the Fall, 1987 entering freshmen class, use of the academic selection index based on high school graders and test scores, which had been the criterion for admitting 50% of entering classes in recent years. The new criteria articulated unequivocally UCLA's intention to emulate the subjective, flexible, admissions policies of highly selective private institutions.

The enrollment of Asian Americans will probably decline as a result of the new policies and standards, because objective admission standards will be supplemented or supplanted by subjective criteria. These criteria include quality and content of high school courses and difficulty of the high school programs, which are verifiable and would not present serious problems for most Asian American applicants, even immigrants. New criteria also include extracurricular activities and ability of the student to express his or her commitment to such activities in personal essays. These additional criteria will certainly create an unexpected burden for less acculturated immigrants and refugees with limited ability to communicate in English (Roark, 1986). The most troubling aspect of the new UCLA system will be the questions of reliability and quality control of ratings in double reviews of thousands of applications by faculty members and admissions officers. The UC admissions system, developed orginally to select students on the basis of merit, is increasingly being eroded.

A similar change was announced in UC Berkeley's admission standards, with 40% instead of 50% of entering freshmen in 1987 to be admitted by academic index alone. Also, an earlier practice of admitting more students who lived within commuting distance is to be discarded in favor of students from rural areas and high schools that sent fewer graduates to Berkeley. A great number of Asian Americans live in the Bay area, and many attend high schools that have traditionally fed their UC eligible graduates to UC Berkeley. Their chances of being accepted by Berkeley will be adversely affected by these policy changes.

A new, centralized, multiple filing admissions application system was initiated in November 1985, for the Fall 1986 admission cycle of the UC system. Full-page ads were placed in 26 metropolitan and ethnic newspapers in California by friends and alumni of UC as a public service. The purpose of the ads was to inform high school and community college students about changes in subject requirements for admission to UC and the new application procedures. Although Asian Americans were a significant minority in the UC system, no ads were placed in any Asian newspapers (*East/West*, October 30, 1985a). Although it is too early to assess the impact of the new system on Asian American applicants, both Berkeley and UCLA are expected to have significant increases in the number of applicants, including Asian applicants who have traditionally preferred these two campuses to other UC institutions. Other UC campuses also have substantial numbers of ethnic Asian students. UC Irvine in Orange County reported 20.4% of undergraduates and 34% of the freshmen in 1985 were Asian. Any admission or retention policy changes that affect Asian American students' access and progress in the California system would affect the lives of many more Asian American students than changes in the policies of private, highly selective institutions.

On May 13, 1985, UC Berkeley's Assistant Vice Chancellor B. Thomas Travers responded to questions from the Asian American Task Force on University Admissions about the impact of the additional criteria, particularly the essay, on new immigrants by stating:

> New immigrants (if discernable through the essay) who worked hard to overcome English language deficiences and adapt to their new surroundings were certainly given fair consideration. . . . Extra points for exemption from the subject A requirement . . . simply acknowledged applicants who through their English Achievement had reflected mastery of the language. . . . No provisions were made relevant to this consideration to new immigrants and refugees. However, given a campus' objective for all students to be proficient in the English language, students not meeting this particular expectation and redirected are strongly encouraged to consider community college for their first 2 years and then transfer at the junior level. This allows for a strong dose of English instruction in an environment where teaching lower division courses is a strong part of the academic mission. (Asian American Task Force on University Admission, 1985, attachment 3)

Chan (1985a) had observed that in fact, community college transfers had little experience in writing, and remained "dismal" in English communications skills. Furthermore, the future of California's Asian American students, in the UC system and State California Universities (CSU), was also being threatened by legislative mandate that by 1990, the proportion of students classified by racial/ethnic groups in the UC and CSU systems be equal to their proportions in that year's high school graduate proportion. Asian Americans will find it increasingly difficult to gain excess to selective public institutions in California.

ACCESS TO LESS SELECTIVE INSTITUTIONS

In October 1985, United States Education Secretary William Bennett spoke before the Vietnamese Student Association of Orange County. Secretary Bennett assured his predominantly Asian audience that the Department of Education would take action against universities and colleges that assigned admissions quotas to limit Asian American students (*East/West*, October 30, 1985a). The power of the executive branch of government, however, is limited by law.

The United States Congress has deliberated exclusion of Asian American students from Title III of the Higher Education Act, which would have seriously affected Asian American access to developing institutions that could admit Asian Americans who were not eligible for admission to selective schools, such as UC Berkeley and UCLA. Legislation passed in the House subcommittee on Postsecondary Education for Reauthorization of the Higher Education Act did not include Asian American students for purposes of determining institutional minority enrollment and eligibility for Title III federal funds. Title III Programs of Institutional Aid constituted the largest source of direct, discretionary funding under the Higher Education Act. The aim of the Title III program was to help institutions that provide higher education to substantial numbers of students from low-income families develop adequate management, improve academic programs, and improve faculty quality. Title III funding eligibility was governed by a formula that gave minority enrollment twice the importance of low-income (Pell Grant recipient) enrollment. The exclusion of Asian Americans from being counted as minority would not only have served poor, immigrant Asian Americans ill, but would have also affected other minority students and public colleges and universities that served them, primarily in California and other states with large Asian populations.

California State Universities and Community Colleges

Several campuses of the California State University and California Community College system would be at a competitive disadvantage, and perhaps lose eligibility for grant aid under the Title III reservation if Asian American students were to be excluded from institutional minority enrollment counts. Hawaii and some New York state institutions could also be adversely affected. The most seriously impacted institutions would be those state and community colleges in which Asian Americans counted for a substantial proportion of the total minority enrollment. These urban schools usually have the greatest enrollment of Black and Hispanic students as well. Table 5.11 shows minority undergraduate enrollment without Asians, the Asian enrollment, and total minority enrollment in California State Universities and Community Colleges.

Federal relations staff of California State University (CSU) and California Community Colleges mobilized educational organizations and institutions to educate members of Congress and national policy makers about the current status of Asian American students, particularly poor and limited-English immigrants, in postsecondary education. Proposed language to include Asian Americans was drafted by John D. Travina, legislative attorney of the Mexican American Legal Defense and Educational Fund (MALDEF), for an amendment to Title III to be offered by Congresswoman Sala Burton during the Floor consideration of the Higher Education

TABLE 5.11

1985 Percent Minority Enrollment at California State University and California State Community Colleges Classified by Asian and Non-Asian Minorities[a]

College	Percent Minority Enrollment (excluding Asians) %	Percent Asian Enrollment %	Percent Total Minority Enrollment %
California State University:			
CSU, Los Angeles	42.4	27.1	69.5
CSU, Dominguez Hills	51.5	8.8	60.3
CSU, San Francisco	13.7	21.7	35.4
CSU, Fresno	20.4	5.2	25.6
CSU, San Jose	17.5	14.7	32.7
California Community Colleges:			
San Francisco CC District	25.4	44.9	70.3
Rancho Santiago District	30.2	12.2	42.4
Los Angeles CC District	40.3	12.4	52.7
San Jose CC District	23.6	11.3	34.9
Los Rios CC District	17.9	9.1	27.0

[a]From Friedling, Aveilhe, and Travina, 1986

Act (Friedling, Aveilhe, & Travina, 1985). The amendment was passed by Congress in November 1985. The Senate marked up the Reauthorization of the Higher Education Act during spring and summer, while resolution of all differences took the remainder of 1986.

California State University and Community College representatives, who were successful in making the changes needed to reinstate Asian Americans in institutional minority counts, pointed out to legislators that:

> In Los Angeles, San Francisco, Sacramento, and San Jose, schools with large black and Hispanic enrollments also have sizeable Asian American student bodies. Seven out of ten students at CSU, Los Angeles are Asian, black or Hispanic. These black and Hispanic students would be ill-served and their schools largely left out of Title III if their fellow Asian students are "magically" reclassified as white. . . . Asian Americans at the urban public colleges are situated similarly to blacks and Hispanics in terms of first-generation college bound status, language disabilities and income levels. . . . Excluding Asian Americans from the minority enrollment figures under Title III is harmful to those educationally needy Asian American students clustered in community and urban public colleges, the other minority students in those schools, and the developing institutions which serve their needs. (Friedling et al., 1985, p. 2)

Access to less selective institutions has not been easy for Asian American applicants, according to the 1985 national institutional survey. In addition, potential barriers do crop up, as in the case of Title III reauthorization. Being less sophisticated politically than long-term residents, Asian newcomers' interests can be protected only if and when informed and interested parties, such as MALDEF, CSU, and California Community College representatives, with the support of the established Asian American community, intervene on their behalf.

A Title III grant permits developing institutions such as CSU and Community Colleges to strengthen and coordinate academic curricula and enhance faculty resources for teaching growing numbers of immigrant students from Asia, Mexico, and Latin America. Not only do many of the newcomers require strong and innovative instruction in English and mathematics and other basic skills for full realization of their academic promise, but most also need help to pay for college.

FINANCING COLLEGE EDUCATION

Social scientists have documented that educational attainment is strongly associated with socioeconomic status. High school students from poor families planned and went to college less frequently than students from better off families. They were less likely to attend prestigious 4-year colleges even if their basic academic abilities were the same as those of their more advantaged classmates (Jencks et al., 1979). The goal of government and institutional policies has been to identify and provide access for disadvantaged students who have interest and ability for college through grants, scholarships, jobs, and/or low-interest loan programs. Pell Grants, which replaced Basic Educational Opportunity Grants (BEOG), and Supplemental Educational Opportunity Grants (SEOG) are awarded to undergraduates who need money to pay for college. National Direct Student Loans (NSDL) are low-interest loans made by colleges. Colleges also provide scholarships and College Work-Study (CWS) jobs. Guaranteed Student Loans (GSL) are made by lenders such as banks, credit unions, or savings and loan associations for graduate and undergraduate students.

Baird (1984) studied a sample, stratified by family income and SAT scores, of students who took the SAT in 1980–1981. Questionnaires were sent to test takers with complete SAT scores and SDQ information on family income variables in Winter 1981 and again in Spring 1982, asking whether they had entered college part or full time and whether they received financial aid or scholarships. Baird reported that while there was a trend for higher scoring respondents to attend 4-year and private colleges, family income had only modest influence on the type of college attended. Applicants from families of all socioeconomic levels and of different ethnic groups all obtained admission to college. Financial support came from BEOG to students from poorer families. NDSL and GSL were used to about the same extent by all respondents, and college and state scholarships more often supported students from low-income homes who also scored well on the SAT. Asian Americans were not studied as a separate group. The author concluded that the study provided support for the idea that the SAT did help to identify talent that might otherwise be missed, and American society was still trying to help disadvantaged students overcome economic obstacles to higher education.

The HS&B survey, which followed 1980 high school seniors in 1982 and 1984, included Asian Americans as a separate category. Peng (1985) reported that financial resources for Asian American college students were not better than for other students. Half of the Asian Americans used earnings and/or savings for college expenses. About a fourth received Pell grants. Asian American students were less likely than all other students to receive any types of grants. With the exception of Native Americans, Asian Americans were also less likely than others to have received any kind of loans, as shown in Table 5.12.

Asian American commitment to higher education was less likely to be influenced by immediate family financial considerations. More Asian Americans than any other group have gone on with postsecondary education, even though proportionately fewer of them received any sort of financial aid.

ENROLLMENT TRENDS, IMPLICATIONS FOR ACCESS

Higher education enrollment figures for the past decade reflected demographic changes as well as enrollment trends. Table 5.13 shows total Asian American enrollment in institutions of higher education from 1976 to 1984, classified by level of institution, ethnicity, and citizenship. Although the 1984 figures were preliminary tabulations, the 210,000 Asian and Pacific Islanders enrolled in 4-year institutions were almost double their enrollment in 1976. There were 151,000 Asian and Pacific Islanders in 2-year institutions. Proportionately, 42% of all Asian Americans were enrolled in 2-year institutions. These figures are close to the 41% of 1980 HS&B Asian American sample of high school seniors who were in 2-year programs in 1982,

TABLE 5.12

Percent of 1980 HS&B High School Seniors Attending Postsecondary Education Who Received Grants or Loans by Ethnic Group

| Ethnicity | Grants[a] | | | Loans[b] | | |
	Pell	SEOG	All Types	GSL	NDSL	All Types
Asian American	23.9	8.5	38.7	11.8	6.8	25.2
Black	41.5	10.1	54.8	9.8	11.6	28.7
Hispanic	29.5	6.8	42.3	10.8	8.0	27.1
Native American	24.4	4.9	50.6	6.0	7.1	22.8
White	22.0	5.6	41.2	13.0	10.0	30.2
All students	24.5	6.2	42.6	12.4	9.9	29.7

Note: From Peng, 1985

[a]Pell Grants are awarded to low-income undergraduates without a bachelor's degree. SEOG is a grant for undergraduates without a bachelor's degree.

[b]GSL: Guaranteed Student Loans; NDSL: National Disadvantaged Student Loans

TABLE 5.13

Trends in Total Enrollment in Institutions of Higher Education by Level of Institution and Ethnicity: Fall 1976 to Fall 1984

Ethnicity and Citizenship	Number (thousands)					% Distribution				
	76	78	80	82	84[a]	76	78	80	82	84[a]
4-year institutions	7,090	7,187	7,548	7,629	7,453	100.0	100.0	100.0	100.0	100.0
White, non-Hispanic	5,984	6,013	6,359	6,289	6,133	84.4	83.7	82.9	82.4	82.3
Total Minority	930	973	1,048	1,070	1,047	13.1	13.5	13.9	14.0	14.0
Black, non-Hispanic	603	611	633	611	577	8.5	8.5	8.4	8.0	7.7
Hispanic	173	190	216	228	224	2.4	2.6	2.9	3.0	3.0
Asian or Pacific Islander	118	137	162	193	210	1.7	1.9	2.1	2.5	2.8
American Indian/ Alaskan Native	35	35	37	38	36	.5	.5	.5	.5	.5
Non-resident alien	176	200	241	269	273	2.5	2.8	3.2	3.5	3.7
2-year institutions	3,880	4,028	4,490	4,699	4,208	100.0	100.0	100.0	100.0	100.0
White, non-Hispanic	3,077	3,167	3,532	3,657	3,288	79.3	78.6	78.7	77.8	78.1
Total Minority	761	810	894	981	873	19.6	20.1	19.9	20.9	20.7
Black, non-Hispanic	429	443	468	483	419	11.1	11.0	10.4	10.3	10.0
Hispanic	210	227	255	291	262	5.4	5.6	5.7	6.2	6.2
Asian or Pacific Islander	79	97	124	158	151	2.0	2.4	2.8	3.4	3.6
American Indian/Alaskan Native	41	43	47	59	41	1.1	1.1	1.0	1.0	1.0
Non-resident alien	42	52	64	61	49	1.1	1.3	1.4	1.3	1.2
Total	10,970	11,215	12,038	12,328	11,661	100	100	100	100	100
White	9,061	9,180	9,791	9,946	9,420	82.6	81.9	81.3	80.7	80.8
Total Minority	1,691	1,783	1,942	2,051	1,920	15.4	15.9	16.1	16.1	16.5
Black	1,032	1,054	1,101	1,094	996	9.4	9.4	9.2	8.9	8.5
Hispanic	383	417	471	519	486	3.5	3.7	3.9	4.2	4.2
Asian or Pacific Islander	197	234	286	351	361	1.8	2.1	2.4	2.8	3.1
Native American	76	78	84	87	77	.7	.7	.7	.7	.7
Non-resident alien	218	252	305	330	322	2.0	2.2	2.5	2.7	2.8

Note: From American Council on Education, 1985
[a]Bureau of the Census, unpublished preliminary tabulations, January 1986

shown in Table 5.14. In 1984, 3.6% of all students in 2-year institutions were Asian, almost double their proportion in the total United States population. The enrollment of Asian/Pacific Americans in 4-year institutions was also higher than would be expected from census figures (American Council on Education, 1985).

The total of 351,000 Asian Americans enrolled in higher education institutions in 1982 was classified by type of institution:

Doctoral level	26.0%	Comprehensive	19.8%
General Baccalaureate	4.3%	Specialized	4.4%
Two-year	45.1%	New	0.4%

An indication of the quality, or selectivity, of institutions attended was reported by Berryman (1983), who analyzed 1981 full-time first-time freshmen surveyed by the Cooperative Institutional Research Program (CIRP) of UCLA and the American Council on Education by institution type, sex, and ethnicity. Among Asian Americans, 48.0%, 38.2%, and 13.8% were enrolled in universities, 4-year and 2-year colleges respectively. Of the 48% in universities, 51% were in the most selective universities. Of those in 4-year colleges, 53% were in the most selective colleges. Altogether, 45% of Asian American first-time, full-time freshmen were in the most selective 4-year colleges and universities, compared to 22% of white freshmen. These figures were obtained in 1981, before the declining acceptance rates of Asian Americans to the most selective institutions were noticed by the affected groups, and before the increased enrollment of disadvantaged newcomers swelled the proportions of Asians in community colleges.

In 1984, more than half of the Asian Americans in higher education were in just two states, California and Hawaii. The 10 states with highest Asian American enrollments are shown in Table 5.14.

New York State, with more the 330,000 Asian Americans counted in the 1980 census, ranked third among the 50 states in Asian population. New York, like California, is an area of high Asian immigrant concentration. Table 5.15 shows the high school retention and college participation rates of various ethnic groups in New York from 1974 to 1982. Asian American high school retention and college participation rates were almost all higher than 100%. Information from national surveys have shown Asian American high school dropout rates to be below average, about 3%; and college enrollment higher than average, about 85%. The estimated ratio of high school freshmen to college freshmen 4 years later should be about 82%. However, new immigrants and older students who enroll for the first time increased the ratio. New York, particularly metropolitan New York City, has attracted many Asian immigrants, which swelled the college enrollment figures during the past decade (American Council on Education, 1984).

TABLE 5.14
States with the Highest 1984 Asian American Enrollments[a]

	N	% of total state enrollment
California	166,837	10.3%
Hawaii	31,574	68.2%
New York	28,779	2.9%
Illinois	18,918	2.9%
Texas	16,812	2.1%
Washington	10,648	4.6%
Massachusetts	8,701	2.1%
New Jersey	8,005	2.9%
Pennsylvania	7,615	1.4%
Maryland	7,360	3.1%

[a]From Racial and Ethnic Makeup of Colleges and University Enrollments, 1986

TABLE 5.15
New York State High School Retention and College Participation Rates by Ethnic Groups,
Even Years, 1974 to 1982

Year	Asian %	White %	Black %	Hispanic %	Native American %
High School Retention: Twelfth grade enrollment as a percentage of ninth graders 3 years earlier[a]					
1974	113	83	58	47	98
1976	108	83	57	51	68
1978	112	82	56	47	72
1980	101	81	49	40	57
College Participation: New full-time college students as a percentage of twelfth graders 1 year earlier[b]					
1978	100	58	58	58	196
1980	86	64	63	68	160
1982	100	62	65	72	188
New full-time college students as a percentage of ninth graders 4 years earlier[a,b]					
1978	109	48	32	27	140
1980	100	52	33	29	113
1982	107	57	30	29	112

Note: From American Council on Education, 1984
[a]High school retention levels and recent immigrants increased ratios to more than 100 for Asians.
[b]Older students entering college for the first time is believed to be a factor influencing Native American college enrollment rates.

California had 1.3 million Asian and Pacific Islanders counted in the 1980 census. In Fall 1980, 6,949 or 6.5% of California's graduate student enrollment was Asian. Among those who were enrolled in first professional degree programs, 2,310 or 7.3% were Asian. These proportions were slightly higher than the 5.5% of Asians in California (American Council on Education, 1985). The 1984 preliminary counts showed that 10.3% of all California's enrollment was Asian American (Racial and Ethnic Makeup of College and University Enrollments, 1986; U.S. Department of Commerce, Bureau of the Census, 1986).

Hawaii is the only state in which the majority of the population is Asian and Pacific Islanders. According to the 1980 census, 57.6% of Hawaii's population declared themselves to be Asian and Pacific Islanders. The six major Asian ethnic groups: Japanese, Filipino, Chinese, Korean, Vietnamese, and Asian Indian together numbered 450,000 and constituted 47% of the state's population (U.S. Department of Commerce, Bureau of the Census, 1983e). More than one fourth of the Asian and Pacific Islanders were foreign born. In 1984, 68% of Hawaii's higher education enrollment was Asian American.

Although median years of schooling of each of the six Asian American groups lagged from 6 months to 1 year behind that of white residents, younger Asian Americans were enrolled in college at higher than white rates. Only 12% of Filipino

Americans 3 years and over enrolled in school were in college, compared to 22% of white students. The proportion of college students among Japanese, Chinese, Korean, Asian Indian, and Vietnamese enrolled in school were 28%, 33%, 24%, 43%, and 25% respectively. All of these enrollment figures were probably under- estimates, because some Hawaiian students from all groups enroll in colleges and universities on the mainland. Access to higher education in Hawaii does not appear to be a problem for Asian Americans as a whole, although Filipino enrollment rates were about half that of other Asian ethnic groups.

1980 Census school enrollment figures were available by age groups. All Asian Americans in the four age classifications—18–19, 20–21, 22–24, 24–34—were more likely to remain enrolled in school than all other Americans (see Table 5.16). Filipino Americans' enrollment patterns were most like other Americans'. Chinese Americans were most unlike other Americans in that they were more than twice as likely to be in school than total United States populations at 20–21, 22–24, and 25–34 years of age (U.S. Department of Commerce, Bureau of the Census, 1983b). These adult students were unlikely to be retarded in their educational level because other data are available to show Asians are younger than other Americans when they graduate from college and apply to postgraduate institutions (Asian American Task Force on University Admissions, 1985; Smith, 1985).

CHOICE OF MAJOR FIELDS

The choice of major fields by Asian Americans has definitely influenced their chances for being admitted to selective institutions. Selective institutions are more stringent in their evaluation of academically qualified Asian Americans because there were

TABLE 5.16
Percent of 18–19, 20–21, 22–24, and 25–34 Year-Old-Asian Americans and Total
of U.S. Population Enrolled in School, 1980[a]

| | Age Group | | | |
| | 18–19 | 20–21 | 22–24 | 25–34 |
	%	%	%	%
Asian Americans:				
Japanese	77.0	61.6	38.9	14.6
Chinese	83.9	74.0	50.7	21.9
Filipino	62.7	38.3	20.2	9.6
Korean	77.7	54.8	30.5	13.2
Asian Indian	72.0	54.3	39.2	14.8
Vietnamese	66.6	47.5	37.8	22.4
Other	62.4	50.2	41.5	20.2
Total U.S.	52.3	32.4	17.3	8.8

[a]From U.S. Department of Commerce, Bureau of the Census, December 1983b

"too many Asians on (the UC Berkeley) campus" (Wang, 1985), or "We (a Princeton graduate faculty) have enough of them" (Winerip, 1985). The fields of science, mathematics, and engineering, and premedical programs have increasingly been the top choice of Asian Americans. The proclivity for these fields is particularly notable among students from immigrant families. Not only did these students demonstrate unusually well-developed quantitative reasoning abilities and mathematics achievement, but they often did not have complete mastery of English. The humanities and social sciences, which require strong verbal skills, would be difficult for them. The proportion of college-bound Asian Americans whose first language is not English will increase because one third of the Asian population in this country is under 18 years of age. The majority of Asian Americans are now newcomers who are younger and have higher fertility rates than native-born Asian Americans, whose fertility rates are lowest of all United States groups.

First Choice Intended Major Fields, College-Bound Students

The ACT assessment program and the SDQ of the College Board's ATP both ask college-bound students to specify their intended major fields of study. Table 5.17 shows the percentages of male and female 1982–1983 ACT and 1984–1985 SDQ respondents who indicated they planned to major in specific fields. Wording of the items in the two questionnaires was different. Therefore, percent distributions by fields of the two programs are not strictly comparable. Similar trends, however, can be seen.

More than half of college-bound Asian American students in both programs intended to major in health sciences, engineering or computer and information sciences. When business and commerce majors are included, 7 in 10 planned to major in these four fields. Biological sciences, art and architecture, and social sciences each accounted for about 5% or less of the intended majors. Other fields attract very small proportions of Asian Americans. The intended major fields of other ethnic

TABLE 5.17

Percent Distributions of First-Choice Fields of Study of Asian American College-Bound High School Students Who Responded to Questions for ACT Profiles, 1982–1983 and ATP Profiles 1985[a]

	Men (%)		Women (%)		Total (%)	
	ACT	ATP	ACT	ATP	ACT	ATP
Health Sciences	19	16	34	24	26	20
Engineering	32	34	10	7	22	21
Computer and Information Sciences	12	12	11	9	12	10
Business and Commerce	9	13	13	22	11	17
Social Sciences	3	4	5	5	4	4
Art and Architecture	5	4	7	6	6	5
Biological Sciences	3	4	2	5	3	5

[a]From American College Testing Program, 1983a, 1983b; Ramist and Arbeiter, 1986

TABLE 5.18
Length of Residence in Relation to Chosen Major Field Length of Residence

Length of Residence	Science (%) N = 102	Nonscience (%) N = 102	Total: N 204
Native born & reared	(40)	(60)	115
Foreign born, American reared (6 years or more)	(51)	(49)	35
Recent Immigrant (1 to 5 years)	(67)	(33)	54

Note: From Bagasao, 1983

groups were more evenly distributed (American College Testing Program, 1983a, 1983b; Arbeiter & Ramist, 1986).

HS&B Science and Nonscience Plans and Decisions

Bagasao (1983) analyzed the planned major fields of 226 HS&B Asian American seniors who planned to begin college in Fall 1980, and a random sample of 384 white college-bound seniors who met the same criteria. She described each of the ethnic groups within the Asian sample: Chinese, Filipino, Japanese, Korean, Vietnamese, and Other Asians. The limited numbers in each ethnic group dictated the use of aggregated Asian American data for most statistical analyses and comparisons with their white peers. Japanese Americans, who were somewhat overrepresented in the HS&B sample, were most like white classmates in that they were native-born Americans, from relatively affluent families, and had both high verbal and mathematics achievement test scores. Japanese and Filipino seniors (whose typical test scores were lower than Japanese Americans, and lower than other Asian groups in mathematics achievement were least likely to plan science majors among the Asian ethnic groups.

Residency history, the length of time the student has lived in the United States, was closely related to plans for major field and subsequent career plans. The shorter the time an Asian American senior student has lived in the United States, the more likely he or she was to plan a science major, particularly in applied sciences such as engineering and computer science, as shown in Table 5.18.

Being male, Chinese, Korean or Vietnamese, and recent immigrants were related to the choice of an applied science major field in college. Being native born, acculturated to American values, of high socioeconomic status, female, and Japanese were related to a pure (as opposed to applied) science or nonscience major field choice.

Actual College Major Fields, HS&B. Once in college, did students actually major in the fields they had planned as high school students? High School and Beyond (HS&B) surveyed national representative samples of high school sophomores and seniors in 1980, and followed samples of them in 1982 and 1984. Table 5.19 shows the actual college majors of the sophomore cohort who were in postsecondary

TABLE 5.19

Percent of Postsecondary Students in 1980 High School and Beyond Sophomore Cohort in Specified
Fields of Study About 2 Years after High School Graduation, by Ethnicity February 1984[a]

Field of Study	Hispanic	Native American	Asian American	Black	White
Business and Management	13.6	9.1	20.1	17.3	18.6
Business and Office	9.1	7.3	2.4	12.9	6.0
Marketing and Distribution	1.2	1.0	1.1	1.9	2.0
Communications	3.0	4.9	1.7	3.1	3.1
Computer Science	11.5	4.3	7.1	10.9	6.7
Consumer Service	3.0	2.6	.7	2.5	2.9
Education	5.6	10.8	3.4	3.8	7.7
Engineering	5.1	2.6	14.6	4.1	6.0
Engineering Tech.	4.0	2.3	2.4	3.0	2.8
Allied Health	3.6	3.3	3.0	5.4	3.7
Health Science	7.0	7.2	5.6	9.0	5.8
English	1.1	.2	2.0	.8	1.6
Liberal Studies	3.1	4.5	4.1	3.9	4.0
Life Science	1.3	1.1	8.1	2.2	2.1
Physical Science	.4	.9	4.5	1.1	1.8
Psychology	2.3	2.6	1.9	1.5	2.3
Protective Service	2.1	2.1	1.0	1.2	1.4
Social Science	2.7	.2	4.2	2.5	4.5
Mechanics	1.4	12.4	.8	.8	2.2
Precision Prod.	2.0	6.4	1.1	1.5	1.7
Visual and Performing Arts	2.2	1.2	3.1	2.3	3.5
Agriculture Related	.8	.0	.5	.3	1.7
Other Academic	5.4	3.5	4.6	4.4	4.3
Home Economic	2.2	1.2	.6	1.2	1.5
Other Vocational	3.0	1.6	.7	1.5	1.4
All Other Fields	3.4	6.7	.7	.9	.8
All Fields	100.0	100.0	100.0	100.0	100.0

[a]From Peng, 1985

institutions about 2 years after graduating from high school, by ethnic groups.
Business and Management was the most popular major across all groups with the
exception of native Americans. More native Americans were specializing in Mechanics than in Business and Management. Business and Office, Computer Science, and
Health Sciences were other fields that were ranked among the top five majors for
at least four of the five ethnic groups surveyed.

Asian Americans' five top choices in rank order were Business and Management,
Engineering, Life Science, Computer Science, and Health Science. Twenty percent
were majoring in Business and Management, and 45% in Allied Health Sciences,
Physical Science or Engineering. About 25% of Asian Americans were majoring in
engineering. They were twice as likely as white and 3 times as likely as black and
Hispanic classmates to major in engineering. The percentage of Asian American

women in Engineering, about 9%, was as high as male students of other ethnic groups. Only 2% of Asian American men and 5% of the women were majoring in education (Peng, 1985). The definition for major fields of the HS&B survey did not match those of ACT or SDQ. The base-year survey sample represented all high school sophomores in 1980, not just college-bound students. The postsecondary institutions of the followup sample included vocational/technical institutes, 2-year and 4-year institutions. Nevertheless, the distribution of major fields was quite similar to those reported by the ACT and SDQ profiles.

Increasing proportion of science, engineering, and mathematics majors among Asian newcomers also can be inferred by comparing average numbers of science and mathematics course credits recorded on college transcripts of two cohorts of Asian Americans with bachelor's degrees. Asian American college graduates who were high school seniors in 1972 earned nearly one third of their college credits in science and mathematics. Those who graduated from high school in 1980 and obtained bachelor's degrees by 1984 earned about half of their college credits in science and mathematics. Between 1970 and 1980, Asian immigrants became the majority among Asian Americans. Black, white and Hispanics in the 1980 HS&B survey also recorded higher mean numbers of credits in science and mathematics than the 1972 samples, but the differences were less dramatic. The mean numbers of postsecondary credits earned in science and mathematics was one-fourth or less of total credits for all three groups (Owings, 1987).

The perception among college admissions officers that most Asian Americans were interested primarily in engineering or pre-med programs cannot be dismissed solely as a tendency to stereotype. On the other hand, the development of creative scientists and engineers is considered a national priority. The propensity of Asian Americans to choose quantitative majors ought not constitute grounds for denial of admission if they were otherwise qualified and would have been accepted had they been from any ethnic origins other than Asian American. Newcomers, in particular, may choose quantitative fields because they lack the English necessary for making other choices.

Students choose major fields for economic reasons as well as a result of prior educational interests, career aspirations, work experiences, and the influence of parents and teachers. The HS&B data showed neither Asian Americans, nor other high school students considered guidance counselors' influence to be important to their postsecondary school plans. Relatives and friends and to a lesser degree, teachers, were considered more important to their plans (Rock et al., 1984). Research studies have shown that students' choice of undergraduate majors was significantly related to labor market values associated with various fields, and to changes in earning differentials over time for the fields, job prospects of the major, and the students' GRE scores even before they took the GRE tests (Thomas, 1984). Students from Asian immigrant and refugee families that have not had time to accumulate savings, own property, or acquire a sense of economic security would be prone to be influenced by less than perfect knowledge of labor market forces in making major field decisions.

PERSISTENCE IN COLLEGE

Asian American students' record of persistence through high school graduation continued in college. They stayed in college once they matriculated. The NCES's HS&B survey of high school seniors in 1980 followed the sample that had enrolled in 2- and 4-year colleges by June 1981. Table 5.20 shows the percent of students, classified by ethnicity, who were in the same college through February 1982 or had transferred to another college, completed a short program, or dropped out.

Asian Americans were more likely to stay the course. They were more likely than most other peer groups to have stayed in the same 4-year college. Eighty-six percent were in the same 4-year colleges and 70% in the same 2-year colleges compared to 75% and 57%, respectively, among white students. The transfer rates of Asian American and native American were about the same from 2- and 4-year colleges. Relatively fewer, just over 10%, in these two groups had transferred from 4-year colleges, and more, almost a fifth, had transferred out of 2-year colleges in comparison with the other groups surveyed. The stability of Asian American enrollment is also shown by their low withdrawal rate. A year and one-half after entering 4-year colleges, 2% of the Asian American students surveyed had withdrawn, compared to 10% of all students. Nine percent of Asian Americans who entered 2-year colleges had withdrawn or completed a short-term program, compared to the 27% and 26% withdrawal or completion rates of white and all students, respectively (Peng, 1985).

Considering the low high school dropout rate, high levels of postsecondary aspirations, high college enrollment and persistence rates, as well as the concentration in metropolitan areas of 7 out of 50 states; the number of Asian American students in selective institutions becomes more understandable. When both college

TABLE 5.20

High School and Beyond Survey's 1980 Seniors Who Entered Two- and Four-Year Colleges and Had Persisted, Transferred, Completed Short-Term Programs or Withdrawn by Ethnicity February 1982[a]

	2-Year College			4-Year College		
Ethnic Group	Persisted	Transferred	Completed/ Withdrew	Persisted	Transferred	Completed/ Withdrew
Asian American	70	21	7	86	12	2
Black	61	1	24	71	14	15
Hispanic	65	11	24	66	17	17
Native American	61	21	18	81	11	9
White	57	16	27	75	15	9
Total	59	16	26	75	15	10

[a]From Peng, 1985

enrollment and persistence rates are taken into account, half of the Asian American and a third of white 1980 high school seniors were in 4-year colleges 2 years later. The proportions in 2-year colleges were 34% and 18% for Asian American and white students respectively.

Owings (1987) described 1980 Asian American high school graduates as persisters, because they did not drop out or stop out of college once they began. Seven out of 8 Asian Americans who graduate from high school in 1980 were in some kind of postsecondary institution, 6 out of 8 full-time, for the 1980–1981 academic year. They persisted at higher rates than their black, white, and Hispanic classmates for 8 or 9 months of the year, and re-entered the same school or transferred to another school at higher rates during 1981–1982 academic year. Only 1 percent of successful Asian American persisters failed to go back in 1981–1982. Thirty-three % of Asian American 1980 high school graduates displayed normal persistence in postsecondary education, compared to 20%, 13% and 10% among their white, black, and Hispanic classmates. Among Asian Americans who completed bachelor's degrees by 1984, half of the credits were earned in fields classified as science and mathematics.

ACCESS TO POSTGRADUATE AND PROFESSIONAL SCHOOLS

In Fall 1980, graduate school enrollment of Asian Americans was more than 23,000 or 2.3% of the total United States enrollment. First professional degree enrollment of Asian Americans was about 6,000, or 2.2% of total United States enrollment (American Council on Education, 1985). Asian Americans were 1.5% of total United States population.

Graduate and professional faculties have finite resources and restrict student enrollment. Between 1972 and 1980, during a period when Asian American population was doubling, aspirations for higher education was also increasing. Asian Americans were the only ethnic group whose mean expected level of higher education rose significantly, according to cross-sectional analysis of the 1972 NLS and 1980 HS&B high school senior cohorts (Rock et al., 1984). Since 1980, the intention to pursue a doctoral or other professional degree has continued to rise among Asian American college-bound women who responded to the SDQ. In 1980, 24% expected to obtain doctorate or equivalent. By 1985, the figure had risen to 29%. The percentage of Asian American college-bound men with the same degree goals has hovered around 33%. The tendency of Asian Americans to cluster in a few disciplines, and to seek advanced degrees, has led to stringent selection and admission criteria for them in fields that have more applicants, Asian and non-Asian, than there were places.

A comparison of Asian Americans in graduate schools, law schools, and medical schools demonstrates the differential impact of variations in abilities, achievement, demand, and access.

Graduate Schools

Graduate facilities admit students and award financial aid primarily on the basis of academic criteria and promise of future scholarly and research productivity. Increasingly, teaching assistantships are requiring demonstration of fluent spoken English as well. In 1983–1984, 2,982 United States citizens, Asian Americans, 2.2% of the test-taking population, took the Graduate Record Examinations (GRE) as a part of the graduate school application process. Four years earlier, Asian Americans had constituted 3.2% of the 1979–1980 SAT test takers. Almost 90% of all Asian American high school graduates did go on to postsecondary education. College persistence data are available to discount the possibility of a high college dropout rate. The relatively smaller proportion of Asian Americans who took the GRE in 1983–1984 suggests that graduate school as an option was not being selected by this group as frequently as other postcollege plans. The majority of ethnic Asians who registered for GRE have been nonresident and resident aliens.

Asian Americans, who are United States citizens and who took the GRE in 1983–1984 were typically younger than all test takers by about 1 1/2 years. They graduated more recently from college. They came from families with parents who were considerably better educated than all other ethnic groups. Their average family income was close to whites' and total average family incomes. Two-thirds of them came from metropolitan areas, and more than a half were from the West. Seventeen percent reported English was not their best language, compared to 27% of SAT test-takers in the same year. About 41% planned a Ph.D. or beyond, compared to 37% of all GRE test takers.

When planned graduate major fields were taken into account, distribution of Asian American students was not even across fields. Asian Americans were 2% or less of all GRE test takers in 8 of 11 graduate major fields. In these fields, Asian Americans would not be viewed by others as being overrepresented. Asian Americans were more than population expectations in three fields: Biological Sciences, Mathematical Sciences, and Engineering, in which they were 2.7%, 4.3%, and 6.5% of all GRE test takers, respectively (Smith, 1985).

Table 5.21 shows the GRE scores of Asian American, white, and total GRE test takers in these fields. Asian Americans who planned graduate majors in Biological Sciences had average GRE scores that were competitive with white and total mean GRE scores. The mean GRE quantitative scores of Asian Americans who planned graduate majors in Mathematical Sciences or Engineering were as high as or higher than typical scores of white and all graduate school applicants. GRE verbal and analytical scores of Asian Americans were lower than white test takers'. Competition for places in highly selective graduate faculties of Mathematical Sciences or Engineering would come not only from white peers but also from resident and nonresident alien Asian applicants. Average GRE quantitative scores of alien Asian test takers have been consistently higher than scores of all American groups, although their GRE verbal and analytical scores were lower (Wilson, 1984).

Centra (1979) analyzed graduate degree aspirations of GRE test takers by test score levels. Among Asian Americans, GRE verbal scores and undergraduate GPAs

TABLE 5.21

GRE Scores of Asian American (AA), White (W), and Total (T) Test-Takers 1983–1984 by Planned Graduate Major Fields[a]

Graduate Major	GRE Verbal			GRE Quantitative			GRE Analytical		
	AA	W	T	AA	W	T	AA	W	T
Biological Science									
Mean	518	533	522	622	586	575	569	584	570
SD	118	99	106	97	101	109	118	107	116
Mathematical Science									
Mean	471	551	537	658	666	653	554	632	615
SD	135	111	121	97	92	105	129	108	121
Engineering									
Mean	473	533	523	680	682	674	561	623	610
SD	120	98	104	84	78	86	126	103	111

[a]From Smith, 1985

were the only variables that significantly predicted degree plans. GRE quantitative scores may have been restricted to higher score ranges, and therefore, limited as predictors. The higher the GRE verbal score and undergraduate grades, the more likely they were to plan a Ph.D. degree. Even in the natural sciences, where GRE quantitative scores carried the greatest weight in predicting graduate degree plans, GPAs and GRE verbal scores were significant predictors. Declining GRE verbal scores among all test takers have been cause for considerable concern (Adelman, 1984). Strong writing ability has been reported to be very important during graduate training, but even more important to success in careers after degree award (Bridgeman & Carlson, 1983). Graduate school applicants chose graduate major fields with awareness of their own developed verbal and other abilities. Examination of Fig. 3.6 shows similarity of Asian and white GRE test takers by fields. Degree attainment data, presented in the next chapter, supports the observation that Asian Americans have not experienced significant difficulties in obtaining access to graduate studies, even in the Engineering, Mathematics, and Science fields where they tended to cluster. Separate data on Asian American graduate enrollments were not available before 1976–1977. The number of Asian Americans in graduate schools has increased modestly (under 100) each year between 1977 and 1981 (American Council on Education, 1985).

Financial Support for Graduate Studies

Admission to graduate faculties without concomitant financial support is tantamount to rejection for many applicants. The 1981 data on doctorate recipients showed that proportionately more Asian Americans, including United States citizens and permanent residents, received financial support from universities than all other groups in all fields of doctoral studies as shown in Table 5.22. They were less likely than other groups to obtain support from the federal government or national fellowships. Only 20% of Asian American doctorate recipients supported themselves primarily and 1.1% borrowed money for their doctoral degrees (Syverson, 1982).

Without "overrepresentation," Asian Americans have not apparently encountered institutional barriers in access to or financing postgraduate education.

Law Schools

In 1983, there were 173 American Bar Association (ABA) approved law schools that conferred the J.D., the first degree in law. These ABA-approved schools enrolled about 41,000 first-year students and had a total enrollment of over 127,000 (American Bar Association, 1984). Law school admissions committees rely heavily but not exclusively on an admission index based on an applicant's grades and LSAT

TABLE 5.22
Primary Sources of Support of 1979–1981 Doctorate Recipients by Ethnicity and Field[a]

Support Source	Total (All Fields) %	Physical Sciences %	Engineering & Computer Science %	Biology & Medical Science %	Psychology %	Social Sciences %	Humanities %	Education %
University								
Asian American	62.6	83.3	74.8	55.1	38.4	52.4	54.8	21.7
Black	24.2	57.0	41.8	31.8	28.3	37.9	36.1	14.8
Hispanic	36.0	67.2	55.7	55.1	27.3	34.5	46.7	15.5
Native American	29.5	69.2	33.3	38.7	22.9	39.3	48.7	12.9
White	41.5	74.2	55.6	44.8	31.8	44.2	47.6	18.4
Self								
Asian American	19.9	5.1	12.3	14.2	31.3	33.8	33.8	56.7
Black	45.5	9.0	12.7	20.8	28.3	28.6	29.3	62.7
Hispanic	34.7	8.6	19.7	15.9	34.0	24.8	36.7	51.6
Native American	47.7	15.4	33.3	29.0	42.9	39.3	38.5	64.0
White	37.7	11.1	19.3	16.6	40.8	33.9	38.4	67.6
Primary Source Reported	N	N	N	N	N	N	N	N
Asian American	2,823	564	803	514	112	231	157	254
Black	2,858	100	55	154	290	269	280	1,532
Hispanic	1,365	116	61	107	150	145	289	426
Native American	325	26	12	31	35	28	39	139
White	62,992	7,683	3,693	9,207	7,442	6,184	8,598	15,609

[a]From Syverson, 1982

scores (Willingham & Breland, 1977). The ABA requires law schools to demonstrate "full opportunities for the study of law" to members of minority groups as a condition for accreditation (Greenhouse, 1980, p. 13). Law school admissions decisions are guided by two key considerations: predicted first-year grades based on the admissions index, and ethnicity (Klitgaard, 1985). Asian Americans have benefitted from affirmative action programs of ABA-approved law schools.

As a group, Asian Americans have not demonstrated developed verbal reasoning abilities of the same level as they have other cognitive dimensions, such as quantitative reasoning and spatial relations. The law is a profession that requires verbal skills and fluency in English. Recent Asian immigrants would encounter difficulties if they studied law, unless they had already mastered the English language.

The law is a highly regarded profession in the Philippines. Most Filipino Americans, unlike other Asian linguistic groups, consider their best language to be English. Also unlike other Asian Americans, Filipino Americans are no better in quantitative reasoning tasks than other Americans. Chan (1985c, 1985d) has postulated that Filipino Americans would be more likely than other Asians to study law. No data are available on Asian subgroups, but data on Asian or Pacific Islander American enrollment in ABA-approved law scores have been collected since 1971. Until 1972–1973, Asian American law school enrollment was less than 1% of the law student population. There has been a steady increase in Asian American law school enrollment since 1973–1974. The total number of first-year students has doubled in a decade from 327 to 711. Their proportion in the first-year law student population, however, has decreased from 2% in 1973 to 1.5% between 1975–1976 and 1983–1984, as shown in Fig. 5.4. Their proportion in the total law school enrollment has been consistently lower than first-year figures, probably due to fewer part-time students who inflate total enrollment figures (American Bar Association, 1984).

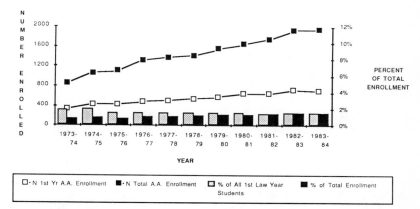

FIG. 5.4 Asian American first year and total enrollment in ABA-approved law schools (from American Bar Association, 1984).

Evidence from test data shows consistently that economically disadvantaged and/ or recent immigrant Asian American test takers do particularly poorly on verbal items. The University of California at Berkeley's Asian American Law Student Association (1978) reported that for Asian students at Boalt Hall, the length of time to attain a bachelor's degree predicted law school performance better than the LSAT in 1976. Particularly for economically disadvantaged Asian Americans, access to law school may still be difficult, due to their limited English proficiency, prior educational experiences, and low LSAT scores. This was the argument set forth by the Boalt Hall Asian American Law Students' Association in favor of a targeted affirmative action program for recent immigrants and low-income Asian Americans. Table 5.23 shows that most Asian American law school applicants in 1978–1979

TABLE 5.23

Law School Data Assembly Service (LSDAS) Asian American Application and Acceptance Data, 1978–79 Number of Candidates and Estimated Number of Candidates Who Were Offered Admission to at Least One LSDAS-ABA Law School

Undergraduate GPA	Average Law School Admission Test Score											
	Below 300	300 349	350 399	400 449	450 499	500 549	550 599	600 649	650 699	700 749	750 and over	TOTAL
Above	0	0	0	1	1	11	15	10	12	13	1	64[a]
3.74	0	0	1	1	1	11	16	11	13	13	1	68
3.74-	0	0	0	4	10	31	29	25	27	9	2	137
3.50	0	1	1	7	10	31	31	25	30	9	2	147
3.49-	0	0	0	5	24	27	26	28	27	12	2	151
3.25	1	0	1	9	29	34	37	30	28	13	2	184
3.24-	0	0	2	9	15	29	28	32	17	0	1	133
3.00	0	0	8	18	23	34	33	34	17	3	1	171
2.99-	0	0	1	3	15	27	15	9	2	3	0	75
2.75	0	4	7	17	24	32	16	11	2	3	0	116
2.74-	0	0	1	5	5	10	17	11	3	0	0	52
2.50	1	4	8	15	17	12	21	12	3	0	0	93
2.49-	0	0	1	3	2	7	5	4	2	0	1	25
2.25	3	5	5	10	6	9	12	4	2	0	1	57
2.24-	0	0	0	0	3	1	0	0	0	0	0	24
2.00	0	5	1	3	9	4	0	0	0	0	0	22
Below	0	0	0	0	0	1	0	0	0	0	0	1
2.00	0	0	0	1	0	1	1	0	0	0	0	3
TOTAL	0	0	5	30	75	144	135	119	90	37	7	642
	5	19	32	81	119	168	167	127	95	41	7	861

Note: From Law School Data Assembly Service, 1975–1979

[a]The top number in each cell is an estimate of the number of offers of admission. The bottom number in each cell is the number of candidates.

were likely to be admitted to at least one Law School Data Assembly Service, LSDAS-ABA law school. Acceptance rates of Asian Americans and other minorities were higher than for white applicants during a period of increasing competition for law school seats. The impetus for increasing minority enrollments came from a consideration of the numbers of minority lawyers in comparison with the total number of lawyers in the United States (Willingham & Breland, 1977).

As in the case of graduate schools, Asian American access to ABA-approved law schools has been facilitated by both ABA and law school admissions policies. The proportions of first-year Asian American law students in ABA approved law schools remained slightly lower than general population figures. Total law school enrollment had reached a plateau of 127,000 by 1981 and was beginning to decline. Given these conditions, it is not likely that access to law schools will become difficult for qualified Asian Americans in the near future.

Medical Schools

Admission to medical school is highly competitive, in academic terms as well as with respect to "personal qualities." Most medical schools have also aggressively pursued affirmative action to recruit and admit underrepresented minorities. Studies have shown that the most powerful predictors of being admitted were grades in science courses and scores on the science portion of the Medical College Admission Test (MCAT). However, medical school admissions committees want to select not only applicants who are most likely to become good physicians: clinicians, teachers, or researchers, but also promising individuals for serving societal needs for health-care delivery (Schmidt, 1986). Letters of recommendation and essays are solicited. Interviews remain the preferred means for assessing personal characteristics, despite a body of research that challenges the reliability and validity of personal interviews (Klitgaard, 1985; Willingham, 1985; Willingham & Breland, 1977).

Medicine has traditionally been an honored profession in Asia. The study of medicine continues to be held in high esteem by Asians who immigrate to the West. Since the mid-1970s, Asian American applications to United States medical schools have doubled, keeping pace with the Asian American population growth rate. Total medical school application has declined during this period. The number of Asian Americans offered acceptances has more than doubled between 1978 and 1984, when 1,203 Asian Americans were offered acceptances (Randlett, 1982, 1984). Nevertheless, the Asian American acceptance rates during this period have consistently remained below those of all applicants and of white applicants, as shown in Table 5.24. In 1978, Asian American acceptance rate was 36%, compared to 47% and 45% for white and total acceptance rates respectively. By 1984, Asian American acceptance rate had risen to 43%. White and total acceptance rates were 49% and 47%, respectively (Association of American Medical Colleges, Division of Student Services, 1974–1985).

TABLE 5.24
U.S. Medical School Applicant Pool and Accepted Applicants for Asian American, White, and All
Applicants Entering Classes 1978 to 1984[a]

	1978	1979	1980	1981	1982	1983	1984
Total Applicants	36,636	36,137	36,100	36,727	35,730	35,200	35,944
N Accepted	16,527	16,880	17,146	17,286	17,294	17,209	17,194
% Accepted	45.1	46.7	47.5	47.1	48.4	48.9	47.1
Asian American/ Pacific Islander Applicants	1,520	1,660	1,774	1,976	2,222	2,325	2,775
N Accepted	546	636	720	824	973	1,020	1,203
% Accepted	35.9	38.3	40.6	41.7	43.8	43.9	43.4
White Applicants	29,709	29,333	28,645	28,998	27,816	27,474	27,826
N Accepted	13,963	14,160	14,025	14,030	13,941	13,828	13,723
% Accepted	47.0	48.3	49.0	48.4	50.1	50.3	49.3

[a]From Association of American Medical Colleges, 1982, 1984; Randlett, 1982, 1984

Asian Americans are a visible minority in medical schools. In academic year 1979–1980, they constituted 3% of first year and 2.8% of total medical school enrollment. By 1984–1985, Asian Americans were 6.6% of first year and 5.6% of total medical school enrollment. Aggregated underrepresented minority students were 9.8% of first year and 8.5% of total enrollment as shown in Table 5.25 (American Medical College Application Service, 1979–1984).

Asian Americans were and are not underrepresented in medical schools. Nor are they targets of affirmative action programs. A legitimate question, however, is whether medical school admissions policies and processes have been fair to Asian American applicants, given their lower acceptance rates. There is evidence that higher than average proportions of some minority students have repeated a year or more of medical school or failed the National Board of Medical Examiners (NBME) tests (Association of American Medical Colleges, 1985; Klitgaard, 1985). Asian American repeat statistics available from 1977–1978 to 1983–1984, have been close to majority (white, non-Hispanic) figures, varying by no more than a fraction of a percent in either direction.

The Medical College Admission Test (MCAT) scores, undergraduate grades, undergraduate college selectivity, medical school grades, and other variables have been used to predict scores on two parts of the NBME, which is used by many medical schools to certify their students (Rolph, Williams, & Lanier, 1978). Other variables being constant, a 100-point increase on the discontinued MCAT scale for each of the four parts of MCAT was estimated to correspond to about 60–79 points, or two-thirds of a standard deviation gain on NBME. A 1-point increase in GPA

TABLE 5.25

First Year and Total U.S. Medical School Enrollments of U.S. Citizens by Ethnic Groups from 1979–1980 to 1984–1985

| Years | 1979–80 | | 1980–81 | | 1981–82 | | 1982–83[b] | | 1983–84 | | 1984–85 | |
Ethnic Group	N	%	N	%	N	%	N	%	N	%	N	%
					First Year Enrollment[a]							
Asian Americans	502	3.0	572	3.3	765	4.4	936	5.4	983	5.7	1,124	6.6
Underrepresented minorities	1,961	11.6	1,548	9.0	1,671	9.7	1,626	9.4	1,658	9.7	1,672	9.8
White	14,259	84.2	14,262	83.0	14,218	82.4	14,085	81.6	13,909	81.1	13,606	80.0
					Total Enrollments							
Asian Americans	1,777	2.8	1,924	3.0	2,518	3.8	2,936	4.4	3,290	4.9	3,763	5.6
Underrepresented minorities	6,351	9.9	5,209	8.0	5,503	8.3	5,544	8.3	5,600	8.3	5,707	8.5
White	54,853	86.0	55,434	85.0	56,201	84.8	56,032	83.9	56,167	83.4	55,232	82.4

Note: From Association of American Medical Colleges, 1978–1979, 1984–85

[a]First year enrollment includes new entrants and those repeating first year

[b]In 1983 the definition of U.S. citizens expanded to include permanent residents

corresponded to a gain of 32 to 35 points on both parts of NBME. MCAT scores and college grades were shown to be good predictors of success in medical school.

Asian American 1981 mean MCAT scores in comparison with white and total mean scores were shown in Table 3.14 in chapter 3. Asian American applicants' average scores were consistently lower than whites' and total means in only one of the six assessment areas—Skills Analysis: Reading. In Biology and Skills Analysis: Quantitative, Asian American means were higher than total means and lower than white means. In Chemistry, Physics, and Science Problems, Asian Americans were higher than white and total means. The increased Asian American applicant pool has not been due to growing numbers of marginal applicants. The 1984 mean total and science scores and undergraduate GPAs were higher than the 1981 scores for all applicant groups, as shown in Table 5.26. In 1984–1985, Asian American applicants were academically competitive with white applicants, but were less likely to be accepted. Because nonacademic, subjective judgments enter into admissions decisions in situations where many applicants are qualified academically, Asian Americans were more likely to have been rejected on nonacademic grounds. At the same time, less qualified white and underrepresented minority applicants were being accepted on personal qualities, with relatively less weighting on academic qualifications.

Did medical school admissions committees, deliberately or unconsciously, employ more stringent criteria on Asian American applicants? The 1984–1985 acceptance data showed that Asian American female applicants' acceptance ratio, 42.8%, was lower than white females' 48%. Asian American males' accepted ratio of 43.6% was also lower than white males' 50%. Table 5.27 shows the differences in academic criteria between Asian and white applicants and accepted students by sex. The figures suggest that Asian American female applicants may have been perceived slightly more favorably than males by medical school admissions committees. They were accepted with slightly lower mean academic credentials than white females. Accepted Asian American males' academic credentials, on the other hand, were equal to or better than white accepted males' in eight out of nine areas. Aggregated data on quality of undergraduate school were not available. It is possible, but not likely, that Asian American and white men and women applicants differed in undergraduate institutions. It is also possible that Asian women applicants presented themselves better than Asian men in medical admissions interviews. However, favorable stereotyping of Asian females is a plausible rival hypothesis. It is a psychological phenomenon that has been observed in the past. Asian American male applicants outnumbered female applicants by 1.75 to 1. White male to female applicant ratio was 2 to 1—so the relative proportion of males to females was not a crucial factor. Unlike the most selective colleges, medical schools do not add many points to admissions evaluations of athletes', musicians', or alumni legacy folders. A pervasive practice, if not a deliberate policy to rate Asian Americans, particularly the males, more stringently on nonacademic grounds remains a tenable explanation for the observed lower overall Asian American medical school acceptance rates.

TABLE 5.26

Average MCAT Area Scores and GPAs of Asian American, White, Underrepresented Minorities, and Total American Medical School Applicants Offered Acceptances Classified by Sex and Ethnicity, 1984

	Asian American		White		Underrepresented[a] Minorities	Total	
	F	M	F	M	F + M	F	M
N	431	771	4,395	9,328	1,533	5,731	11,463
%	2.5	4.5	25.6	54.3	8.9	33.3	66.6
Area Scores							
Biology							
Mean	10.0	10.6	10.1	10.4	8.2	9.7	10.2
S.D.	1.7	1.7	1.6	1.7	2.0	1.9	1.8
Chemistry							
Mean	10.2	11.0	9.6	10.3	7.6	9.3	10.1
S.D.	1.9	1.8	1.8	1.8	2.0	2.0	2.0
Physics							
Mean	10.2	11.3	9.5	10.6	7.5	9.2	10.4
S.D.	2.0	1.9	1.9	2.0	2.1	2.1	2.2
Science Problems							
Mean	10.0	10.9	9.6	10.4	7.5	9.3	10.2
S.D.	1.9	2.0	1.8	1.9	2.0	2.0	2.1
Skills Analysis Reading							
Mean	8.8	8.7	9.6	9.3	7.3	9.2	9.0
S.D.	2.0	2.1	1.5	1.6	2.1	1.9	1.8
Skills Analysis Quantitative							
Mean	8.8	9.6	8.9	9.6	6.5	8.5	9.3
S.D.	2.0	2.0	1.9	1.9	2.0	2.1	2.1
BCPM GPA[b]							
Mean	3.47	3.53	3.50	3.49	2.92	3.42	3.44
S.D.	0.35	0.34	0.33	0.35	0.52	0.41	0.40
Total GPA							
Mean	3.52	3.56	3.55	3.52	3.06	3.49	3.48
S.D.	0.29	0.29	0.27	0.31	0.42	0.34	0.34

Note: From Association of American Medical Colleges, 1984

[a]Not available by sex

[b]Biology, Chemistry, Physics, Mathematics Undergraduate Grade Point Average

TABLE 5.27

Differences in Acceptance Rate and Average Academic Qualifications in Standard Deviation Units between Asian American and White Medical School Applicants and Acceptance Offers by Sex 1984–1985 Entering Class[a]

| | AA Applicants | | AA Acceptance Offered | |
	Female	Male	Female	Male
Biology	−.13	0	−.06	+.12
Chemistry	+.22	+.26	+.32	+.39
Physics	+.26	+.35	+.36	+.29
Science Problems	+.09	+.12	+.21	+.25
Skills Analysis: Reading	−.64	−.33	−.47	−.39
Skills Analysis: Quantitative	−.18	−.09	−.05	0
BCPM GPA	−.16	+.06	−.09	+.11
AU GPA	−.15	0	−.03	+.06
Total GPA	−.19	+.03	−.07	+.13
N (acceptance rate) AA:	1,006	1,769	431 (42.8%)	772 (43.6%)
White:	9,158	18,668	4,395 (48.0%)	9,328 (50.0%)

[a]From American Medical College Application Service, 1984

The significant percentages of Asian American students accepted for each recent medical school entering class, despite lower acceptance rates than white applicants, suggests a liberalizing of earlier policies that might have limited proportions of some minority students in accordance with their numbers in the total population pool. Data from the 1975–1976 entering class reported by Willingham and Breland (1977) suggested that Asian and Cuban American medical school applicants were treated differently in terms of academic credentials, but shared the lowest acceptance ratio, 31.7%, of all applicant groups. At that time, Asian Americans were 2.8% of the applicant pool, and 2.5% of the accepted students. Cubans were 0.48% of the applicants and 0.39% of accepted medical students. Examination of academic credentials of accepted groups showed that accepted Asian American mean MCAT scores were slightly lower in two areas, and higher in two areas than accepted white scores. Their undergraduate GPAs were the same as accepted white GPAs. Accepted Cuban mean MCAT scores and GPAs were lower than white and Asian accepted students', but higher than all other Hispanic groups, each of which had higher acceptance rates. Data are no longer kept separately for Cubans, who are now grouped with Other Hispanics in Association of American Medical Colleges statistics. But in the mid-1970s, and continuing in mid-1980s, acceptance rates appear to have been based not only upon academic credentials, but also on personal qualities, including ethnicity.

A 1985 announcement by Johns Hopkins Medical College to abandon the requirement of MCAT scores in the application process may mean greater academic and non-academic hurdles for future Asian American applicants. The policy was described by administrators as an effort to "combat the pre-med syndrome" by "wanting applicants with a broad general education," (Anderson, 1985; Biemiller, 1985b; Schmidt, 1986). The pre-med syndrome was described as taking too many sciences, avoiding extracurricular activities and shortchanging themselves during the undergraduate years. For many Asian Americans, particularly newcomers whose mother tongue is not English, adoption of the Hopkins policy by other medical schools may lead to additional barriers to access and lower admission rates in the short run. In the long run, however, increased attention to a liberal undergraduate education and communications skills may prove rewarding to Asian American careers.

For extremely well qualified high school seniors committed to medicine, there are accelerated honors programs in medical education. Such programs generally accept a limited number of outstanding students straight from high school, and aware them both B.S. and M.D. degrees within 6 or 7 years. Several honors programs in medical education are beginning to enroll high proportions of Asian Americans. University of Miami reported that 60% of the fall, 1986, first-year students in the accelerated program were Asian Americans. The proportion at Boston University was 30%. Northwestern's Honors Program in Medical Education reported that 50% of its second-year, and 63% of first-year students were Asian American. At Northwestern Medical School, Asian Americans were 19% of the total enrollment in 1986–1987.

The number of Asian American applicants has been increasing steadily since the early 1980s. Dean Harry W. Linde of Northwestern's Honors Program noted that most of the students were foreign-born, and United States reared. They were of Chinese, Korean, Asian Indian, and other Asian heritage: and usually came from families in which one or both parents were professionals. Honors students are an outstanding group, in terms of persoanl qualities as well as academic credentials. Criteria for admission include not only a demonstrated record of high performance and interest in facing tough academic challenges, but also evidence of leadership, ability to write and speak well, strong recommendations, and follow-through in extracurricular activities. The extracurricular activities of the Asian American honors students ranged from professional caliber performing arts and Olympic level athletics to developing voluntary health-care programs for local Asian communities (Soo Hoo, 1986–1987).

The rising proportions of Asian Americans in some medical honors programs show clearly that Asian American applicants, particularly those from professional immigrant families, constitute an exceptionally strong group of candidates. The Asian American applicant pool for both accelerated and regular medical education programs manifest considerable breadth of interests as well as depth in academic abilities and achievement. Strictly merit-based selection and admission policies and practices on the part of a few programs, while the majority of institutions opt for a "balanced" entering class, could result in high proportions of Asian American matriculants in the few programs that adhere strictly to merit principles.

CONCLUSIONS AND DISCUSSION

Asian Americans, even recent immigrants, have been applying for college in unprecedented numbers. The most up-to-date population projections predict continuing growth and increased diversity of Asian American college-age youth. It is not only demographics that influence college attendance figures. Low dropout rates among Asian American high school students, high proportions that plan postsecondary education, high college retention and completion rates, traditional Asian proclivity for scholarly and healing pursuits, and current United States immigration policy's preferential categories for skilled workers and professionals have all contributed to Asian American staying power along the higher education pipeline.

Not only do Asian Americans want higher education, they are willing to make sacrifices to obtain the very best. It is this demand for quality that has put pressure on admissions offices of the most selective institutions. Many have admitted 3 to 5 times the number of Asian Americans that would have been expected from 2 percent of the total population. Nevertheless, Asian American acceptance rates remain lower than all other groups.

Neither national enrollment statistics, nor overall state figures from California, Hawaii, and New York suggest there have been systematic barriers placed in the way of Asian Americans who planned higher education. However, many Asian American applicants will be disappointed by being turned down by their top choice institutions more frequently than their peers. Students who hoped for a 4-year college may have to settle for a 2-year institution instead. Highly academically talented students, who aspire to one of the most selective public or private colleges, may have to attend a second choice, not quite so highly selective institution. In California, the gateway for Asian immigrants, future Asian American applicants may experience greater difficulty in gaining admission to selective public institutions, which are adopting the flexible, personal admissions practices of selective private institutions.

There is evidence that English-proficient Asian American students are more likely to be rejected by the most selective institutions on nonacademic, personal grounds, or on the basis of planned major fields rather than on inadequate grades, high school rank or test scores. Asian immigrants, particularly those with limited English proficiency, will be more likely to be turned down on the basis of their inability to communicate, and because too many wanted to enroll in engineering or physical science programs. Competition for finite resources, laboratory space and equipment or financial aid, has been cited by some university faculty and admission officers as a deterrent to Asian American applicants. University administrators and policy makers in general, however, did not always agree with their staff on the resource issue.

Asian Americans have expressed skepticism about the validity of academic and nonacademic criteria used by institutions to evaluate applicants. Information presented in earlier chapters confirmed the validity of grades, rank in class and test scores for predicting academic success in college. However, low verbal scores alone have not prevented recent immigrants from doing well in fields that required quantitative skills and above average performance in high school or in college. There is evidence to support policies that consider nonacademic, personal qualities of applicants along with academic predictors for optimal selection of applicants who will succeed in the broadest sense in college. Reliance on ascriptive personal qualities for admissions decisions may be a deterrent for some academically qualified Asian American applicants.

There is very little evidence for supporting the existence of widespread, collusive, or systematic exclusionary admissions policies. However, the aggregated result of a series of independent decisions by the most selective institutions has been inequity in standards being used to judge one particular group of academically qualified and highly motivated Americans. Furthermore, the burden of exclusion has been borne disparately by disadvantaged immigrants.

Asian Americans being denied admission to the most prestigious colleges and medical schools each year are a mere handful compared to their total enrollment in higher education. But there is more at issue than equality of access. Other pernicious problems may surface in these institutions if current admissions policies are continued over time by:

1. Perpetuating the Super Asian myth. If prestigious institutions use more strict criteria in selection and admission of Asian Americans, particularly when classes also include academically able and motivated self- or government-selected Asian foreign students. More students may conclude: "some students say if they see too many Asians in a class, they are not going to take it because the (grading) curve will be too high." The statement above was made by 1985 UC Berkeley student body president, Pedro Noguera (Mathews, 1985).

2. Exacerbating divisiveness among ethnic groups. When greater than average selectivity is being exercised in admitting one visible group such as Asian Americans, those admitted would very likely perform academically or even all around at higher than average levels. Resentment could build up among all other groups. The atypically high performances, due to extreme selectivity rather than typical distribution of talents even at the right tail, would alienate Asian Americans from each other and from their majority and minority classmates.

3. Discouraging qualified and motivated Asian Americans denied access to first-choice institutions. Asian Americans are the only group being taken out of consideration for admissions to the most selective institutions because there were too many who were pre-med, engineering, or science/mathematics oriented. There are programs to recruit and encourage all other American youth to enter these fields. Evidence in later chapters will show that most Asian American science and engineering academicians and researchers come from the ranks of immigrants rather than the native-born. The drive for excellence, particularly notable among immigrant youth, may be blunted or deflected if they must settle for second best. The loss

will be not only to the individuals, but will be felt by a nation that is striving to keep its ever narrowing edge in science and technology.

Aside from the most selective institutions, Asian Americans apply to and are being admitted to 2- and 4-year undergraduate institutions, graduate, and professional schools in unprecedented numbers. The numbers do not suggest any overall barriers to access. In the humanities and law, fields that require strong English communications skills, Asian Americans have been counted as underrepresented minorities and sometimes admitted under affirmative action programs with lower than average academic credentials. Enrollment and applications to professional schools are declining, but not among Asian Americans (Maeroff, 1985). As qualified but visible minorities, Asian Americans will continue to be regarded as being overrepresented by some selective colleges and professional schools.

In conclusion, the stringent admissions criteria for Asian American applicants observed among some of the most selective colleges, universities, and professional schools, have developed within the last decade as institutional responses to pressure from the right tail of the Asian American, postsecondary student distribution. Asian American competition has not diminished the acceptance of underrepresented minority groups. The latter are treated as separate pools. Nor have white applicants who are athletes, alumni offspring, or have other special talents or connections been seriously affected. The competition seems to be limited to within Asian groups, citizens, permanent residents, and nonresident aliens, with recent immigrants being at considerable disadvantage; and between Asian Americans and White applicants who could present no special talents or social connections.

Most selective institutions have experienced similar pressure for admission from new groups in the past: by southern- and middle-European immigrants, Catholics, Jews, other minorities and by women (Hechinger, 1987; Kempner, 1985; Oren, 1985). Institutional memories or archives could provide policies and practices found to have been successful in the past. There are historic precedents appropriate for dealing with the wave of qualified Asian American applicants in rational, fair, and culturally sensitive ways without undue ire from coaches, alumni, academic senates, or administrators, most of whom may be white and establishment, but must also be dedicated to maintaining institutional stability, balance, and excellence.

There are, in addition, actions that can be considered by Asian Americans as individuals, as groups with common interests and goals, and in coalition with other groups, majority and minority, to serve not only the educational interests of Asian Americans, but a shared belief in institutional policies dedicated to excellence and equality.

6

Achievement in Higher Education

More Asian Americans each year since the late 1970s have been enrolling in higher education institutions than would be expected from population counts, as was shown in Tables 5.13 and 5.16 of chapter 5. The growth in proportions as well as numbers of Asian Americans at each level of postsecondary education indicated that students from immigrant families that arrived after 1968, and from refugee groups after 1975, demonstrated as great as or greater propensity for higher education than native-born, third-, or fourth-generation Asian Americans.

In 1980, when Asian and Pacific Islanders were 1.6% of the total United States population, Asian and Pacific Islander higher education enrollment was 2.4%. The 1980 census reported that Pacific Islanders represented about 7% of the Asian and Pacific Islander population. Pacific Islanders (Hawaiian, Guamanian, and Samoan), who enrolled in large numbers in institutions located in Hawaii and Guam, had lower overall college attendance rates than white and Asian ethnic groups (U.S. Department of Commerce, Bureau of the Census, 1983b, 1983f). Aggregated statistics of Asian and Pacific Islander higher education enrollments and degree awards, excluding data from Guam, are presented here as Asian American with the understanding that a fraction of the total would identify themselves as Pacific Islanders. Data from NCES and the Office of Civil Rights (OCR) of the Department of Education included permanent residents and excluded nonresident aliens in making Asian American counts.

By 1984, when Asian Americans were approaching 2% of the population, there were 382,000 Asian Americans enrolled in higher education institutions. Asian Americans were 3.2% of total United States undergraduates, 2.6% of graduate students, 3.3% of professional school enrollment, and 3.2% of unclassified institutions (Racial and Ethnic Makeup of College and University Enrollments, 1986;

U.S. Department of Commerce, Bureau of the Census, 1986a). Asian Americans in 4-year institutions were following through to earn a degree, and substantial numbers continue in graduate or professional school.

THE GAP BETWEEN ENGLISH AND MATH/SCIENCE ACHIEVEMENT

In order to maintain good academic records and earn a degree, Asian Americans, particularly individuals with limited English proficiency, have resorted to a variety of strategies to optimize their chances for success. These strategies included avoiding courses that required fluency in the English language and choosing fields that can capitalize on their strength in mathematics and sciences. These are essentially the same strategies that college-bound Asian American high school students used to maintain their grade point averages. The combination of high school and postsecondary course choices could only increase the gap between Asian American students' verbal and quantitative achievements. There is evidence that Asian Americans, particularly disadvantaged immigrants, have earned degrees from selective institutions in demanding science, engineering, and mathematics fields without commensurate improvement in their ability to speak or write English. GRE scores of Asian Americans continued the trend of relatively lower verbal and higher quantitative developed abilities observed in college, in elementary and secondary schools, and even among preschool children.

Reports of Limited English Proficiency

When Asian immigrants were crowded in ethnic ghettos and attended segregated schools, poor command of the English language was often the reason given to keep Asian American college students from entering fields that demanded verbal ability. A typical example was San Francisco State College, (now University), the major teacher-training institution in the Bay Area. Chinese Americans had to overcome two hurdles before they could become elementary school teachers. First, applicants had to pass the college's oral screening procedures before graduating. Speech courses were required of all Chinese American students. After completing all course requirements, teacher applicants to the San Francisco school district were evaluated by oral interviews before being accepted for jobs. Until 1930, only three American-born Chinese managed to make the grade. After 1950, the number of Chinese American teachers increased. Low (1982) interviewed 45 Chinese American teachers who began to teach in the San Francisco school district after World War II. He also obtained permission to review many of their files. Supervisors generally evaluated Chinese American teachers as being cooperative, hard working, conscientious, quiet, and unassuming. Four out of 10 evaluations also included remarks about their accents or other speech deficiencies. Japanese Americans, even English-fluent Nisei, were not hired as teachers until after World War II (Kitano, 1976). Asian Americans are underrepresented in the teaching profession to this day.

During the 1960s and 1970s, observers of second- and third-generation Asian American college students' verbal behavior continued to record significant differences from that of mainstream Americans. Counts of the number of contributions by white and Japanese American male and female students to classroom discussions, in three psychology classes at the University of Hawaii, showed that men were twice as likely to speak as women. Whites of both sexes were 10 times more likely to contribute to classroom discussions than Japanese Americans of the same sex (Hutchinson, Arkoff, & Weaver, 1966). Records showed that Asian American students at the University of Hawaii and UC Berkeley were required to sign up for remedial English courses more often than white classmates, even before the influx of Asian immigrant and refugee students (Meredith, 1965; Watanabe, 1973).

Although the observations of non-Asian educators and researchers might be discounted as biased, evaluations by fellow Asian Americans have been, if anything, more severe. Russell Endo (1974) described Asian American students as tending

> to fear and avoid verbal classroom participation, and to be hesitant, disorganized and nervous when called upon to speak. Written work is often weak, rambling and unimaginative. . . . Part of the problem is a deficiency in language skills. . . . Cultural patterns of obedience and acquiescence, backed by a racism that generated fear and denied the worth of Asian cultures and communities . . . all contributed to the development of weak, unassertive individuals. (pp. 6–7)

Takeuchi (1974) described academically disadvantaged Asian American Educational Opportunity Program (EOP) students at the University of Colorado as being reticent to the extent that there was seldom enough professor–student discourse for learning to take place on the student's part or for evaluation of student verbal performance by their instructors. The university initiated a remedial program for Asian Americans to improve verbal skills and develop self-confidence considered necessary for future job interviews and community activities. Similar EOP programs were developed for Asian students enrolled in the University of Washington (Hodgson & Lutz, 1975) and Sacramento State College (Maykovich, 1972). The compensatory programs were designed for Asian American college students during the early 1970s, before the recent waves of immigrants and refugees from Asia. Contemporary Asian American college students are more ethnically as well as linguistically diverse than ever before. They are also more likely to be limited in English proficiency.

Suchang Chan (1985a) described the "dismal" essays written by native- as well as foreign-born Asian students in her UC Berkeley Asian American history class. She had taught th same course annually since 1974, but noticed serious deterioration in both speaking and writing for the first time during the 1980–1981 academic year. Her students claimed they had never been taught basic skills for oral or written discourse in high school but worked mainly on English as a Second Language (ESL) workbooks. Chan was a history professor, but she decided to offer a special English course for Asian students to teach them to write and speak with clarity. Her students made remarkable progress in a few weeks of intensive work.

In order to discover how Asian students with such poor study skills managed to get admitted and stay at Berkeley long enough to earn a degree, Chan looked into the academic background of Asian-ancestry undergraduates in 1980 and 1981. With the exception of Japanese Americans, the bulk of Asian American students was born abroad. Most of the foreign-born Chinese, Korean, and Vietnamese students scored below 400 on the SAT-Verbal test. Yet they earned higher than average GPAs when they were majoring in difficult fields, such as engineering and the physical sciences.

Chan diagnosed her students as having differential encoding and decoding skills. They did well in school because they were used to absorbing and regurgitating large and complex bodies of information. But most could not write essays by using their own format and choosing their own words. Turning her classroom into an anthropological research laboratory, Chan analyzed her students' backgrounds and followed their progress. She concluded that there were environmental factors that limited English proficiency. These factors included Asian home languages, almost exclusively Asian friends, discomfort in the presence of even well-liked and respected non-Asian faculty, lack of familiarity with American society, and general ignorance about the social and political world at large. Her students were modern in the sense that they shared the pop culture of American youth. However, they rarely read for pleasure in any language and remained ignorant of the literary and cultural traditions of Western as well as their own Far Eastern civilizations.

Asian ancestry students reported they chose science and engineering as majors because these rigorous fields provided them the greatest intellectual challenge. Their earlier ESL or regular English courses in high schools and community colleges offered them little challenge or practice in writing. Lack of confidence in their own verbal abilities led many Asian students to fulfill their UC Subject A and English 1 A-B requirements by taking an ESL sequence or equivalent course at less demanding UC, CSU, or community colleges. Many students regarded English requirements as obstacles, rather than as life-enhancing skills essential for reaching their ambitious career goals.

Chan concluded that Asian American students, particularly immigrants, did arrive in college with language handicaps (Chan, 1981). But she was convinced that they could be helped by "creating a learning environment where the students' own strengths can be tapped as a resource to be used to overcome the disabilities they bring with them" (Chan, 1985a, p. 29).

An earlier report by Tang (1983) also cited as problem areas the underpreparation of immigrant Asian students in basic English language skills and limited choice of majors due to parental pressure. Administrators and staff at UC Berkeley were also faulted in the report for pervasive negative stereotyping and lack of interest in integrating Asian immigrant students into the mainstream of campus life to prepare them better for future work settings.

Achievement in Quantitative Fields

Although Asian Americans, particularly recent immigrants, encountered difficulties with college-level courses that required mastery of English, they manage to do well in major fields that maximized their strength in mathematics and sciences (Sue, 1985). Berryman (1983), in *Who Will Do Science?* hypothesized that having parents who went to college would equalize the percent of students from all racial ethnic groups who chose quantitative majors. She tested a causal model by analyzing survey data of 1981 full-time, first-time, college freshmen collected by the Cooperative Institutional Research Program (CIRP) at UCLA and the American Council on Education. For whites and all minority groups, having at least one parent with some college increased the percentage of quantitative majors to 20–22%. More than 40% of Asian Americans chose quantitative majors, and those whose parents had no college were more likely to choose quantitative majors. Berryman concluded that Asian Americans did not behave like whites or other minority groups:

> educational plans increase as parental education increases, and their choice of quantitative majors increase as high school performance and postsecondary educational plans increase. However, each level of parental education translates into higher high school grades and postsecondary educational expectations for the Asian American than for the other freshmen groups. Each level of high school performances and expected educational attainments also translates into higher rates of choosing quantitative majors. (p. 88)

The enrollment and degree attainment data presented earlier showed that Asian Americans succeeded in gaining the educational credentials necessary for careers in scientific and technological fields. Bagasao (1983) showed that the newcomers majored in applied science and technology, whereas the native-born were more likely to choose basic sciences. For recent immigrants, academic success could be achieved, despite limited English proficiency, by the use of several strategies during their undergraduate years.

Asian American Adaptive Strategies

Concentrating in subjects that demanded limited classroom participation and few writing assignments, and taking required English courses in less academically demanding departments or institutions were strategies adopted by some Asian American students who were not confident about their English. They also made use of other strategies that improved their chances for academic success.

In Sue (1985) and Sue and Zane's (1985) study of 177 Chinese American students at UCLA, the students were classified according to their length of residence in this country: American born (AB), early immigrants (EI) who have resided in the United States for more than 6 years, and recent immigrants (RI) who have lived in this country for 6 years or less. There were no significant differences in their cumulative GPAs. Mean Chinese American GPA was 2.99, above the mean university cumulative GPA of 2.87.

Strategies used by RI students to maintain their grades included taking significantly lighter academic course loads, after controlling for differences in class membership and socioeconomic status; restricting academic choices to majors in mathematics or computer sciences; and spending more hours per week studying than AB and EI students. The investigators confirmed earlier work (Sue & Morishima, 1982) that found recent immigrants' academic success was not come by easily, but gained at personal and psychological costs.

East Coast Asian American students whose best language was English have used similar adaptive strategies to remain in good standing at college. Preliminary findings have been reported on Asian American students at a private, selective college in New England. Toupin and Son (1985) compared the academic performance of Asian Americans and a matched control group of non-Asian classmates. The majority of Asian Americans were native born and came from well off suburban and urban families. The groups were matched by class, gender, choice of college (Arts and Science or Engineering), parental education, type of high schools, SAT scores, and other socioeconomic factors. Contrary to the investigators' expectations, these Asian Americans of higher socioeconomic status were not more likely to major in science and mathematics than the comparison group. Nor did they perform better academically. In fact, they were more likely to be placed on academic probation than the control group.

These middle-class, English-proficient, Asian American students, with mean SAT Verbal scores of 550 and SAT Mathematical scores of 620, used the following strategies more frequently than non-Asian comparison group members: dropping science and mathematics courses, completing freshman year with less than the normal course load, taking more courses in summer school, taking nine semesters to graduate instead of the normal eight, and withdrawing from college. Lack of congruence between parents' aspirations and students' interests or abilities was one possible explanation for the Asian American students' behavior. The investigators concluded that the model minority image may have impeded diagnosis of student needs and the development of appropriate services.

Adoption of mainstream values, with lower motivation for educational achievement, observed among some third-generation Japanese Americans (Sansei), could be generalizable as an explanation to the behavior of other third-generation Asian Americans. Acculturation is another possible explanation for the defensive behavior strategies that were used by second- or later generation Asian Americans as described previously (Feagin & Fujitaki, 1972; Kitano, 1976).

DEGREES CONFERRED BY STATES

There were seven states with 100,000 or more Asian Americans in 1980: California, Hawaii, New York, Illinois, Texas, Washington, and New Jersey, in rank order. These states were among the top 10 states with the highest Asian American enrollment. In 1984, California had almost 167,000 Asian Americans, more than 10% of the total state enrollment, in its institutions of higher education. Hawaii had more than 31,000 Asian American higher education students, 68% of the state's total. Massachusetts, Pennsylvania, and Maryland also enrolled 7,000 to 9,000 Asian American college and university students (Racial and ethnic makeup of college and university enrollments, 1986). Except New Jersey, these states were also among the top 10 states with institutions that conferred the highest number of Bachelor's degrees upon Asian Americans. Table 6.1 shows states that conferred the highest numbers of Bachelor's, Master's and Doctoral degrees upon Asian Americans. At the doctoral level, Asian Americans, like other students, were more likely to receive their degrees from institutions with the highest numbers of degree recipients rather than from institutions in their home states (U.S. Department of Education, Office of Civil Rights, 1986a, 1986b, 1986c, 1986d). Californian and Hawaiian institutions conferred doctoral degrees on Asian Americans at no higher than population proportions.

Major Fields of Bachelor's, Master's, Doctoral, and Professional Degrees Conferred

Degrees conferred by United States institutions in 1980–1981 have been recorded by major fields of study, sex, and ethnicity. The source of data was the U.S. Department of Education, Office for Civil Rights (OCR), which receives degrees conferred reports from higher education institutions. Two percent of all Bachelor's, 2.1% of Master's, 2.7% of Doctoral, and 2% of first professional degrees conferred by United States institutions of higher education in 1980–1982 were to Asian Americans (National Center for Education Statistics, 1984a). These figures are close to those of Asian American citizens and permanent residents, who were 2.1% of the total enrollment of 4-year institutions in Fall 1980 (American Council on Education, 1985).

Distribution of Asian American degree recipients in 1980–1981 by major fields is shown in Figs. 6.1–6.4. Distribution among major fields by sex is detailed in Table 6.2. There were just under 19,000 Asian American Bachelor's degrees recipients. Business and engineering were top undergraduate major field choices of Asian Americans. Business and engineering counted for 21% and 16%, respectively, of Bachelor's degrees conferred in 1980–1981. Women and men received degrees in business in equal proportions. Engineering degrees were conferred upon 27% of male and 4% of female Asian American graduates. Among all engineering Bachelor's degrees conferred, 14% were to males and 1.7% to females. Bachelor's degrees in

TABLE 6.1

States with Highest Numbers of Bachelor's, Master's, and Doctor's Degrees Conferred Upon Asian Americans, 1982–1983[a]

Degree Level	State	Degrees to Asian Americans N	% of All Degrees Conferred
Bachelor's			
	California	7,322	8.6
	New York	2,216	2.6
	Hawaii	2,006	61.4
	Illinois	1,066	2.3
	Washington	766	4.2
	Texas	647	1.2
	Massachusetts	544	1.4
	Pennsylvania	541	0.9
	Oregon	405	3.6
	Arizona	305	2.6
Master's			
	California	1,647	5.3
	New York	1,013	3.1
	Illinois	560	3.3
	Hawaii	460	46.4
	Texas	407	2.5
	Pennsylvania	263	2.0
	Ohio	247	1.9
	Massachusetts	230	1.7
	Michigan	222	1.7
	District of Columbia	197	3.6
Doctor's			
	California	231	5.6
	New York	124	3.9
	Illinois	111	5.9
	Hawaii	49	40.8
	Pennsylvania	49	2.8
	New Jersey	45	5.5
	Kansas	38	10.5
	North Carolina	37	5.1
	Ohio	36	2.4
	Texas	31	1.8

[a]From U.S. Department of Education, Office for Civil Rights, 1986a, 1986c, 1986d

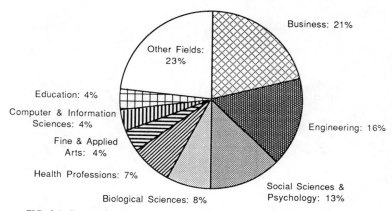

FIG. 6.1. Percent distribution of U.S. Bachelor's degrees conferred upon Asian Americans by fields of study, 1980–1981 (2.1% of total conferred in the U.S.; from National Center for Education Statistics, 1984a).

the health professions were earned by 12% of Asian American and 11% of all females. Social sciences degrees were awarded to 9% of Asian American men and women, compared to 12% of all men and 10% of all women. As the proportion of recent immigrants rises, the proportion of mathematics, science, and engineering degrees also increases (Owings, 1987).

At the Master's level, business and management or engineering degrees were earned by 56% of Asian American males. The top choice fields among women were education, 27%; business and management, 19%; and health professions, 11%. There were more than 6,000 Master's degrees in all.

Doctoral-level degrees were awarded to 655 Asian American men and 222 women in 1980–1981. Men earned Doctoral degrees primarily in three disciplines: engineering, 28%; and biological and physical sciences, each with 14%. Three fields in

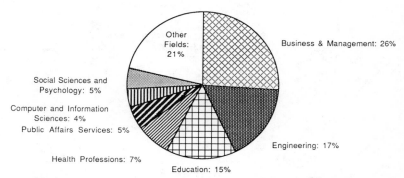

FIG. 6.2. Percent distribution of U.S. Master's degrees conferred upon Asian Americans by fields of study, 1980–1981 (2.1% of total conferred in U.S.; from National Center for Education Statistics, 1984a).

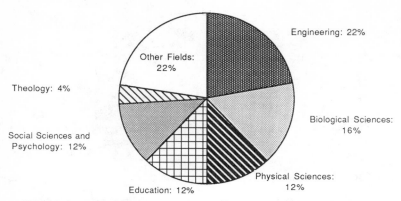

FIG. 6.3. Percent distribution of U.S. Doctor's degrees conferred upon Asian Americans by fields of study, 1980–1981 (2.7% of total conferred in the U.S.; from National Center for Education Statistics, 1984a).

which women concentrated were education, 26%; biological sciences, 21%; and social sciences, 11%.

First professional degrees were conferred upon 1,456 Asian Americans. Law and medicine were the most popular fields. Thirty-two percent of Asian American men and 45% of women received law degrees. When the fields of medicine, dentistry, pharmacy, and optometry were combined, 57% of the men and 50% of women received professional degrees in these fields.

Current population and enrollment figures suggest that numbers of Asian American degree recipients will increase through the 1980s, and on into the 21st century.

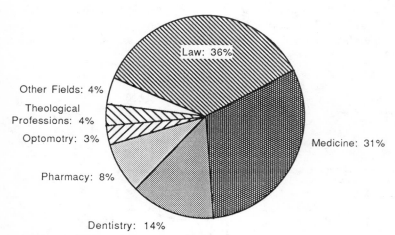

FIG. 6.4. Percent distribution of U.S. first professional degrees conferred upon Asian Americans by field of study, 1980–1981 (2.0% of total conferred in the U.S.; from National Center for Education Statistics, 1984a).

TABLE 6.2

Percent Distribution by Major Fields of Study of Asian American Bachelor's, Master's, Doctoral, and First Professional Degree Recipients by Sex, United States, 1980–1981[a]

	Men	Women	Total
Bachelor's Degrees:	*N = 10,107*	*N = 8,687*	*N = 18,794*
	%	%	%
Business	21	21	21
Engineering	27	4	16
Social Sciences	9	9	9
Biological Sciences	8	8	8
Health Professions	3	12	7
Psychology	3	6	4
Fine and Applied Arts	3	6	4
Master's Degrees:	*N = 3,773*	*N = 2,509*	*N = 6,282*
	%	%	%
Business and Management	30	19	26
Engineering	26	4	17
Education	8	27	15
Health Professions	4	11	7
Public Affairs and Services	4	6	5
Computer and Information Sciences	5	3	4
Social Sciences	4	3	4
Doctorates:	*N = 655*	*N = 222*	*N = 877*
	%	%	%
Engineering	28	4	22
Biological Sciences	14	21	16
Physical Sciences	14	7	12
Education	7	26	12
Social Sciences	7	11	8
Psychology	3	7	4
Theology	5	—	4
First Professional Degrees:	*N = 991*	*N = 465*	*N = 1,456*
	%	%	%
Law	32	45	36
Medicine	33	25	31
Dentistry	16	10	14
Pharmacy	6	11	8
Theological Professions	5	2	4
Optometry	2	4	3

[a]From National Center for Educational Statistics, 1984a

United States and Foreign-Born Ph.D.s

Among 2,704 Asians who received Ph.D.s in 1980–1981 from United States universities, 460 were United States citizens, 602 had permanent resident status, and 1,559 had temporary visas. Citizens may have been United States or foreign born. The 1980–1981 data are not comparable with earlier National Research Council (NRC) surveys because there have been changes in the survey question on racial/ethnic groups. The 1973 Summary Report included data for racial and ethnic groups for the first time. That year, about 9,000 respondents did not provide racial or ethnic data. The item was revised in 1977 to conform with Office of Management and Budget format for federally sponsored surveys. In 1978, Asian Indians were changed from white to Asian category. The item was again revised in 1980 to limit the respondent to the choice of one racial/ethnic category only (Commission on Human Resources of the National Research Council, 1980).

The 1980–1981 figures showed that Asians who were not United States citizens obtained Ph.D.s in far greater numbers than Asian American citizens, who represented 1.8% of all doctorate recipients. The number of United States-born Asian Americans who obtained doctorates in earlier surveys has consistently been a fraction of the foreign-born Asian Ph.D. recipients. The 1979 NRC survey provided estimates of all United States Ph.D. recipients from 1936 to 1978 by fields and ethnic groups. Table 6.3 shows estimated numbers of foreign- versus native-born Asian

TABLE 6.3

U.S.- and Foreign-born Asian American Science, Engineering, and Humanities Ph.D.s by Year of Doctorate, 1936–1973[a]

	Total U.S.		Asian American			
			Native-Born		Foreign-Born	
	N	%	N	%	N	%
Science/Engineering Ph.D.s—1936–1978						
	324,335	100	1,812	0.6	19,576	6.0
1936–1949	23,984	100	54	0.2	110	0.5
1950–1959	49,299	100	248	0.5	1,212	2.5
1960–1969	98,118	100	686	0.7	5,737	5.8
1970–1978	152,934	100	824	0.5	12,517	8.2
Humanities Ph.D.s—1936–1978						
	71,171	100	147	0.2	575	0.8
1936–1949	5,032	100	—	0.0	—	0.0
1950–1959	9,395	100	19	0.2	48	0.5
1960–1969	19,608	100	51	0.3	145	0.7
1970–1978	37,139	100	77	0.2	382	1.0

Note: From Maxfield, 1981

[a]Estimates based on data from 1979 Survey of Doctoral Recipients conducted by Commission on Human Resources of the National Research Council

Americans who earned Doctoral degrees between 1936 and 1978. In the science and engineering fields, foreign-born doctorates outnumbered native-born 11 to 1. Together, Asian Americans constituted 6.6% of all science and engineer doctorates earned during the 43-year interval, but the native-born were only 0.6% of the total.

From 1936 to 1949, native-born Asian Americans earned about 0.2% of the science and engineering (S/E) Ph.D.s. Asians were about 0.4% of the population in the 1940 and 1950 census. Between 1950 and 1959, native-born Asian Americans earned 0.5% of S/E doctorates, about the same as the proportions of Asians in the total United States population in 1960. The 1970 census estimated about 0.7% of Americans were Asian. Asian Americans who earned their S/E doctorates during the 1960–1969 interval were 0.7% of the total. Only 0.5% of 1970–1979 Asian American S/E doctorates were native-born. Asians had risen to about 1.6% of the 1980 census. The "overrepresentation" of Asians among science and engineering doctorates had never been due to high rates of participation on the part of native-born Asian Americans. Foreign-born Asian American S/E doctorates, on the other hand, have increased in numbers and proportion during each decade since 1950. They were 2.5%, 5.8%, and 8.2% percent of all S/E doctorates for 1950–1959, 1960–1969, and 1979–1978, respectively. In 1984, almost 24% of ethnic Asian scientists and engineers in the United States were not United States citizens. More than one third of ethnic Asian scientists and engineers with doctoral degrees were not citizens (National Science Foundation, 1986).

Participation of Asian Americans in advanced studies in the humanities has been low. In the 1979 NRC survey, foreign-born Asian Ph.D.s in the humanities outnumbered native-born 4 to 1. Together, they made up 1% of all United States humanities doctorates from 1936–1978. There were too few respondents for reliable estimates to be made prior to 1949. Native-born Asian American doctorates in the humanities accounted for 0.2% to 0.3% of the United States total for each decade since 1950 (Commission on Human Resources of the National Research Council, 1974; Gilford & Snyder, 1977; Maxfield, 1981).

Choice of fields was different between native- and foreign-born Asian Americans. Among 1,812 native-born Asian Americans with science and engineering doctorates earned between 1939 and 1978, two-thirds obtained their degrees in life sciences or behavioral sciences. Two-thirds of 19,576 foreign-born Asian American S/E doctorates were in engineering, mathematics, or physical sciences. In the interval between 1970 and 1978, choice of fields by native-born Asian Americans approached that of native-born white S/E doctorates, whereas foreign-born Asians avoided behavioral sciences as shown in Table 6.4.

Too Many Doctors and Engineers?

Distribution of degree recipients by fields within the Asian American population fails to put in perspective the impact of their numbers upon the total degree recipients in any single discipline or profession. At the Bachelor's level, Asian Americans

TABLE 6.4
1970–1978 S/E Ph.D.s, Percents by Field and Ethnicity[a]

	Native-Born		Foreign-Born	
	Whites	Asians	Whites	Asians
	%	%	%	%
Engineering/Mathematics/Physics	39.2	33.7	48.0	70.0
Life Sciences	26.0	32.6	21.7	29.7
Behavioral Sciences	34.8	33.6	30.3	9.3

[a]From Maxfield, 1981

received 18,794, or 2% of all degrees conferred in 1980–1981. In 7 out of 24 major fields, Asian Americans received one half of 1% or more over their expected 2% share of Bachelor's degrees: area studies, 4.6%; computer and information sciences, 4.4%; engineering, 4.1%; mathematics, 3.5%; biological sciences, 3.4%; architecture and environmental design, 3.1%; and physical sciences, 2.5%. The total number of Bachelor's degrees conferred upon Asian Americans exceed 1,000 in the following fields: biological sciences, business and management, engineering, health professions, and social sciences.

At the Master's level, Asian Americans received more than one-half of 1% over their expected share of degrees (2.1%) in 8 out of 23 fields: computer and information sciences, 6.7%; engineering, 6.6%; area studies, 5.3%; mathematics, 3.8%; architecture and environmental design, 3.6%; physical sciences, 2.9%; business and management, 2.8%; and health professions, 2.7%. Business and management and engineering were two fields in which more than 1,000 Asian Americans received Master's degrees.

At the first professional degree level, Asian Americans received more than one-half of 1% over their expected share of degrees (2%) in 4 of 10 fields; pharmacy, 17.3%; dentistry, 3.7%; optometry, 3.6%; and medicine, 2.9%. Among 71,340 first professional degree recipients, there were 805 Asian Americans who received degrees in one of these four fields. Recent medical school enrollment figures indicate that the proportion of physicians will increase substantially through the 1980s.

At the Doctoral level, Asian Americans received more than one-half of 1% over their expected share of degrees (2.7%) in 8 out of 23 fields: engineering, 7.5%; computer and information sciences, 5.6%; architecture and environmental design, 5.4%; mathematics, 4.3%; library science, 4.2%; area studies, 3.8%; biological science, 3.8%; and physical sciences, 3.4%. Engineering, biological sciences, education, and physical sciences were fields in which more than 100 Asian Americans earned Doctoral degrees (National Center for Education Statistics, 1984a).

The Office of Scientific and Engineering Personnel of the National Research Council (NRC) conducts annual surveys of earned doctorates from United States universities. Students who earned doctorates between July 1, 1980 to June 30, 1981 were asked by their graduate deans to fill in a survey questionnaire after they had completed all requirements for their doctoral degrees. The 1980–1981 summary figures from NCR were different from those of NCES. Methods for collecting data and definitions of categories were independently designed. The NRC information was collected from individual degree recipients, whereas NCES data were collected from institutions. NRC included only United States universities. NCES included institutions in Puerto Rico and outlying areas. NRC included history under humanities instead of social sciences, and psychology under social sciences. Mathematics and computer science were included under physical sciences. The total number of doctoral recipients were 32,834 according to NCES and 31,319 according to NRC. The number of Asian American doctorates, including citizens and permanent residents, was 877 or 2.7% of the total according to NCES and 1,062 or 3.4% of the total according to NRC. The number of doctorates in engineering and physical sciences were 282 and 214, respectively, in the NRC summary and 151 and 191 in the NCES report. NRC figures would increase total percentages of Asian American engineers and physical sciences doctorates to 11.2% and 5.1% of doctorates in each field, respectively, for 1980–1981. Increase in Asian Americans in the NRC summary report was offset by a decrease in the total number of nonresident aliens (Syverson, 1982). An explanation for the differences could be that cumulative institutional records may not have fully reflected changes in citizenship status of students who received permanent visas or became naturalized citizens during their graduate years.

Engineering, computer and information sciences, physical sciences, and mathematics have been fields of choice by Asians and, to a lesser degree, by Asian Americans at all degree levels. These fields are also being chosen by many immigrant and refugee students who are entering higher education institutions in the 1980s. These students typically presented academic records that showed high performance in quantitative areas, and limited proficiency in English. They major in fields that minimize need for English, maximize their strength in mathematics, and are likely to lead to well paying jobs after graduation. This group may produce more than their share of scientists and engineers to meet national economic, educational and national security needs. The coming shortage of physical scientists, mathematicians, and engineers for carrying out basic research and university teaching has been an issue of continuing concern to United States science and technology research and development policy-making bodies. The National Science Foundation and National Academy of Sciences have been monitoring the nation's stock of scientists, engineers, and mathematicians (National Science Board, 1983; National Science Foundation, 1986). In 1984, about 5% of all employable scientists and engineers were of Asian origins. Among those holding doctorates, Asians were 8% of all employed scientists and engineers. Between 1982 and 1984, the rate of increase of ethnic Asians (39%) was double that of whites (22%). Immigrant Asian Americans will be a significant proportion of future scientific stock.

CONCLUSIONS AND DISCUSSION

Between 1970 and 1985, the Asian American population has more than tripled, mainly due to the influx of Asian immigrants and refugees. Recent immigrants have changed the character of Asian American participation in United States higher education. The newcomers' propensity for higher education is as high as if not higher than the native-born. Absolute numbers of visually identifiable Asian American students have increased on major campuses. The relative proportion of Asian Americans in postsecondary enrollment has also increased, to a higher percentage than would have been expected from their numbers in the age-relevant population. Asian Americans, particularly recent arrivals, are not spread out evenly across all 50 states, but tend to concentrate in a few metropolitan areas. The higher education institutions in areas of high Asian population are enrolling Asian American students in unprecedented numbers. Recent immigrants also tend to major in subject areas that maximize their strength in quantitative fields, minimize their weakness in English, and could lead to good jobs. The high proportions of Asian Americans observed in selective institutions and specific faculties are a function of their distribution. Their absolute numbers remain a small fraction of the total United States higher education enrollment.

Despite encountering academic and personal difficulties common to all newcomers, Asian American immigrants in a variety of higher education institutions have managed to achieve respectable academic records and earn college and advanced degrees. They have kept up academically, even in demanding major fields at selective institutions, by making use of several strategies. These included majoring in subjects that limit classroom participation and written assignments, taking lighter course loads than other Asian Americans, and spending much more time studying.

Not only recent immigrants but also native-born Asian Americans whose families have lived in America for two, three, or more generations still manifest limited communicative skills in higher education environments. Immigrants, of course, are worse off because they are more likely to be socioeconomically disadvantaged, speak a language other than English at home, live in ethnic ghettos, have only Asian friends, and attend schools with limited English proficient classmates. The contrast between Asian Americans' achievement in quantitative fields and their avoidance of and difficulties with fields that demand well developed verbal skills is stark among recent immigrants and still noticeable after several generations among the native born.

The strategies that Asian American students have used to reach their educational and career goals have interacted with institutional policies and educational practices. Together, these reinforce a pattern of differential achievement in engineering, mathematics, and sciences in contrast to the humanities that probably began well before Asian American students entered first grade (Lesser, 1976; Lesser et al., 1965). However, there is evidence at the college level that Asian Americans, including recent immigrants, can improve their speaking and writing ability with appropriate effort, given high-quality instructional programs. If these students are to fully realize their academic and personal promise and to achieve the ambitious educational and career goals set by themselves and their families, mastery of English is an essential tool that cannot be foregone during their college years.

Immigrants, children of professional and scientific immigrants, and other foreign-born Asians are most likely to obtain advanced degrees in engineering, mathematics, and physical sciences. Eleven out of 12 Asian American doctorates in these fields were granted to the foreign born. Asian Americans in science and engineering fields are growing both in absolute numbers and relative proportions. They will contribute significantly to the training of future scientists and engineers, as well as to basic and applied research that is needed for economic growth and national defense. The potential usefulness of Asian American scientists and engineers for contributing to future scientific and technological teaching, research, and development can be enhanced by improving their communicative skills.

The next chapter summarizes the career achievements of Asian Americans who have had the benefit of higher education and provides a rationale for Asian American demand for postsecondary education.

7

Education, Occupation, and Income

Like all Americans, education has been the primary key to Asian American success. By investing time, energy, and resources in higher education, Asian Americans have been able to move up steadily in the hierarchy of occupations. With the exception of recent immigrants or refugees who arrived after 1975, Asian Americans have attained occupational status about equal to that of white Americans. Above-average education has also been crucial to raising income levels of Asian Americans. Only by being better educated could they hope to reach economic parity with the majority. Without investment in education, Asian Americans would still be limited to jobs in industries with low wage scales, to poorly paid service work, or to small businesses where risk of failure is high, hours are long, and profits limited. Asian Americans have managed to approach socioeconomic parity with white Americans through overachievement in education, by higher participation in the labor force, and by pooling family or household resources.

LABOR FORCE PARTICIPATION

The 1980 census asked men and women age 16 and over if they were working or looking for work during the week before the census count. Asian American men and women were recorded as having participated in the labor force at higher rates than other racial/ethnic groups. Participation rate was 66.6% for Asian Americans, and 62.2% among white persons. There were variations in labor force participation rates among Asian ethnic groups, depending on their educational level, immigration status, and mastery of English. With the exception of 57.3% labor force participation by Vietnamese, who only began to arrive in large numbers after 1975, all major

Asian ethnic groups reported higher labor force participation rates and lower unemployment rates than white Americans. Sixty-three percent of Asian American families had two or more workers, compared to 54% of white families. Only the Vietnamese had relatively fewer families with two or more workers than whites. Labor force participation rates, percent of families with two or more workers, and unemployment rates of Asian ethnic groups and whites are shown in Table 7.1 (U.S. Department of Commerce, Bureau of the Census, 1983).

Asian American Women Participating in Labor Force

The majority of Asian American women work. Asian American women participated at higher rates than white, black, or Hispanic women, 57.7% to 49.6%, 53.3%, and 49.3%, respectively. By Asian ethnic groups, Asian Indian and Vietnamese women participated at slightly lower rates, and Japanese, Chinese, Filipino, and Korean women at higher rates than white women. At 68.1%, Filiipino women's labor force participation rate was highest, higher than those of Asian American and white men. The section on income later in this chapter shows that Filipinos earned less than most other full-time Asian American workers, so that Filipino households needed more workers to achieve the same level of income as other Asian Americans.

The family situations of Asian American women, like other women's, influenced their labor force participation rate. Wives living with their husbands were less likely to work than women who were female householders. However, like other Americans, Asian American women were likely to work even when they had children under 18 living at home. Proficiency in English influenced all Asian women's ability to participate in the labor force. In general, the better their English, the more likely they were to work. However, about half of Chinese and Korean women, and a third of Filipino, Asian Indian, and Vietnamese women who spoke English "not well" or

TABLE 7.1

Asian American and White Labor Force Participation, Unemployment, and Families with Two or More Workers in 1980[a]

	White	Asian American	Japanese	Chinese	Filipino	Korean	Asian Indian	Vietnamese
% Persons age 16 and over in labor force	62.2	66.6	67.8	66.4	72.5	63.9	65.4	57.3
% Unemployment	5.8	4.6	3.0	3.6	4.8	5.7	5.8	8.2
% Women age 16 and over in labor force	49.4	57.7	58.5	58.3	68.1	55.2	47.1	48.9
2 or more workers in family	54	63	64	66	72	60	58	41

[a]From U.S. Department of Commerce, Bureau of the Census, 1983a, 1983b

"not at all" were working or looking for work in 1980. The kinds of jobs open to these women would have been among the least rewarding.

Native-born Asian American women were more likely to work than the foreign-born or recent immigrants and refugees who arrived after 1975. However, foreign-born Filipino and Asian Indian women were more likely to work than their native-born sisters. Asian Indian and Filipino women were the best educated among all Asian women; 41% of Filipino and 36% of Asian Indian women age 25 and over had at least 4 years of college, compared to 27% of all Asian American women and 13% of white women. Filipinos and Asian Indians were also the most likely to have arrived with a good command of English. Selective migration via third or sixth preference immigrant status, those with professional, technical skills or workers needed for the United States labor market, could account in part for the higher labor force participation rate among these two groups of women. Table 7.2 shows labor force participation of Asian American women classified according to their ethnicity, family situation, nativity, and English language proficiency (Gardner, Robey, & Smith, 1985).

TABLE 7.2

Labor Force Participation Rate of Asian American Women by Ethnicity, Family Situation, Nativity, and English Proficiency 1980[a]

	Japanese	Chinese	Filipino	Korean	Asian Indian	Vietnamese
	%	%	%	%	%	%
Family Situation						
Female/spouse of households	55.9	61.2	71.9	56.2	51.9	52.7
With own children under 18	76.6	75.4	78.3	71.2	73.1	53.5
Female households with no husband present	72.7	69.8	78.5	72.9	57.3	57.6
With own children under 18	77.8	76.3	77.2	73.6	74.9	56.6
Nativity						
Native-born	68.3	65.0	64.5	59.1	29.4	56.1
Foreign-born	42.7	56.0	68.8	54.8	53.6	48.7
Living abroad in 1975	26.0	46.9	60.5	30.9	51.6	44.1
English Proficiency						
Speaks English at home[b]	71.8	67.8	67.3	59.7	36.0	56.0
Speaks another language at home[b]	48.2	57.9	70.3	55.8	53.6	50.2
Speaks English "not well" or "not at all"	26.8	48.5	32.2	50.5	30.9	34.1

Note: From Gardner, Robey, and Smith, 1985

[a]Percent of women age 16 and over who worked or looked for work in week before 1980 census

[b]Data for women age 18 and over

TABLE 7.3

Labor Force Participation and Employment of White, Black, Hispanic, and Foreign-Born Asian American Men, 1979[a]

	Percent in Labor Force Who Worked	Percent Who Worked 50–52 Weeks	Percent Who Worked Full-Time 50–52 Weeks	Percent Who Had Some Unemployment	Average Weeks of Unemployment
	%	%	%	%	%
White	99.0	67.1	63.1	16.7	13.9
Black	95.5	55.4	51.3	26.1	17.8
Hispanic	97.6	57.0	54.0	23.9	14.4
Foreign-Born Asian American Men by Country of Birth					
Japan	98.9	64.1	59.2	13.5	11.7
Taiwan or Hong Kong	98.1	54.9	48.0	19.2	11.8
Philippines	98.1	59.8	56.3	18.9	13.3
Korea	98.7	54.6	50.2	21.4	10.6
India	99.0	70.0	67.0	14.4	11.5
Vietnam	93.4	46.7	43.1	32.6	13.5

[a]From Gardner, Robey, and Smith, 1985

Labor Market Participation of Immigrant Asian Men

Except for substantial proportions of Asian Indians and Filipinos, Asian immigrants usually landed in the United States with limited proficiency in English. Even if they had completed university or held professional licenses in their homelands, these credentials were not usually accepted by United States employers. Men who had families to support could seldom afford the luxury of immediate retooling. They settled for what work they could find while they studied or negotiated for transfer of credentials. The 1980 census recorded that nearly all foreign-born Asian men who wanted to work did work at some time during 1979, but they were less likely to have worked for 50–52 weeks, and even less likely to have worked full time throughout the year. Unemployment at some time during the year ranged from 13% among foreign-born Japanese to 33% among Vietnamese men. The average weeks of unemployment for each group was no higher than those of white, black, or Hispanic Americans, as shown in Table 7.3. Like all immigrants, Asian men who come to the United States must overcome initial difficulties in order to become established in a full-time job. The fact that so many of their wives worked, even when they had little or no English, may be due to the reality of needing two breadwinners per family to make ends meet. Labor force participation by multiple members of the Asian immigrant family or household was crucial to group welfare. Southeast Asian refugee households became economically self-sufficient and ceased to rely on public assistance when a second family member found a job (Gardner, Robey, & Smith, 1985).

Asian immigrants have always worked hard and long. Chinese, Japanese, and later Filipino laborers came to this country to find work. The only kinds of work open to them were hard, dirty, menial, and poorly paid or dangerous jobs that no one else wanted. Later, even those undesirable jobs in mining, railroad building, and agriculture were closed to Asians. They then turned to domestic service or started small-scale enterprises. They created their own ethnic niches in the labor market, such as the hand laundries and cheap restaurants of the Chinese and the contract gardeners and tenant truck farms of the Japanese. Second- and third-generation Asian Americans benefitted from hard work, frugality, and respect for education on the part of their forebearers. Through education, they gained competitive power—the ability to compete as individuals with the majority in certain occupations in the labor market.

OCCUPATIONS OF ASIAN AMERICANS

During and after World War II, Asian Americans gained access to a variety of occupations previously closed to them. Even before the war, Chinese and Japanese Americans were earning college degrees, although they were aware that they would have a hard time finding jobs commensurate with their education levels. However, when opportunities arose as a result of the manpower shortage, they were prepared. Political changes in Asia beginning in the late 1940s stranded thousands of Asian students in American universities. In time, they too entered the United States labor market. Changes in immigration legislation during the 1960s and the influx of political refugees since 1975 have added more Asian workers to the labor force. Most Asian Americans were foreign born. Even educated Asian immigrants had little or no English. Most native-born Asian Americans invested in higher education. As a result, Asian Americans have not been distributed evenly across all occupations in the same proportions as the majority. They tended to cluster at both ends of the occupational scale: professionals and technical workers at the high end, and operatives or service workers at the bottom of the scale.

According to the 1980 census, more than one third of Asian Americans were in professional, managerial, or technical jobs. Just over one quarter of white workers were in these categories. Asian Americans also concentrated in service jobs, particularly in food services. They were less likely than whites to be in sales jobs, which requires verbal and persuasive skills; or in unionized, skilled blue-collar jobs, traditionally closed to Asian workers. There were differences among Asian ethnic groups. Asian Indians had the greatest proportion of professionals, 37%; and the recently arrived Vietnamese, the least at 9%. Twenty percent of Chinese Americans were professionals, and 19%, service workers. These variations reflected in part differences between the native-born and immigrants. The native-born have occupation patterns more similar to white Americans'. The immigrants' occupations depended on the transferability of their skills and credentials and their proficiency in English (U.S. Department of Labor, 1974). Among foreign-born Chinese, about half were in service occupations, and 30% in managerial, professional, and executive positions. These occupation choices also reflected differences between immigrants who entered the United States for family reunification and those who were given occupational preferences. The discrepancy in jobs also marked the kinds of work open to English speakers and those with limited English proficiency. Japanese Americans, who have the smallest proportion of immigrants, were most like whites in their occupational patterns. Table 7.4 shows the percent of Asian Americans by major ethnic groups and of whites in major occupational categories (U.S. Department of Commerce, Bureau of the Census, 1983b; Gardner, Robey, & Smith, 1985).

Most professional, managerial, and technical occupations require higher education credentials before entry-level jobs can be obtained. More Asian Ameicans work in these occupations than would have been expected from population counts. Their high rates of enrollment and degree attainment in higher education institutions for several decades, and the educational levels of recent Asian immigrants accounted for their numbers in these occupations. Asian Americans were not disributed evenly across all professional, managerial, and technical occupations. Table 7.5 shows the representation of Asian American men and women in selected occupational categories relative to their representation in the total civilian labor force in 1980. A representation index (RI) of 100 means Asian men or women were represented in that category according to statistical expectations. An RI of 200 means that Asian American workers in the category were twice the statistical expectation. An RI of 50 means there were half the statistically expected numbers.

In managerial occupations, Asian American males were chief executive officers

TABLE 7.4

Percent of Employed White and Asian American Persons Age 16 and Over by Major Occupation Categories, 1980[a]

	White	Asian American	Japanese	Chinese	Filipino	Korean	Indian	Vietnamese
	%	%	%	%	%	%	%	%
Professional	12.8	18.3	15.7	19.6	17.3	15.0	36.6	8.8
Managerial	11.1	10.6	12.8	12.9	7.7	9.9	11.9	4.5
Technical	3.1	5.5	4.3	6.3	6.0	3.7	7.6	8.0
Sales	10.7	8.4	10.3	8.6	5.8	13.4	7.0	5.6
Administrative support, clerical	17.3	16.9	19.6	15.2	21.5	10.2	13.4	13.0
Service	11.6	15.6	12.8	18.6	16.5	16.5	7.8	15.3
Farmers	2.9	2.1	4.4	0.5	2.8	0.9	0.9	0.9
Precision production, craft	13.4	8.4	10.0	5.6	8.3	9.8	5.2	14.5
Operators, laborers	17.1	14.2	10.1	12.7	14.0	20.5	9.6	29.3

[a]From U.S. Department of Commerce, Bureau of the Census, 1983b

TABLE 7.5
Representation Index of Asian American Participation in Selected Occupations by Sex, 1980[a]

	Men	Women
CEOS and general administrators, public	60	101
Salaried managers and administrators (not specified)	104	82
Self-employed managers and administrators	190	221
Accountants and auditors	202	228
Architects	251	249
Engineers	293	232
Mathematical and computer scientists	219	194
Physicists and astronomers	357	185
Chemists	421	646
Biological and life scientists	316	375
Medical scientists	372	386
Physicians	537	1,098
Registered nurses	236	188
Pharmacists	256	366
Postsecondary teachers	249	138
Teachers, except postsecondary	70	58
Lawyers	41	77
Judges	35	21
Legislators	109	76

Note: From U.S. Department of Commerce, Bureau of the Census, 1983b

[a]Representation Index (RI) is the percent of Asian Americans in occupation divided by percent of Asian Americans in total civilian labor force × 100. RI of 100 means Asian American men or women, were in the occupation according to statistical expectations; 200 means twice the proportion expected; 50 means half the proportion expected.

or general administrators in lower than expected numbers, with an RI of 60. They worked as unspecified salaried managers and administrators in proportion to population expectations. Twice the expected numbers were self-employed managers or accountants and auditors. Double the expected number of Asian American women were also self-employed managers or accountants and auditors. Self-employment as sole proprietors of small businesses has historically been the Asian immigrant's strategy for accommodating to labor market barriers (Bonacich, Light, & Wong, 1976; Bonacich & Modell, 1980; Light, 1972; Light & Wong, 1975). There were more than 80,000 Asian American-owned firms in 1977 (U.S. Department of Commerce, Bureau of the Census, 1980a).

In the professions, Asian American men worked as architects, mathematicians, computer scientists, registered nurses, pharmacists, and college and university professors at 2 to 2.5 times the expected numbers. They were 3 times more likely to be physicists and astronomers, biological and life scientists, and medical scientists. Asian American men were quadruple the expected numbers of chemists and 5 times their expected share of physicians. Asian American women were overrepresented by about the same proportions in most professions. However, they represented more than 6 times as many chemists, and 10 times as many physicians as would have been predicted from the total number of Asian American women in the work force. Most of the women in natural sciences and engineering were Chinese Americans. The vast majority of women physicians were Asian Indian or Filipinos. These two groups were most likely to have been fluent in English, to have received their training before immigrating, and then to have entered this country under the third preference.

Asian American men and women were underrepresented as elementary and secondary teachers, lawyers, and judges. Asian women were also underrepresented among legislators. These are fields that require well-developed communicative skills in addition to the necessary credentials. There were only one third the expected number of male judges, and one fifth of female Asian American judges. Earlier chapters on academic abilities, achievements, and higher education enrollments provided figures that suggest that these fields will continue to attract relatively fewer Asian Americans for some time to come. These are also the fields in which Asian American aspirants are least likely to be denied access due to "overrepresentation."

Asian American community leaders still maintain that in spite of superior educational credentials, Asian Americans have not increased their numbers among the ranks of managers and executives in industry or government. The high proportions in the professional, managerial, and technical occupations were due to professionals or technical workers and self-employed managers. Among Asian Americans employed by private firms in 1984, 4.1% were professionals, 2.9% were technicians, but only 1.3% were officers or managers (U.S. Commission on Civil Rights, 1986). White executives in major private firms, on the other hand, claimed that although Asian Americans were desirable employees as technicians and researchers, they lacked the personal qualities for "sorting through the complexities of big business here" (Yu, 1985, p. 35). In 1984, among scientists and engineers, about 20% of Asian Americans reported their primary activity to be management or administrative, compared to 29% of white scientists and engineers (National Science Foundation, 1986).

Results from an experimental study support the hypothesis of differential access for Asian American women to management jobs in health care institutions. A series of ficticious professional resumes were mailed in response to openings for middle management nursing positions advertised in selected major Sunday newspapers across the country during a 6-month period in 1977 and 1978. The resumes systematically varied surname (Anglo or non-Anglo), birthplace (United States or Philippines), and place of education and work experience (totally United States or partly United States). Institutional responses demonstrated discrimination at the resume-review phase of job competitions. Positive responses were related to education and experience totally in the United States, and to Anglo surnames. The disadvantage of a non-Anglo name was found to be more significant for native-born applicants (Macaranas, 1979).

A theory of competitive power and minority access to higher status occupations was developed by Blalock (1967). The theory postulated that if job prestige levels and labor market conditions were held constant, visible minorities would be most likely to gain access to prestige occupations if certain conditions prevailed. It would be difficult to prevent the minority from acquiring the necessary skills, individual performance is positively related to productivity of a work team of various specialists, the work group would share in the rewards of productivity, individual performance is relatively independent of skills in interpersonal relations, high individual performance does not lead to power over other members of the team, individual performance can be readily assessed, productivity is not strongly limited by consumer demand, and there is competition among employers for outstanding personnel. Sports and entertainment were two areas cited as possessing characteristics of fields amenable to integration by visible minorities. Rossi (1965) and Perrucci (1973) have shown that women's entrance into science-based professions fitted the Blalock model fairly closely. The professional occupations of third and later generations of Asian Americans and of well-educated, contemporary Asian immigrants and their children may represent other reasonable fits to the Blalock model.

Trends in Asian American Occupations

Asian Americans as a group have improved their occupational status over time. Record-keeping methods have changed, as have the rules of who may call themselves Asian Americans. The population composition of Asian Americans has been transformed since the late 1960s. Nevertheless, some occupational trends can be observed from longitudinal data or cross-sectional data on different generations of Asian Americans.

Cross-Sectional Analysis of 1980 Census Data

How have Americans of different ancestry fared over generations in terms of occupational status? Neidert and Farley (1985) used interview data obtained by the Bureau of the Census in November 1979 from a national sample of 170,000 respondents. They were asked birthplace, ancestry, and language questions that appeared on the Census of either 1970 or 1980. It was therefore possible to study educational and occupational achievement in 1979 not only by ancestry groups, but also by generation. First generation was identified as foreign born. Second generation was native born with one or both parents born abroad, and third and subsequent generations were native born with parents who were also native born. There were two measures of educational attainment: median years of school completed and the proportion who finished at least 1 year of college. Average socioeconomic occupational score for each group was estimated by the Duncan socioeconomic index (SEI). The Duncan SEI ranges from 96 assigned to dentists; to 3 for mine-equipment operatives. The Census Bureau survey recorded the detailed occupations of employed men, and their usual jobs for those who were out of work.

Because the majority of Asian men were first generation, those who were employed were likely to have been in residence for some time, to have acquired some degree of English proficiency, and to have been admitted via the third or sixth preference because they possessed marketable skills. The less reliable first-generation respondents were more likely to have been unemployed, and responded to the survey with their former occupations in Asia, or been unable to respond due to limited command of English. The SEI estimated for first-generation Asians may therefore have been spuriously high, because income was low. For the entire sample, Mean SEI for first-generation men age age 20 to 64 in 1979 was 35. Average SEI was 42 for the second generation, and 39 for the third and subsequent generations.

Men of English ancestry were designated the standard "core culture" group against whom all other groups with at least 50 in the sample were compared. Table 7.6 shows education, occupation, and per capita household income by generations with men of English descent as the standard group. Characteristics of selected groups of immigrant Americans included Asians with a separate group for first-generation Filipinos, Russians grouped with East Europeans for the first generation only, and Mexicans. Information about occupation indices of selective ethnic groups across three generations follows.

First-generation English men had an advantage in the labor market over all other groups in 1979. Their mean SEI was 50. Immigrant Asians were significantly better educated but held lower status jobs than men of English ancestry. Mean SEI of Asians was 44. The estimated SEI of first-generation Asians may have been spuriously high due to the format of the survey item, which asked for the former occupation of the unemployed. Few first-generation Asians could obtain employment in the United States at occupational levels comparable to the jobs they held in their countries of origin. Filipinos also were significantly better educated than the English but reported jobs with mean SEI of 38. Filipinos were more familiar with American culture and more likely to have been able to communicate in English than all other Asian immigrants except Asian Indians. Their responses would have been more likely to be reliable. The Asian SEI of 44 was probably confounded by prior occupations of the unemployed, by nonresponses from those who have not yet learned English, by reluctance of newcomers to deal with officials, and possible sampling bias due to the concentration of immigrants within a few metropolitan centers rather than even distribution across all states.

Median years of education demonstrated selective migration on the part of college educated Asians. A college education is a rare privilege in most Asian countries. Yet 64% of Asian immigrants had some college. Many immigrants entered under the third preference by having a profession that was considered to be in short supply in the United States. However, most immigrants drop downward in occupation for years before they regain their pre-migration job levels. There have been a number of studies that used 1970 census data to demonstrate the typical span of years necessary for the foreign born to reach the same earning power as native-born adults of the same ethnic group, sex, age, years of schooling, and other factors related to occupational success. Chiswick (1980) reported that foreign-born white adults required 13 years from migration to earnings cross-over. For Japanese, Filipinos, and Mexicans, years to cross-over were 18, 13, and 15 years, respectively. Even after 30

TABLE 7.6

Education, Occupation, and Per Capita Household Income and Return for Education of Selected Groups of Men Age 20 to 64 Classified by Ancestry, Generation, and Nativity, 1979

Generation/Nativity	Population	Characteristics of Ethnic Groups				Regression Analyses Returns for Education[a]		
		Median Years of Schooling	Percent With Some College	Mean Duncan Occupation Score	Per Capita Household Income	R^2	b	S.E. of b
	(000)		(%)	(3 to 96)	(000)	%		
First/Foreign-Born								
English	123	13.2	43	50	$ 9,400	39	4.5	0.8
Russian/E. Europe	271	13.1	47	44	8,000	49	4.5	0.4
Asian	202	14.2**	64**	44	5,200*	46	5.4	0.5
Filipino	88	13.9	76***	38*	5,300*	36	3.8	0.8
Mexican	587	6.9*	9*	18*	2,700*	16	0.9*	0.2
Second/Native-Born Sons with at Least One Foreign-Born Parent								
English	318	13.8	56	50	9,000	41	5.5	0.5
Russian	259	14.4	64	55	10,900	30	4.5	0.6
Asian	108	13.6	56	44*	8,400	42	7.2	0.9
Mexican	371	10.1*	21*	30*	5,000*	21	2.6*	0.3
Third or More/Native-Born Sons of Native-Born Parents								
English	6,162	13.3	50	44	8,600	36	5.3	0.1
Russian	396	15.1**	78**	58**	11,400**	49	7.0**	0.5
Asian	71	14.8**	69**	51**	11,800**	50	7.4	1.0
Mexican	459	11.7*	29*	32*	5,200*	25	3.4*	0.4

Note: From Niedert and Farley, 1985.

[a]The value of b indicates the change in occupational status associated with a one-year change in educational attainment.

*Value is significantly smaller than parameter for the English standard group (0.05 level).

**Value is significantly greater than parameter for the English standard group (0.05 level).

years, foreign-born Chinese men had not equaled the earnings of the native-born Chinese American males when other variables were held constant.

Except for Japanese immigrants, who worked for Japanese international firms in the United States, even well-educated Asian immigrants who arrived within 5 years of the 1980 census were less likely to be ranked higher in occupational scale than earlier immigrants. Asian immigrant physicians, pharmacists, and nurses often had to work as interns, laboratroy assistants, and technicians. Language problems and differences in professional standards contributed to their descent along the occupational ladder, but labor market discrimination was another likely factor (Cheng, 1984).

The 1979 occupation and income data of adult men collected for the 1980 census was analyzed by Neidert and Farley (1985). Using a covariance model, they regressed 1979 male SEI upon years of education and a series of control variables that influence achievement: age, marital status, region of residence, and English proficiency. Rate of return for education varied by ancestry groups and over generations. For first-generation Englishmen, each year of schooling netted a gain of 4.5 SEI points. Asian men gained 5.4 SEI for each additional year of schooling, and Filipinos, 3.8 points. These values were not different statistically from the English. Statistical differences were found for only two groups: other Southern Europeans and Mexicans, who received significantly lower returns from their education.

In 1979, the estimated number of Asian and Filipino first-generation men was 290,000, compared to 108,000 second-generation Asian American men age 20 to 64. Second-generation Asian American men were not quite as well educated as their peers of English ancestry, with a median of 0.2 years less schooling but about the same proportion with some college. Mean Asian SEI remained at 44, but it was significantly lower than the English men's SEI of 50. Return on education for second-generation Americans of Russian ancestry, however, had forged ahead. They had more education, better jobs, and higher income than those of English ancestry. Second-generation Mexican and other Hispanic Americans remained significantly below the English in education, occupation, and income. Regression analysis showed that for second-generation Asian Americans, returns on education was high. An extra year of schooling was associated with 7.2 points on the Duncan scale, compared to 5.5 points for English men, and 2.6 points, a significantly lower rate of return on education, for Mexican Americans.

Data on occupational achievment relative to education was more encouraging for third- and subsequent-generations of Asian American men in 1979. There were 71,000 third- or later generation Asian American men. Third-generation Asian Americans were significantly higher than English ancestry peers in median years of education. Their median years of schooling was 14.8 against 13.3 for the English, and 69% had some college, compared to 50% of the English. Asian American mean SEI of 51 was significantly higher than the English ancestry's 44. Each additional year of schooling for third-generation Asians was associated with 7.4 SEI points in occupation. Rank order of occupational returns for investment in education among

10 immigrant groups found Asian Americans at the top for all three generations. Asian American persistence in the educational pipeline and demand for quality higher education can thus be regarded as rational decision making in favor of maximal occupational returns.

Ethnicity was significantly related to occupational attainment even in the third generation and beyond. Russians, largely Jews according to earlier census counts, continued the trend of success observed among the second generation by being significantly higher than the English in education, occupation, and income. Their mean SEI was 58. Each year of additional schooling translated into 7 more points on the SEI.

For Mexican and other Hispanic Americans as well as Afro-Americans who have been in this country for three generations or more, education, occupation, and income remained significantly lower than those of English, Russian, and Asian ancestry. One more year of school was associated with 3.4 and 3.9 SEI points for Mexican and Afro-Americans, respectively. American Indians were no better off than most of the other minorities. Their median years of schooling, occupation, and per capita household income remained significantly lower than the English "core culture" group's. In the rank order of 10 immigrant groups' occupational returns on education, Mexican Americans came in tenth for all three generations. For third- or later generation Mexican Americans, the mean SEI was 30, 5 points lower than the average for all first-generation men in the study sample. For Mexican Americans, obtaining educational credentials was not associated as consistently with better jobs as among other ethnic groups.

There were limitations to the 1979 survey data. Income figures were per capita family income, which would be overestimates for individual Asian American worker's income, because Asian families have more workers. There was no way to evaluate the location or quality of education of first-generation immigrants. The assumption that one additional year of education at any level anywhere in the world could be related linearly to an index of occupational status may not have been warranted. Cross-sectional analyses are limited for generalizing about the future. The sons and grandsons of contemporary immigrant parents may not behave in the same patterns as second- and third-generation men did in 1979.

Although the data supported the inference of higher occupational returns on education with each subsequent generation, intergenerational occupation status did not increase across all ancestry groups, as shown in Fig. 7.1. Third-generation Englishmen recorded a mean SEI of 44, lower than mean SEIs of 50 recorded by first- and second-generation Englishmen in 1979. German and other Western European mean SEIs remained about the same across all three generations. Other Southern Europeans, however, had raised their mean SEI with each generation, so that the third generation was about the same as the other Europeans. The Asians' occupational gains seemed to be between the second and subsequent generations, due to limitation of survey instrument.

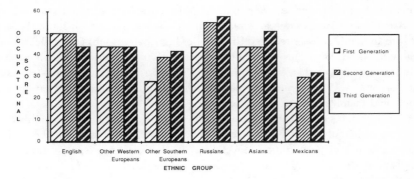

FIG. 7.1. Intergenerational comparisons of mean occupational scores of men age 20 to 64 classified by selected ancestry, 1979. The Occupational score = Duncan socioeconomic index, range from 3 to 96. Russians in study were predominantly Jews (from Neidert & Farley, 1985).

Asian American Women's Education and Occupation, 1970

Carliner (1977) reported information on immigration, education, labor force participation, occupational status, and median income of adult women by ethnic groups from the 1970 census. The Duncan SEI scores of Japanese, Chinese, and Filipino women were 40.6, 42.2, and 41.5, respectively, compared to 42.6 for white women. Asian women were better educated than white women. Carliner concluded from results of regression analyses that the occupational differences between Asian and white women may have been due to labor market discrimination. The differences were statistically significant for Japanese and Filipino women. The differences between white and all other groups of women were greater for wages than for Duncan scores. Gaining access to high-status occupations was easier for educated Asian American women than obtaining equal pay. For other minority women, but not Asian women, lack of education was considered to have been a significant factor in limiting access to high-status occupations. Asian American women have made gains in education since 1970. However, Asian American women, like all women, earn less than men of the same ethnic group.

EDUCATION, OCCUPATION, AND INCOME

Asian American families, according to all accounts, have invested single-mindedly in higher education. These human capital investments have resulted in returns in the form of professional, managerial, and technical jobs for their offspring. United States media have broadcast to the world the news that as of 1980, median Asian

American family income had risen to $23,600 for the six groups that comprise 95% of Asian Americans, above the white families' median income of $20,835. Real growth in family income reflected the trend of higher status jobs accessible to well-educated Asian Americans since World War II. Asian American households and families were larger than white families'. The mean number of persons in Asian families was 3.75, compared to 3.19 in white families. More Asian family and household members were in the labor force.

Asian ethnic groups varied substantially in their size of families, numbers of workers per family, avarage age, region of residence, generations in the United States, recency of immigration, educational level, work experience, command of English, and other factors that influence occupation level, individual income, and family income. The Vietnamese family averaged 4.68 persons. Their median income of $12,840 was close to the median income of black families' $12,598. The Japanese, who were almost three-quarters native born, behaved most like whites. Japanese American families averaged 3.24 persons with a median income of $27,354. Table 7.7 shows median income of whites, other minorities, and Asian Americans by ethnic groups as year-round and full-time workers, separately for foreign-born and female workers, and as families. Family income statistics can be misleading when applied to the foreign born and particularly for recent immigrants and refugees. These latter groups live in households with more individuals amd more workers in order to share the limited resources of each to improve the living standards of all. Asian immigrants have historically depended on the community, and later, when familites were allowed, on their families for mutual support and assistance (Bonacich, 1972, 1980; Bonacich & Modell, 1980; Nee & Sanders, 1985).

The median incomes of Japanese, Chinese, Filipino, and Asian Indian families were higher, of Korean families very close to, and of Vietnamese families much lower than white families'. The median income of a full-time, year-round worker also varied by Asian ethnic groups. Asian Indians, who have the highest education levels and solid grounding in English, reported median income of $18,707 per year. Full-time Vietnamese workers, on the other hand, reported median incomes of $11,641, close to Hispanic Americans' median income of $11,650 and black full-time workers' $11,327. Filipino full-time workers, with income of $13,690, were the only other Asian group who had lower income than the white median of $15,572. Filipino families' higher median family income was achieved through having more workers per family and smaller differential between the income of male and female workers. Full-time women workers earned much less than men in each group. However, Japanese, Chinese, Filipino, and Asian Indian women earned more than white women. Korean women's median income was close to white women's. Vietnamese women, however, earned less than white, black, and Hispanic women. Foreign-born workers earned less than the native born, and workers with limited English proficiency earned less than those fluent in English (Chiswick, 1978, 1979). These aggregate income figures do not fully elucidate the role of higher education

TABLE 7.7

Median Family and Full-Time Worker Incomes and Family Poverty Levels of White, Black, Hispanic, and Asian Americans by Ethnic Groups in 1979[a]

	White	Black	Hispanic	Japanese	Chinese	Filipino	Korean	Asian Indians	Vietnamese
Median family income	$20,835	$12,598	$14,712	$27,354	$22,559	$23,687	$20,459	$24,993	$12,840
Median income of year-round full-time worker	$15,572	$11,327	$11,650	$16,829	$15,753	$13,690	$14,224	$18,707	$11,641
Median income of foreign-born worker				$ 9,937	$11,818	$12,715	$ 9,589	$13,138	$ 9,256
Median income of full-time female worker	$10,512	$ 9,583	$ 8,923	$11,916	$11,891	$12,007	$10,263	$11,799	$ 7,261
Percent of families below poverty level	7.0	26.5	21.3	5.6	11.8	5.3	7.9	5.0	30.3

[a]From Gardner, Robey, and Smith, 1985, U.S. Department of Commerce, Bureau of the Census, 1983a, 1983b

in raising the earnings of Asian Americans. Trends in returns on investment in education provide a fuller explanation.

Trends in Returns on Investment in Education

By 1980, with the exception of recent immigrants and refugees, typical family and per capita income of major Asian American ethnic groups was close to that of white Americans. Third-generation, college-educated Asian ancestry men and women have been particularly successful in using their education to enter prestigious occupations with high earning potentials. The largest income discrepancies remained those between men and women of all ethnic groups. The trend toward approaching family and per capita income parity could be seen from census figures. Much of the economic improvement had been due to investment in higher education and improved occupational returns on investment.

Young (1977) provided an economic model for describing the comparative advantages of Asian Americans. These included high productivity perception by the majority group, group unity, maximization of group rather than individual utility, small entrepreneurial specialization, and preference for education. Education has a high value in Asian individual as well as group utility functions. These high utillity values have led to investment in higher education by Asian American students and their parents. Education is deemed by Asians to be a capital asset that cannot be expropriated. Japanese Americans families, for example, lost much of their accumulated physical assets during the World War II evacuation and relocation, but they retained and even added to their human capital investments during the war years (Daniels, Taylor, & Kitano, 1986).

Young's model was based on a theoretical framework for economic analysis of discrimination in the market place formulated by Becker (1971). If economic discrimination against human capital investment is high, an individual who makes an investment decision perceives limited opportunities in the open labor market and would be less likely to make additional investments beyond the minimum. However, if perceived productivity of a minority group is high, and economic discrimination is moderate, then concentration in small ethnic enterprises that employ their own people would result in a more elastic labor supply curve. Thus, shielded partially from the open labor market, that minority group can work and live together to maximize opportunities to accumulate capital for investment in education. The minority group expects to equalize their income to that of the majority by overinvestment in human capital. Over time, aggregated investments in education would have an effect on occupational choices, which in turn influence income.

Each group of Asian immigrants, to a greater or lesser degree, has invested in education even when there were few immediate prospects for better jobs. Their education credentials prepared them to move up to higher status occupations when opportunities arose. Even in the face of moderate levels of discrimination, Asian Americans tried to offset prejudice by offering compensating advantages in the form of education. They have been able to offer a more educated group to the labor market by raising their educational levels at an accelerated rate compared to the U.S. population as a whole. In 1940, the median years of education of Americans 14 years and over was 8.3 years. It was 8.8 years for Japanese Americans and 5.6 for Chinese Americans. By 1960, both Chinese and Japanese Americans had surpassed total United States population in median years of schooling and had a high percentage in the professions.

There is abundant evidence that discrimination against nonwhites increases systematically with education and age. Becker (1971) predicted that increase in the education of American minorities would only increase paartially their incomes relative to those of whites, given greater discrimination against the older and better educated. Career patterns and income trends of Asian Americans to date have not provided evidence for refuting Becker's prediction (Harman & Maxfield, 1979).

Fogel (1966) and Young (1977) investigated returns to education for Asian Americans in 1960. Fogel limited Asian Americans to Japanese in California, and concluded that they received a lower rate of return in terms of median income for investment in median years of education. Young studied the returns on investment in education by calculating an expected education by income matrix for Chinese, Japanese, and black Americans if they had received the same returns to education as the total United States population. He found significantly smaller numbers of Asian and black Americans in the upper income ranges. From the middle-income range onwards, there were significantly fewer Chinese, Japanese, and blacks than expected. The drop reached a maximum at 70% of expected numbers in the highest income cells for Asian Americans. The number of blacks was lower throughout the upper income ranges, to only 10% of expected numbers in the top income cell. Returns to education in 1960 was lower than average for Chinese and Japanese Americans, even lower for the foreign born, who concentrated in the middle income brackets, and lowest of all for black Americans. Chi (1972) also used multivariate regression models to study the relationship between education and income among diverse ethnic groups recorded in the 1960 census. He concluded that education affected income only indirectly through its influence on occupations. Education alone was not enough to equalize income among groups.

The situation was different in Hawaii, where Asian Americans were a majority of the population, and where the war had opened up unions traditionally closed to Asians. In 1960, whites continued to dominate the highest income ranges, but Chinese Americans, 92% native born, urban, and with higher proportions of professionals, were overrepresented in the other upper income groups. Japanese Americans, who arrived in Hawaii later than the Chinese and who had higher proportions of craft and rural workers, also were approaching the expected numbers in all but the highest income levels (Young, 1977).

Young postulated that the returns on education for Asian Americans should rise also on mainland United States, due to their stress on investment in higher education and consequent entry in professional occupations. He predicted the rise would be rapid for Japanese Americans, because of the greater numbers of native born and limited immigration. Returns to education for Chinese Americans would remain below average because of the high proportion of foreign born and continuing influx of immigrants.

Initial examinations of 1970 census income figures suggested that Japanese American males, at least, were indeed approaching parity with whites in earnings. However, multiple regression analyses by detailed occupations conducted by independent investigators, who used somewhat different models to control for factors related to earnings, yielded separate conclusions that Chinese, Japanese, and Filipino American males still earned less than their white peers. More investment in higher education had not closed the earnings gap.

Taable 7.8 shows national median earnings of white and Asian Americans classified by ethnic groups, sex, and education levels in 1969. For men and women in all groups, each additional level of schooling—elementary school, high school, and college graduation—was associated with higher earnings. Wide differences in earnings among ethnic groups were reduced when education was taken into account. Women earned about half as much as men at all educational levels. Japanese men with elementary and high school educations had slightly higher earnings than white men. White and Japanese men earned more, and Filipino men less, than men of other groups at all educational levels. Returns on investment in college education was lower for both Filipino men and women (Wilber, Jaco, Hagan, & del Fierro, 1975).

Asian Americans were not distributed evenly across the nation. Most lived on the West Coast. The 1970 Asian American earnings in California (the state with the largest number of Asian Americans) have been compared with earnings of whites

TABLE 7.8

Median Earnings of White and Asian Americans by Ethnic Group, Sex, and Education Level in 1969[a]

	Japanese	Chinese	Filipino	Korean	White
Males					
8 years elementary	$ 7,575	$ 5,567	$ 6,041	$ 5,900	$ 7,001
4 years high school	8,675	7,441	6,632	7,687	8,332
4 years college	11,762	10,975	7,171	8,111	12,143
Percent college above elementary graduate	55.3%	97.1%	18.7%	37.5%	73.4%
Female					
8 years elementary	$ 3,478	$ 2,725	$ 3,616	$ 3,250	$ 3,154
4 years high school	4,564	4,400	3,676	3,600	3,854
4 years college	6,666	5,705	4,793	5,076	5,943
Percent college above elementary graduate	91.4%	109.4%	37.5%	56.7%	88.4%

[a]From Wilber, Jaco, Hagan, and del Fierro, 1975

TABLE 7.9

Average Age, Education, Occupational Status, and Annual Earnings[a] and Multiple Regression Analysis[b] of Earnings of Native-born Whites, Blacks, Chicanos, Chinese, and Japanese Men Age 24 through 62 in California, 1970

	Whites	Blacks	Chicanos	Chinese	Japanese
N	21,362	2,033	2,403	137	396
Age					
Mean	41.7	40.6	39.8	39.7	42.5
S.D.	10.8	10.5	9.7	9.2	9.3
Education					
Mean	14.6	13.0	12.2	16.0	15.2
S.D.	3.0	3.2	3.7	2.7	2.6
Occupational Status[c]					
Mean	3.7	2.6	2.8	4.3	3.8*
S.D.	1.6	1.6	1.5	1.7	1.9
Annual Earnings					
Mean	$10,550	6,678	8,077	10,626*	10,358
S.D.	7,093	4,493	4,811	7,551	6,850
Multiple Correlations	.39	.29	.43	.45	.40

$ Change in earnings associated with unit change in an independent variable when all other variables in the equation are held constant

Age $	79	33	76	174	84
Education $	522	284	340	320**	438
Occupational Status $	969	471	752	1,501	1,088
Intercept	−4,003	422	−1,179	−7,803	−3,969

Note: From Jiobu, 1976
[a]1970 public use sample, 15% state file for California
[b]Unstandardized partial regression coefficients are shown
[c]Edwards type scale: 1 = laborers, service workers to 6 = professional and technical workers
*Not significantly different from white mean at .05 level, all other means significantly different
**Less than twice standard error, and other coefficients exceed twice the S.E.

and other minorities. Jiobu (1976) used a multiple regression model to estimate the net cost of minority status in 1969 when age, broad occupational status, and education were taken into account for earning of native-born black, Chicano, Chinese, and Japanese men age 24 through 62 in comparison with white men's. Chinese and Japanese had higher average education and occupational status, and black and Chicano lower, than white men, as shown in Table 7.9. The two Asian American groups' dollar earnings were close to white means.

When earnings were regressed against age, education, and occupational status for each group, regression equations of blacks, Chicanos, and Chinese were significantly different from the white equation, whereas the Japanese equation was not. Japanese data were excluded from further analyses. Regression coefficients in Table

7.9 represent the net rate that each independent variable was related to earnings. One year of education was worth $522 for whites, $438 for Japanese, $340 for Chicanos, $320 for Chinese, and $284 for blacks. Differences in quality of education was one possible explanation advanced for differences in worth in terms of earnings. However, other data from the same period, such as the Equality of Educational Opportunities Survey, have shown that the developed academic abilities and investment in education of Asian Americans were not below white levels. Chinese earnings were related more positively to their occupational status than whites, Chicanos, and blacks in that order. If Chinese were to have the same mean educational level and occupational status as whites, their mean earnings would have been lower than the 1969 actuals. Chinese–white parity in mean earnings was due to high Chinese level of education and their level of as well as value of occupational status. Blacks and Chicanos would have increased their earnings substantially had they had the same mean educational and occupational levels as whites. Jiobu concluded that on the basis of a fixed minimum educational level, Chinese incurred the greatest "cost" through their ethnic group membership by more than $1,600 not explained by age, education, or occupation levels. The reasons behind the hidden cost of being Chinese American continues to be a focus of concern to Asian American scholars (Leong, 1985).

A different conclusion was reached by Roos (1977), who used the same data base as Jiobu, but employed a different regression model that refined occupations into 400 detailed categories. Roos concluded that Japanese Americans, in fact, had not yet reached earnings parity in 1970. Roos compared incomes of currently employed Japanese, Mexican American, and white males age 25 to 64 who were working for government, wages and salary in private firms, and self-employed. Table 7.10 shows mean income, school years completed, and income adjusted for age and education. Accounting for age and education differences increased the income discrepancy of the Japanese relative to whites from 93% downward to 87%, and substantially

TABLE 7.10

Average Income, Education, and Income Adjusted for Age and Education Differences of White, Japanese, and Mexican American Men Age 25 to 64 in California, 1970[a]

	White	Japanese	Mexican American
N	7,175	473	3,943
Years of schooling	12.5	13.2	9.6
Mean income ($)	$11,075	10,250	7,570
Income as percent of white income (%)	100	93	68
Income adjusted for age and income ($)	$11,075	9,618	9,304
Adjusted income as percent of white income (%)	100	87	84

[a]From Roos, 1977

reduced the Mexican American discrepancy from 68% upward to 84% of mean white income. Education did not close the gap between Japanese American and white earnings. Multiple regression and regression standardization procedures supported an occupational structural explanation of the white, minority income difference as well as the existence of a differentiated dual reward system based on socioeconomic status and ethnicity.

Mexican Americans were in blue-collar jobs and concentrated in low-paying employment. The lower income return was due primarily to inferior schooling rather than job-specific discrimination. Japanese Americans had more than closed the education gap with whites and therefore offered direct competition to whites in the labor market for white-collar jobs. The primary consequence of high-education attainment for the Japanese was to gain access to relatively high-status occupations. Self-employment benefitted Japanese less than whites or Mexican Americans. Japanese Americans earned less not only because they were concentrated in low-paying employment rather than the better paying occupations, which whites dominated, but also because they did not receive equal wages in the same detailed occupations. The lower income of native-born Japanese American males in California was related to structural underemployment and minimal upward mobility. Foreign-born Japanese were even more segregated into low-income employment and had a greater gap in loss of earnings unaccounted for by the variables included in the analysis. Japanese Californians were not receiving the income payoff in 1970 that they would have had for their education had they been white (Roos, 1977).

The quality of education, occupation choices, and income status of Filipino Americans in 1970 was different from those of the Chinese and Japanese. Macaranas (1979) postulated that "conventional wisdom relating education and income appears valid on a straight cross-sectional or even on intergenerational cross-section basis. However, this statistical relation does not explain whether Asian Americans have achieved their educational levels because of or in spite of the predetermining environmental variables" (p. 4). Macaranas believed that much of the college education Filipino immigrants received before coming to the United States was of a consumption type rather than the investment type of education that would prepare them for higher earning occupations when they reached the more advanced United States economy. Private, for profit institutions of higher education in the Philippines provided low-cost college diplomas as status symbols rather than as transferable preparation or credentials for careers. Three out of four Filipino family heads with college degrees were working in low-status sales, clerical, or service jobs in a 1973 survey of Asian Americans in low-income urban areas. Given their own work experiences, it was little wonder Filipino immigrant parents would place relatively less value than other Asians on higher education. College enrollment rates of Filipino youth were and remain lower than those of Chinese and Japanese Americans.

Regression analyses of mean or median earnings of Chinese, Japanese, and Filipino Americans were undertaken, using as independent variables eduaction, sex, labor force participation, and other socioeconomic data. In addition, a survey of educational attitudes and work/income opportunity perceptions among Filipino American youth was conducted in 1977 and 1978. Macaranas concluded that, unlike the Chinese and Japanese, education was not a significant explanatory variable for income levels of Filipinos. Filipino males age 20 to 24 have to work longer hours to equal earning levels of their Chinese and Japanese age cohorts, because fewer Filipinos were in the occupational categories of professional, technical, or managerial workers.

Occupations and Earnings in 1960, 1970, and 1976

Despite evidence of lingering labor market discrimination, the socioeconomic gains made by Asian Americans that was recorded by the population census of 1960 and 1970 have continued. The 1976 Survey of Income and Education by the Bureau of the Census provided a third data point for analysis of occupational and income trends among United States ethnic groups during the 15 years between 1960 and 1975. Hirschman and Wong (1984) used data from 1960, 1970, and 1976 of all Chinese, Filipino, and Japanese males age 25 to 64 with reported occupation and industry and of representative samples of whites, blacks, and Hispanics. The composition of Asian and Hispanic populations had changed during the 15-year span. By 1976, the foreign born in the study sample had risen to 83%, 81%, and 48% for Chinese, Filipinos, and Hispanics, respectively. Occupational status was measured by the Duncan SEI, and annual earnings were reported in constant 1975 dollars.

Average SEI scores of Chinese and Japanese were above whites' for all 3 years. Filipinos, augmented by educated immigrants, had closed the occupational gap very substantially by 1976, as shown in Table 7.11. Mean annual earnings of the Japanese were more than white means for 1969 and 1975. Blacks and Hispanics had also reduced their occupational and income gaps, but remained substantially below white attainments.

Multivariate regression equations were used to estimate the effects of ethnicity on socioeconomic status both directly and indirectly, mediated by intervening variables. When age composition and birth place were controlled, Asians had occupational status approximately equal to that of whites. If educational composition was held constant across populations by lowering the educational attainment of Chinese and Japanese, Asian occupation achievement would have been lowered by 5 to 6 SEI points relative to white men. The direct ethnic effect on occupational attainment with all other variables in the equations held constant would result in all minorities being below the white SEI level. Except for a decline in the black–white gap, the investigators observed no significant trend in the occupational data.

Direct and indirect ethnic effects in earnings were expressed as deviations from white mean earnings in thousands of constant 1975 dollars and summarized in Table 7.12. Gross differences showed that black and Hispanic men earned on the average about $4,000 less than white men in 1975, although they had narrowed their earnings disadvantage. Japanese and Filipino men had made gains in earnings, but not the Chinese. Japanese men's earnings had been $1,100 less than whites in 1960,

TABLE 7.11

Average Occupational Status and Earnings in Constant 1975 Dollars of Men Age 24–64 by Ethnicity: 1960, 1970, 1976[a]

	Mean Duncan Socioeconomic Index (Ratio to White SEI)					
	1960		1970		1976	
White	38.0	(100)	41.1	(100)	42.5	(100)
Black	18.8	(50)	23.8	(58)	27.4	(64)
Hispanic	24.7	(65)	31.0	(75)	29.6	(70)
Japanese	38.3	(101)	41.9	(102)	43.6	(103)
Chinese	43.0	(113)	44.8	(109)	46.2	(109)
Filipino	22.0	(58)	34.3	(83)	39.8	(94)
	Mean Annual Earnings in Thousands of 1975 $s (Ratio to White Earnings)					
White	11.2	(100)	14.4	(100)	13.5	(100)
Black	5.5	(49)	8.5	(59)	9.1	(67)
Hispanic	7.1	(63)	10.5	(73)	9.7	(72)
Japanese	10.2	(91)	14.7	(102)	15.1	(112)
Chinese	9.4	(84)	13.1	(91)	11.7	(97)
Filipino	6.8	(60)	10.2	(71)	12.6	(93)

[a]From Hirschman and Wong, 1984

but they rose to about $1,600 more than whites' in 1976. Filipinos were still $600 below whites in 1976, but they had been $4,500 below in 1960. Chinese men received, on the average, about $2,000 less than whites at all three points in time. Japanese and Filipino men had reached parity with whites, once differences in foreign origins were taken into account.

Education was the primary determinant of ethnic earning differences. About $1,500 of black and Hispanic earnings disadvantage could be explained by lower educational attainment. Education also accounted for a substantial share of Asian Americans' economic gains. If Asian educational levels were adjusted downward to match the rest of the population, average earnings would have declined by about $1,500 in 1975. It has been only through overachievement in education that some Asian Americans have reached socioeconomic parity with white men. Net of the other independent variables in the regression model, there were substantial direct ethnic differences in earnings. Japanese men earned about $1,000 more than white men when all factors were held constant. Chinese men continued to receive about $2,300 less than white men in 1975, even when their backgrounds were equivalent. With the exception of Chinese men, the direct negative effect of ethnicity on earnings had declined for all groups. Hirschman and Wong (1984) believed that discrimination alone could not explain these trends in differential earnings for the Chinese. They postulated that continuing concentration of immigrants in Chinatowns and holding jobs in ethnic enterprises, strategies that had been necessary for survival in the days of legal discrimination and overt racial hostility, may now actually be

TABLE 7.12

Direct and Indirect Effects of Ethnicity on Occupational and Earning Attainment of Men in the Labor Force Age 25–64 in 1960, 1970, and 1976

	Occupation: White-Minority Differences in Duncan SEI Points								
	Total Effects Net of Age and Birthplace			Indirect[a]			Direct Effects of Ethnicity		
Year	1960	1970	1976	1960	1970	1976	1960	1970	1976
					Years of Schooling				
Ethnicity									
Black	−20**	−18**	−15**	−7**	−8**	−7**	−13**	−11**	−8*
Hispanic	−14**	−11**	−13**	−7**	−6**	−8**	−6**	−5**	−5*
Japanese	0	1	2	5**	6**	6**	−4**	−3**	−3
Chinese	7**	3**	5**	3**	5**	6**	1	−1	−2
Filipino	−12**	−8**	−1	0	1	8**	−10**	−6**	−8*

	Earnings: White Minority Differences in Thousands of 1975 $s								
	Total Effects Net of Age and Birthplace			Indirect Effects[a]			Direct Effects of Ethnicity		
Year	1960	1970	1976	1960	1970	1976	1960	1970	1976
					Years of Schooling				
Ethnicity									
Black	−5.7**	−6**	−4.4*	−1.3**	−1.7**	−1.5**	−2.5**	−2.2**	−1.4**
Hispanic	−3.5**	−3.7**	−3.4*	−1.3*	−1.4**	−1.8**	−1.6**	−1.8**	−1.0*
Japanese	−0.9	0.2	1.7*	0.8	1.4**	1.1	−2.8**	−2.0**	1.1*
Chinese	−1.0*	−0.8*	−1.2*	0.7	1.4*	1.1	−2.6**	−2.6**	−2.3**
Filipino	−3.2**	−3.5*	0.2	—	0.3	1.3	−2.9**	−3.1**	−0.7

	Occupation		
Ethnicity			
Black	−0.9**	−1.0**	−0.8**
Hispanic	−0.4	−0.4	−0.5
Japanese	−0.3	−0.3	−0.3
Chinese	0.2	−0.1	−0.2
Filipino	−0.7	−0.6	−0.8

Note: From Hirschman and Wong, 1984

[a]Only independent variables with significant indirect effects are included

*Statistically significant at the 0.5 level

**Statistically significant at the 0.1 level

contributing to the slow progress of the Chinese. The remaining inequities are subtle in expression and probably based upon differential access to institutional settings. Hirschman and Wong (1984) and Wong (1982) concluded that except for the Japanese, there remained a cost associated with being a mainland Asian American. The cost was highest for the Chinese. These findings supported earlier findings on California Chinese by Jiobu (1976) and of Chicago Chinese by Li (1977).

Hirschman and Wong's conclusion that Japanese and Filipino Americans had attained earning parity with whites of similar background has been challenged by Nee and Sanders (1985). They contended that the national socioeconomic advantages reported for Japanese Americans in 1976 was due to a number of artifacts: their concentration on the West Coast, where per capita income was higher than the national average; and the limited proportion of Japanese immigrants, most of whom arrived with college degrees or marketable skills and had jobs waiting for them in Japan-based firms. They attributed the Chinese American disadvantage, on the other hand, primarily to the high proportion of immigrants and the cost of immigration rather than to ethnicity. Limiting their analysis to Californian men, age 25 through 64, who were employed in 1979 in the 1980 census 5% public use sample, Nee and Sanders concluded that native-born whites retained a modest earnings advantage over comparable Chinese and Japanese Americans.

Investment in education remained the most important mechanism for socioeconomic mobility for Chinese and Japanese Americans. The capital for making educational investments originated from strong ethnic enclave enterprises, which have gained renewed vigor from the influx of recent Asian immigrants. Filipinos, who did not develop small business bases, have not fared as well. Filipinos in California have remained in blue-collar jobs and still earned less than other Asians. They invested less in American education and received much lower returns on their education. Immigrant Filipinos, who arrived with more years of schooling, earned more than the native born.

Except for native-born Filipinos and Chinese immigrants, Asian Americans were better educated than white-native Californians. Mean years of schooling are shown in Table 7.13.

Nee and Sanders (1985) used a multiple regression model that included two measures of age to control nonlinearity of earnings with age, education, marital status, hours worked, sector of employer, occupation status, English skills, citizenship and proportion of new immigrants as independent variables. With all other

TABLE 7.13

Mean Years of Schooling for Native and Immigrant Chinese, Japanese, Filipino, and Whites.[a]

	Chinese	Japanese	Filipino	White
Native	17.2	16.4	15.3	16.0
Immigrants	15.1	16.7	16.2	13.5

[a]From Nee and Sanders, 1985

factors held constant, native-born white, Japanese, and Chinese males received $904, $900, and $770 in earnings for each additional year of schooling. Native-born Filipino Californians received $217 for each year of schooling. Returns on education among immigrants were lower for white, Chinese, and Filipino immigrants, who received $494, $334, and $300, respectively, for each year of schooling. Japanese immigrants were better paid than the native-born and all other immigrants, probably because they worked for Japan-based international firms. Mean earnings are shown in Table 7.14 by ethnic groups for native-born, immigrant, and college-educated men. Filipinos were disadvantaged socioeconomically in 1980. College graduates earned less than immigrant whites. Typically, a white worker in California with a college education still earned more than Japanese, Chinese, or Filipino college graduates in 1980.

The role of ethnic enterprises in the economic progress of Asian Americans was reinforced by these analyses. Self-employment was associated with higher earnings for Chinese and the small proportion of Filipinos who owned businesses. Self-employed whites enjoyed a greater earnings advantage. For self-employed Japanese, many of whom owned truck farms of modest acreage, the earnings advantage was not as notable.

English skills and Unites States citizenship were also associated with higher earnings for immigrants. The cost of being a new immigrant, however, was twice as much for the Filipino and Chinese as for whites. Despite modest earnings differentials, the 1980 California census data supported the generally held view that Asian Ameicans as a group were on the road to earnings parity through investment in higher education.

REWARDS IN ACADEME

Asian Americans have approached income parity with the majority through their investment in higher education. Since the 1950s, Asian Americans, predominantly those who are foreign born, have obtained advanced degrees and entered academic ranks of post-secondary institutions. Evidence from national surveys conducted by the American Council on Education (ACE) in 1968-1969 and 1972-1973, by the National Research Council in 1979, and a 1983 Northeastern regional survey show

TABLE 7.14.
Mean Earnings for Native-Born, Immigrant, and College-Educated Men[a]

	Chinese	Japanese	Filipino	White
Native	$20,841	$20,164	$15,482	$21,506
Immigrant	$15,675	$20,310	$14,058	$17,958
College Graduates	$21,000 +	$23,000 +	$16,000 +	$25,000 +

[a]From Nee and Sanders, 1985

TABLE 7.15
Frequency Distribution and Quality of Degrees and Mean Annual Salaries of Full-Time Faculty by
Ethnic Groups, 1973[a]

	Total N	Distinguished or "Strong" Ph.D.s	Lower Ranked Ph.D.s	Unranked Ph.D.s	Less Than Doctorates
		%	%	%	%
Degree Quality					
White	359,828	11.0	14.3	12.3	62.4
Black	9,273	3.8	5.9	7.9	82.4
Asian Americans	4,678	15.8	26.7	16.8	40.7
Salary					
White		$17,991	$17,414	$18,179	$15,981
Percent of White Salary		%	%	%	%
White		100	100	100	100
Black		113	126	113	95
Asian American		101	98	92	80

[a]From Sowell, 1975

that salaries of Asian Americans, adjusted for quality of degree and productivity, lagged behind salaries of fellow black and white faculty academicians. There are more Chinese than Japanese Americans in academic work.

Sowell (1975) analysed the mean annual salaries of full-time faculty in 1972-1973 by ethnic groups. Black faculty with Ph.D.s earned more than whites when degree level and quality were held constant. Asian Americans earned $2,000 to $3,000 less than either black or white faculty with the same qualifications. Their overall mean salary was only a little lower than whites and blacks because Asian Americans were concentrated in the higher degree levels, held higher quality degrees, taught primarily natural sciences and engineering, and had published more than their colleagues. These findings were confirmed by Freeman (1978), who analyzed 1969 and 1973 ACE faculty survey data. Salary as percent of white salary relative to degree quality is shown in Table 7.15, relative to productivity in terms of articles published is shown in Table 7.16. Income relative to white colleagues in most categories had decreased among Asian Americans from 1969 to 1973, whereas relative income of other minorities had increased across productivity levels. Because proportionately more Asian Americans held Ph.D.s, from "distinguished" or "strong" as well as other doctoral programs, and had published more than whites and blacks, Sowell and Freeman agreed with Asian American academicians that Asian American faculty did suffer from some discrimination in the academic market place (Minami et al., 1979).

A 1983 survey of Northeast Coast Chinese American faculty found that the majority of Chinese American faculty were foreign born, received their bachelor's

TABLE 7.16
Productivity and Mean Annual Salaries as Percent of White Salaries of Full-Time, Male, Minority
Faculty 1969–1973[a]

	5 +	1–4	0	Total
	%	%	%	%
1973 Distribution by Number of Articles				
White	35.6	27.6	35.5	98.7
Other Minority	30.5	26.8	42.3	99.6
Asian American	52.4	22.9	24.1	99.4
1973 Salary as Percent of White Salary				
White	100	100	100	100
Other Minority	89.4	90.6	111.9	89.7
Asian American	87.4	100.3	88.7	94.6
1969 Salary as Percent of White Salary				
White	100	100	100	100
Other Minority	81.5	89.7	91.0	84.9
Asian Americans	92.4	93.6	92.4	98.3

[a]From Freeman, 1978

degrees overseas and their doctorates from highly ranked United States universities.
They had high levels of scholarly productivity. The 1969 ACE survey had reported
that 59% of Asian American faculty had more than 10 scholarly publications,
compared to 40% of their white counterparts. In 1983, 78% of the Chinese American
faculty surveyed had published more than 10 articles. One fourth of them had
published more than 50 articles. However, they reported that they were burdened
by heavy teaching loads and did not receive academic rewards commensurate with
their training and job performance (Yun & Nishi, 1986).

Income of Native- and Foreign-born Ph.D.s.

The median 1979 salaries of full-time academically employed science, engineering,
and humanities Ph.D.s are available from respondents of the 1979 biennial Survey
of Doctorate Recipients (Maxfield, 1981). Not all academically employed doctorates
were faculty members. Some worked in research and development, others held
administrative positions. Earnings were estimated by ethnic groups with 50 or more
respondents. Results are shown in Tables 7.17 and 7.18. Relative to native-born
white academics, foreign-born whites earned higher median salaries in all fields
except foreign languages. Black academics in science and engineering, who tended
to concentrate in lower paying behavioral science fields, earned less than the standard
group. Native- and foreign-born Asian Americans earned less than native-born whites
in all fields except life sciences, in which native-born Asian Americans earned a
median salary 15% higher than that of the standard goup. In the humanities, native

black academicians earned more than white peers in all fields. Median salaries of foreign-born Asians in the humanities were about the same as the standard group's, slightly lower in the fields of foreign languages and other humanities.

When years of professional experience was taken into account, native-born Asian Americans earned less, and foreign-born Asian median salary was nearer to native-born white medians at all experience levels. The foreign-born were more likely to have specialized in the better paying fields of physical sciences and engineering (National Science Foundation, 1983; U.S. Department of Commerce, Bureau of the Census, 1980b). Median salaries of most recent black doctorate recipients in science/engineering and humanities were higher than white medians. With the exception of native-born Asian Americans in the life sciences, Asian American median salaries were lower than whites in all fields, and lower than blacks' in the humanities. The differences were not large, except in behavioral sciences, in which native Asian American salaries were lower than foreign-born whites by 22%, and lower than native whites by 11%.

Executive, Management, and Administrative Positions

In addition to lower salaries, Asian American faculty were also less likely to receive nonpecuniary rewards of academic work. These include tenure status, and appointments or election to policy-making bodies or executive positions. The California

TABLE 7.17

Median Annual Salaries as Percent of Median Native-Born White Salaries of Full-Time Academically Employed Science, Engineering, and Humanities Ph.D.s by Nativity, Field of Doctorate, and Ethnicity, 1979[a]

	Native-Born			Foreign-Born		
	White	Black	Asian American	White	Black	Asian American
Science/Engineering	$26,200					
	%	%	%	%	%	%
% of native-born white salary	100	94.3	97.7	109.5	—	95.8
Engineering, math, physical sciences	103.8	99.6	—	110.3	—	98.8
Life sciences	99.6	95.4	114.9	109.2	78.6	94.3
Behavioral sciences	96.6	90.1	85.5	107.6	—	95.8
Humanities	$22,800					
	%	%	%	%	%	%
% of native-born white salary	100	108.8	—	101.8	86.4	100.9
History	106.1	116.2	—	110.1	—	—
English language/literature	98.2	—	—	103.5	—	—
Other languages	94.7	106.1	—	96.9	—	96.5
Other humanities	101.3	111.8	—	105.3	—	97.8

[a]From Maxfield, 1981

TABLE 7.18

Median Annual Salaries as Percent of Median, Native-Born, Whites Salary of Full-Time, Academically Employed, Science, Engineering, and Humanities Ph.D.s by Years of Professional Experience and Ethnicity, 1979[a]

	Native-Born				Foreign-Born			
Years of Experience	White %	Hispanic %	Black %	Asian %	White %	Hispanic %	Black %	Asian %
Science/ Engineer- ing								
2–5	$19,900 (100)	98.5	104.5	94.5	103.5	93.5	—	100
6–10	$22,900 (100)	106.1	99.6	93.4	102.2	109.2	—	98.3
11–15	$26,500 (100)	—	91.7	—	104.5	—	—	97.7
16–20	$29,300 (100)	—	90.1	—	103.8	—	—	100.3
Humanities								
2–5	$17,000 (100)	—	104.8	—	97.1	102.9	—	—
6–10	$19,800 (100)	86.9	114.6	—	97.0	—	—	104.5
11–15	$22,500 (100)	85.8	—	—	96.0	101.3	—	—
16–20	$24,200 (100)	—	—	—	98.3	—	—	—

[a]From Maxfield, 1981

TABLE 7.19

Percent of Asian American Faculty and Administrators at California Public Institutions[a]

Institutions	Year	Full-Time Faculty %	Executives, Managers, and Administrators %
UC—9 Campuses	1983	5.5	3.3
CSU—19 Campuses	1984	6.8	4.2
SFCC—8 Colleges	1983	13.6	21.4

[a]From Wong, 1985

higher education system serves more Asian American students than any other state system. Recent figures on Asian American faculty and administrators in the system showed that there were proportionately more Asian Americans serving as full-time faculty members than as administrators on the 9 UC and 19 CSU campuses. At several of the major campuses, Asian American enrollment exceeded one fourth of the student body.

The policy of the San Francisco Community College District (SFCC), which consists of the City College of San Francisco and seven community colleges, has been to recruit and hire faculty members and administrators representative of the community it serves. SFCC has a higher proportion of Asian American faculty and administrators than UC and CSU, as shown in Table 7.19.

Asian Americans were 5.5% of California's population in 1980. Asian American enrollment in the California system was substantially higher. To date the CSU system has never had an Asian trustee (Wong, 1985).

INCOME OF ASIAN AMERICAN SCIENTISTS AND ENGINEERS

Science and engineering remain favorite fields for Asian Americans, whose strengths lie in quantitative areas. In 1984, almost 5% of all employed scientists and engineers were Asian. More than 8% of all employed doctoral scientists and engineers were Asian. The majority, 63%, were engineers. About 60% were employed by industry, and 15% by educational institutions. Current higher education enrollment figures indicate that there will be more Asian American engineers and scientists entering the labor force. They will increasingly be foreign born. In 1984, one third were not United States citizens. Science and engineering are fields in which salary differences between Asian Americans and white peers are narrow, and for recent graduates, virtually nil (National Science Foundation, 1986).

Ethnicity, nativity, amount of professional experience, degree level, fields of study and employment, employer sectors and other factors influence salaries of scientists and engineers. At entry level, for example, engineers have the highest starting salaries and psychologists the lowest. In 1980, median salary of black engineers with recent bachelor's degrees was $1,100 more than whites', because the stock of black engineers was low in relation to labor market demands (National Science Foundation, 1982b).

Median salaries of Ph.D. scientists and engineers employed full time in nonacademic fields in 1979 are shown by nativity and ethnicity, as percent of median native-born white salary in science and engineering, in Table 7.20. Business and industry and United States government salaries were higher than other types of nonacademic employers. Foreign-born white doctoral scientists and engineers recorded higher median salaries than the native born in government and industry. Black and Asian scientists and engineers, on the other hand, earned median salaries lower than whites in all sectors. Business and industry, in which foreign-born Asian American median salary was about 8% lower than native-born whites', manifested the smallest salary differential. Median salaries for both native- and foreign-born Asians were at least 10% lower in other sectors (Maxfield, 1981).

Entry-level jobs for scientists and engineers with recent Bachelor's or Master's degrees displayed a different pattern, as shown in Table 7.21. In 1980, beginning black engineers, with Bachelor's degrees earned in 1978 or 1979, reported median salaries about 5% higher, and Asian Americans about 1% higher than white engineers. When data of scientists and engineers were aggregated, Asian American median salary was almost 10% higher than whites' and 15% higher than blacks'. Asians' preference for majors in the high-paying engineering, physical sciences,

TABLE 7.20

Median Annual Salaries as Percent of Median Native-Born Whites Salary of Full-Time, Nonacademically Employed, Science and Engineering Ph.D.s by Type of Employer, Nativity, and Ethnicity, 1979[a]

	Median Annual Salaries[b]					
	Native-Born			Foreign-Born		
Type of Employer	White	Black	Asian American	White	Black	Asian American
Business/Industry	100%	—	—	107.3%	—	91.7%
U.S. Government	101.5%	—	90.8%	111.0%	—	89.6%
Elementary/Secondary Schools	76.8%	—	—	—	—	—
Other Nonacademic	82.6%	88.1%	—	98.8%	—	76.5%

[a]From Maxfield, 1981
[b]Percentages are based on the white median, full-time, science/engineering salary of $32,700 (i.e., $32,700 = 100%)

mathematics, and computer science fields was the primary reason for overall higher median salary of beginning Asian scientists and engineers. Blacks, who concentrated in the low-salaried fields of social sciences and psychology, recorded the lowest median salaries. Choice of fields also accounted for the 12% higher beginning salaries reported by Asian Master's-level scientists and engineers. Within detailed fields, computer science or engineering for example, Asian American median starting salaries were actually 3% to 5% less than white peers (National Science Foundation, 1982b).

Salaries rose with professional experience for all groups. However, Table 7.22 shows that the rate of increase was not the same among Ph.D.s from all ethnic

TABLE 7.21

Median Annual Full-Time Salaries as Percent of Median, White, Full-Time Salary of Recent Science/ Engineering Bachelor's and Master's Degree Recipients by Selected Field of Employment and Ethnicity, 1980[a]

	White		Black	Asian
	$	%	%	%
1978, 1979 Science/Engineering Bachelor's Recipients' Median Salaries 1980				
Total science/engineering/all fields	$15,400	100	85.1	109.7
Engineering	$20,700	100	105.3	101.4
1978, 1979 Science/Engineering Master's Recipients Median Salaries 1980				
Total, all fields	$20,700	100	92.8	112.1
Computer science	$23,500	100	—	94.5
Engineering	$24,600	100	—	96.7

[a]From National Science Foundation, 1982b

TABLE 7.22

Median Annual Salaries as Percent of Median, Native-Born, White Salary of Full-Time, Nonacademically Employed, Science and Engineering Ph.D.s by Years of Professional Experience and Ethnicity, 1979[a]

| | Native-Born | | | | | Foreign-Born | | | |
| | White | | His-panic | Black | Asian | White | His-panic | Black | Asian |
Years	$	%	%	%	%	%	%	%	%
2–5	$24,600	(100)	—	93.9	98.0	106.5	—	—	110.2
6–10	$29,400	(100)	102.4	103.4	87.8	103.1	96.6	—	100.3
11–15	$34,400	(100)	—	114.2	119.2	97.7	—	—	96.2
16–20	$36,100	(100)	—	—	—	105.3	—	—	98.1
21–25	$38,300	(100)	—	—	—	106.0	—	—	95.3

[a]From Maxfield, 1981

groups up to 1979. For full-time, non-academic work, native-born black and Hispanic scientists and engineers with more than 5 years of experience earned more than whites. Native-born Asian Americans earned more than whites after 10 years. Foreign-born Asian Americans, who are most likely to be in the higher paying physical science and engineering fields, recorded lower median salaries than comparable whites with 10 years or more of professional experience. Only foreign-born Asians with 5 years or less of work experience received median pay higher than whites; (Maxfield, 1981). The 3% to 10% lower salaries, recorded for less-experienced, native-born; and for more-experienced, foreign-born, Asian American Ph.D. scientists and engineers in nonacademic jobs supported the Hirschman and Wong (1984) hypothesis that labor market discrimination still existed in education, government, and industry; and overinvestment in education continued to be the strategy of choice for Asian American accommodation. The increased gap of foreign-born Asian Ph.D.'s with greater experience also suggests these scientists and engineers received lower salary increases over decades of work than their white peers.

The National Science Foundation (1986) reported mean rather than median salaries for 1984. Table 7.23 shows the average salaries of employed scientists and engineers in the aggregate and by selected fields, classified by ethnicity and years of professional experience. Beginning salaries differed substantially by fields. Engineers with less than 1 year of experience earned $12,500 more a year than physical scientists. However, there was convergence of mean salaries across fields with experience. Across all fields, Asian Americans with less than 15 years of experience earned comparatively higher salaries than those with more experience. Overall, Asian American with 15 years or more of experience earned on the average up to 4% less than whites with similar experience. The patterns of changes in salary in relation to years of professional experience reported by Asian physical scientists and social scientists

TABLE 7.23

Average Annual Salaries as Percent of Mean White Salaries of Scientists and Engineers by Selected Fields, Ethnicity, and Years of Professional Experience, 1984[a]

Years	<1	1–4	5–9	10–14	15–19	20–24	25–29	30–34	35+
Total S/E									
White $s	$20,300	23,300	32,300	36,900	41,600	43,400	44,500	44,900	44,000
	%	%	%	%	%	%	%	%	%
White	100	100	100	100	100	100	100	100	100
Black	77.3	90.6	95.0	93.5	88.7	81.8	98.2	90.9	83.9
Asian	119.7	113.7	108.0	105.4	99.8	98.8	97.8	96.0	95.9
Native American	110.8	96.6	102.2	108.9	118.3	98.8	100.4	98.2	96.6
Hispanic	87.7	73.4	95.0	94.9	92.8	91.9	93.3	96.2	97.0
Physical Scientists									
White $s	$14,800	21,300	32,700	36,800	42,900	43,700	46,700	48,700	45,800
	%	%	%	%	%	%	%	%	%
White	100	100	100	100	100	100	100	100	100
Black	160.8	92.0	83.8	85.0	81.4	93.6	92.3	92.8	94.5
Asian	148.6	118.8	94.8	96.2	80.0	91.1	108.1	95.7	119.0
Native American	—	—	70.3	—	—	115.1	—	—	152.8
Hispanic	125.0	86.9	45.9	82.3	59.7	96.1	114.8	—	109.2

Social Scientist

White $s	$19,000	18,900	30,100	32,600	41,500	40,100	42,900	46,100	45,600
	%	%	%	%	%	%	%	%	%
White	100	100	100	100	100	100	100	100	100
Black	61.6	91.0	94.0	103.4	94.7	85.5	108.9	78.7	78.9
Asian	84.2	150.8	95.0	104.9	84.1	112.2	76.5	80.7	—
Native American	—	116.4	50.8	119.6	96.4	—	91.1	—	98.7
Hispanic	78.9	74.1	72.4	97.2	77.1	90.3	89.3	61.8	—

Engineers

White $s	$27,300	26,500	33,900	38,300	42,300	44,300	45,000	44,400	43,600
	%	%	%	%	%	%	%	%	%
White	100	100	100	100	100	100	100	100	100
Black	75.1	101.9	99.1	93.5	86.3	88.9	91.8	94.6	82.3
Asian	107.3	99.2	110.3	104.2	99.3	97.3	96.2	98.4	88.8
Native American	106.2	57.0	92.6	108.6	119.1	80.8	100	99.3	90.4
Hispanic	91.6	98.9	96.2	98.4	98.3	92.6	94.2	96.8	97.0

^aFrom National Science Foundation, 1986

fluctuated, from a high of almost 50% higher than white beginning physical scientists, to almost 25% lower than white social scientists with 25 to 29 years of experience. Engineering was a field in which Asian American and other minority groups' mean salaries remained close to whites' at all levels of professional experience.

The trend of Asian American salaries becoming increasingly lower than white peers' with additional years of professional experience was observed in academic institutions, in industry, and in government. Lower academic qualifications or lack of productivity were not plausible explanations, because there was evidence from diverse sources that Asian Americans tended to be academically overqualified and professionally as productive as their peers. Asians may have been hired at lower salaries prior to 1970, or they may have received salary increases at slower rates than white colleagues. Culturally based diffidence about salary negotiations over time may have contributed to the increasing gap. Limited verbal fluency in making professional arguments for promotions or raises may have been another explanation. Institutional discrimination in salary administration cannot be ruled out. Entry level salaries have been similar across all ethnic groups in recent years. If salaries of experienced Asian engineers or scientists continue to fall over time across all sectors, institutional policies and practices in salary administration and promotions may need to be monitored. The increasing number of foreign-born Asian Americans, many with limited English proficiency, could also influence future aggregated salary statistics. If highly qualified and productive professionals are not able to communicate fluently, they may not be able to achieve the professional recognition or career advancements they merit.

CONCLUSIONS AND DISCUSSION

Higher education has been the main route for upward mobility among most Asian Americans. Since World War II, they have made steady progress in American society by investing more than all other Americans in education, an investment that has led in turn to better jobs and higher income. By 1980, Asian Americans had surpassed the majority in educational achievement and reached parity in occupational attainment. Individual earnings, however, still lagged behind white earnings for the same jobs. If Asian Americans were to reduce their years of schooling to white levels, their socioeconomic status and earning power would be lower still.

The typical family income of major Asian American ethnic groups, except those of recent refugees, now exceeds that of white families. For most Asian immigrants, one's family and the ethnic community remain bulwarks against a sometimes alien and unfriendly environment. By living frugally together in larger households, by more members of each family working, if only in jobs with long hours and low wages in a marginal business owned by a compatriot or relative, Asian immigrants save and invest in higher education for their children.

Distribution across occupational categories varied by Asian ethnic groups. Japanese Americans, predominantly native born, have an occupational distribution most like the majority. Chinese Americans, majority foreign born, concentrated at both ends of the occupational scale, with high proportions of professionals and managers at the top and concentrations of service workers and operatives at the low end. Many Koreans and first-wave Vietnamese have been following the ethnic enterprise route. Asian Indian and Filipino immigrants were more likely to have a good command of English as well as transferrable professional credentials. Almost half of foreign-born Asian Indian Americans were professionals, executives, or managers. Although Filipino occupational distributions are similar to the majority, more of the former were blue-collar workers.

The uneven distribution of Asian Americans across occupations can also be observed in detailed occupations. Within an occupational area, Asian Americans were more likely to hold jobs in lower salaried categories. Within categories, Asian American earnings were lower than white peers'. Among immigrants who lived in ethnic enclaves, participation in the secondary labor market with lower wages provided plausible explanation for their lower earnings. The lower incomes of Asian Americans in academic jobs and science or engineering, however, could not be attributed to ghetto living.

In academic institutions, Asian Americans were more likely to be in nonteaching, nontenure track jobs and less likely to be in decision-making positions. They were most likely to be faculty members in departments of engineering, physical sciences, and mathematics; less likely to be in social sciences, with the exception of Asian American studies; and least likely to teach the humanities, with the exception of Asian languages. Asian American faculty with stronger academic credentials and more scholarly publications were paid less than average.

Science and engineering have always been and remain the most popular choices for major field of study by Asian Americans, these were fields in which Asian Americans have demonstrated strength. There remained some signs of smaller salary increases for Asian American scientists over time. Entry level salaries of recent graduates have been about the same as those reported by white peers. Engineering has the highest starting salaries for graduates with bachelor's or master's degrees. Engineering is also the occupation in which salary differences between Asian Americans and whites remain the smallest for all experience levels.

All recent education, occupation, and income trends suggest that greater than current investment in education will bring significant returns in the forms of better jobs and higher pay to blacks, Hispanics, native Americans, and to Filipinos in some regions. Other Asian Americans, for example, Chinese Americans, may be approaching a point of diminishing returns for increased investment in education unless there is broader distribution across major fields and occupations. Such choices and decisions may be feasible for English proficient, acculturated, native-born Asian Americans. In the short run, Asian immigrants will be limited in their higher education and occupational choices unless deliberate efforts are made by students, their parents and the educational institutions that serve them to substantially improve their developed verbal abilities and English language skills.

8

Summary, Conclusions, and Recommendations

The most visible minority student groups on many of our nation's prestigious college and university campuses today are Asian Americans and Asians (Salholz, Doherty, & Trans, 1987). Recent immigrants and refugees from Asia are also crowding the classrooms of less selective and open-door urban institutions. Asian Americans are the United States's fastest growing minority. Between 1970 and 1985, their numbers more than tripled from 1.4 to 5.1 million. About 85% of 18-year-old Asian Americans took either the SAT or ACT for college admissions, more than double the rate of all students. Asian Americans are now about 2% of the total United States population and may reach 4% by the end of the century. But they constitute 10% to 20% or more of the entering classes at the best colleges and universities. The growth has been due mainly to enactment of a liberalized United States immigration law in 1965, and the admission of refugees from Vietnam, Cambodia, and Laos after 1975.

Not only have the numbers increased, but the demographic structure of the Asian American population has also altered. In 1970, Japanese Americans were the largest group of Asian Americans, followed by Chinese and Filipinos, with Koreans far behind. By 1985, Filipinos had become the largest Asian American group, followed by Chinese, Japanese, Asian Indian, Korean, Vietnamese, and more than 20 smaller Asian national groups from Bangladeshi to Thai. The newcomers are younger than established Asian Americans such as the Japanese. All immigrants and refugees are generally younger than typical Americans. They also bear more children than average. The diversity of Asian Americans is manifest not only by national origins but also in ethnicity, language, culture, socioeconomic status, age and sex composition, family size, education, occupation, income, geographic concentration, and acculturation to American customs and values.

The central role of the family and traditional belief in hard work and education as the route to individual success, family prosperity, and community respect are values shared by virtually all Asians. Asian American students, in all their diversity, are literally changing the faces of Unites States campuses and in turn being influenced by American education at every level. Their presence and performance demand new viewpoints to established concepts of minorities in higher education. The foregoing review of available information about Asian American experiences in higher education, and careers that require higher education credentials, has brought together data that describe the ongoing evolution of Asian Americans.

ABILITIES, ASPIRATIONS, AND ACHIEVEMENTS

There are differences among Asian American groups in developed abilities important for school. These differences are associated with language, location, length of residence, socioeconomic status, prior educational experiences, English proficiency, and a host of other background factors. Similarities outweigh differences, however, when the academic performances of Asian Americans are compared with other Americans under standardized, objective, assessment conditions. In comparison with the majority of Americans, the pattern of abilities shown by most Asian Americans is one of relative strength in performing tasks that demand quantitative reasoning abilities, combined with difficulties in performing tasks that require verbal fluency in English. The pattern of relatively low verbal and high quantitative performance held without regard to ethnicity, socioeconomic status, level of the test, selectivity of the test-taking population, command of English, or quality of earlier education. It is true of educationally and socioeconomically advantaged, third-generation Japanese Americans and of recently landed "boat people" refugees, some of whom have hardly ever been exposed to formal education. Because of their diversity, Asian Americans' performance on standardized norms-referenced tests manifests greater than average variability.

Among Asian American high school students and college-bound seniors, including the one quarter whose best language was not English, typical scores on quantitative aptitude and mathematics achievement tests were higher than white peers'. With the exception of 1 in 5 Asian Americans from economically and educationally advantaged families, verbal aptitude and English achievement test scores of Asian Americans whose best language was English were somewhat lower than whites'. The more economically disadvantaged the student, the lower the verbal score in comparison with white students with the same family income. Nine out of 10 college-bound Asian Americans whose best language was not English fell below the twenty-fifth percentile of all test takers in verbal aptitude tests.

Validity studies have shown that standardized, norms-referenced test scores predicted English proficient Asian Americans' future academic performance about as well as for white test takers. There have been instances of slight underprediction of grades, more likely related to grading practices or time devoted to studies rather than to test characteristics. However, findings from recent studies suggest that for recent Asian immigrants, standardized quantitative test scores are likely to be under-estimates of their true developed mathematical abilities, even though their typical performance was better than all other groups'. Their low scores on verbal aptitude tests and indirect tests of standard written English, on the other hand, probably failed to reflect fully their inarticulateness in spoken or written English. Recent Asian immigrants are likely to do relatively better in quantitative subjects and encounter more problems with language-related subjects than their test scores would indicate. Students who have mastered the mechanics of English, even those who could organize and order their thoughts, still could not write essays as well as other American students.

Asian American test scores, high school grades, and rank in class taken together are typically better than that of their white classmates. They make plans for higher education early, and prepare for college by choosing college preparatory programs, taking more academic courses and earning more credits in the "new basics" and advanced science and mathematics courses, devoting more time to homework, and spending less time on part-time jobs. Recent immigrants do not do as well in subjects that require English, but manage to keep up their better-than-average grades by limiting the number of English and social studies courses and concentrating on subjects that rely on their strength in mathematics and sciences. Asian Americans, including recent immigrants, garner more than their share of academic honors.

Eight out of 10 Asian American high school students hope to go on to college. Six out of 10 aspire to 4-year colleges. Most succeed in gaining admittance, but not always to their top-choice institutions. Almost 9 out of 10 Asian American high school graduates continue with higher education. In part because they still seek admission to the most selective institutions, Asian Americans admission rates are lower than all students'. More than half enroll in 4-year institutions. They enroll, remain in good academic standing, transfer but do not drop out, and stay through to graduate from public and private 2-year and 4-year colleges and universities.

Academic criteria, including test scores, have not been significant barriers to higher education for Asian Americans. Indeed, test scores and grades have been key factors that led to increased proportions of Asians in higher education. Even recent immigrants gain admission to selective colleges and universities. However, they are more likely than other students to be denied admission on the basis of personal qualities; criteria that are judged subjectively, and sometimes biased by unconscious sterotypes or conscious perogative requirements. Compared to white students, more Asian American college students come from families of modest means. Yet, fewer Asian American undergraduates receive financial aid. Their families invest willingly in higher education because they expect significant returns in terms of occupational status and a stream of future income to benefit the family.

Asian Americans with a limited command of English are restricted in their choice of majors to one of the quantitative fields if they want to do well academically.

Many Asian Americans, including recent immigrants, plan graduate or professional studies after college. Earlier patterns of relatively low verbal and high quantitative admissions test performances continue to be observed among applicants to graduate or professional schools. Asian American students' focus upon science, mathematics, and engineering during their undergraduate years may actually serve to widen the gap between their subsequent verbal and quantitative performances.

The majority of Asian Americans, particularly the foreign born, plan to concentrate in the sciences and engineering in graduate school, or in medical and allied health professions. The majority of ethnic Asians in United States graduate school are foreign nationals who received their undergraduate training abroad. There is ample evidence that the latter are highly selected students who not only benefitted from rigorous mathematics and science curricula in elementary and secondary schools, but gained admission to undergraduate institutions in their homelands through a series of highly competitive examinations. Asian American and Asian graduate students have been most frequently supported by institutional funds. With the exception of the humanities and law, fields that demand strong verbal abilities, Asian Americans apply to and are accepted by graduate and professional institutions and earn advanced degrees at rates commensurate with or exceeding their numbers in the population.

ACCESS AND DISTRIBUTION

The majority of college-age Asian Americans are students in good standing at accredited institutions. They are enrolled in the most selective colleges and universities in numbers several times higher than could be expected from two percent of the total United States population. Why then do many Asian American students and their families, with the support of Asian American faculty and community leaders, still express concern about access to the most selective institutions? Asian Americans look at their own admittance rates, which are often the lowest of all applicant groups, and conclude they are being judged more harshly than anyone else. When sudden drops occur in the number of new admissions, or when accepted students seem to need substantially stronger academic credentials than average, the specter of Asian quotas arises. College and university officers, on the other hand, point to the visible presence of Asian Americans and Asians on their campuses, with increasing numbers of freshmen each year, as proof of fairness in admissions policies.

Owing to a variety of international and domestic causes, the 1980s have seen signs of rising anti-Asian sentiment across the nation. Asian Americans regard any hints of inequality in access to higher education as subtle but pernicious expressions of racial prejudice. These are considered to be no less deplorable than recent acts of harassment, intimidation, vandalism, and violence against Asian Americans. Widespread racially motivated hostile acts have been documented in a 1986 clearinghouse report from the U.S. Commission on Civil Rights. Barriers of access to quality

higher education, limitation of access to the best, perhaps the only route to occupational and income parity, is regarded as a vital blow to the values Asians hold
most dear.

Higher education access issues are complex. Institutional objectives and admissions policies and practices appear to be at odds with Asian American educational
abilities, achievements, aspirations, and strategies. Selective institutions want stability, balance, and excellence in building an entering class. Academically qualified
Asian Americans are pressing selective institutions for entry not only because they
value and pursue excellence; but also because they are aware that they must be better
qualified educationally, in order to be competitive in finding and keeping jobs after
graduation. Mutual understanding and accommodation on the part of institutions
and Asian Americans will be necessary to minimize future misunderstandings that
will inevitably arise as ever greater numbers of Asian American youth reach college
age and press for admission to the most selective institutions.

FUTURE CONSIDERATIONS FOR ASIAN AMERICAN
STUDENTS, PARENTS, AND COMMUNITIES

Asian American families have always taken a long view of education. They invested
in higher education when there were few jobs for Asian Americans with college
degrees. Now that a broad range of careers is open to all, Asian Americans begin
early to prepare for the future. It is possible that in focusing on academic preparation
for college and careers, Asian American students and their parents have overestimated
the importance of academic credentials and overlooked the crucial role of personal,
nonacademic qualities in admissions decisions. When so many applicants are well-
qualified academically, as in the case of Asian Americans, acceptance to the most
selective institutions will most likely turn on nonacademic factors. These include
the quality of personal essays, the manner in which applicants present and express
themselves during interviews, the content and sources of letters of recommendation,
evidence of sustained interest and commitment to worthwhile extracurricular activities, or demonstrated interpersonal skills, leadership, or scholarly, creative, athletic,
or artistic talents. These unique personal qualities distinguish outstanding individuals from an applicant pool full of excellent students. Such promising students are
the most likely to succeed in the broadest sense, by contributing to campus life as
students and later to society as adults. For Asian American students who aspire to
the most selective colleges or universities, and outstanding academic record will
increasingly become a necessary but hardly sufficient prerequisite. Equally, or perhaps more important, will be the ability to write a strong personal essay, to develop
a track record in extracurricular participation that reflects a sustained interest and
evidence of leadership, a special talent in a sport or the performing arts, as well as
the ability to communicate with others in an interview situation. These qualities

will become increasingly important as students progress through higher education and enter their chosen careers.

The importance of developing fluency and style in speaking and writing English cannot be overstated. The United States is a multilingual and multicultural society. But the nation's books, laws, and contracts, are written in English. Everyday affairs are conducted in English. For most immigrants, learning English is key to finding a decent job. A scientist or engineer who does not have mastery of English will lack the confidence to speak out and thus can never reach his or her full professional potential.

Asian American high school or college students who avoid courses in English and other subjects in the humanities and social sciences in order to maintain an A average are being short-sighted. Only by frequent practice in speaking and writing English, and by benefitting from constructive criticism from instructors, can one acquire in youth the communications skills necessary for adult life in America. Having a command of English need not mean denial of one's ancestral language or culture. After all, it has been these very cultural traits that have helped Asian immigrants survive, and in time, prosper. The challenge for each Asian American ethnic group will be to balance dual cultures in order to maintain the strengths of each.

In applying to selective higher education institutions, a qualified Asian American applicant will find his or her chief competitors to be other Asian Americans with comparable abilities, achievements, and interests, and similar Asian nationals and White applicants. Some applicants may have an advantage because of institutional connections—an employee's or potential donor's relative. Other applicants may have special talents that fit institutional needs—needs for a lacrosse goalkeeper or an oboist. Underrepresented minority applicants are usually treated as separate pools. Asian Americans are not underrepresented, except in law and some humanities and social science subjects.

As the numbers of Asian American applicants increase, driven by demographics and cultural patterns, admittance rates will inevitably fall. The number of highly selective institutions is limited, and each institution has places for only so many students a year. Asian American acceptances may increase, but probably not at the same pace as the growth of qualified applicants. In the same way, the supply of some professionals such as physicians is increasing at a rate higher than the current labor market can absorb. Professional organizations are moving to limit admissions to medical school and to specialty training programs, and to further restrict licensing of the foreign trained. Such policies are bound to affect Asian Americans adversely. In addition to taking individual interests and abilities into account, students and their families need to be objective and realistic about evolving higher education and labor market conditions in making choices concerning institutions, major fields, and professions.

Asian American students and their families can best prepare to face coming changes in higher education and the job market by maintaining their long view and by gaining a broad understanding of American society and the role played by higher education in allocation of important societal resources. Unlike other nations, the array of United States institutions and major field choices is enormous and deserves exploration. Another difference is that American youth have not just one, but multiple opportunities to enter higher education at various levels, to change fields, institutions, and later on, careers. The need for flexibility means that one should not decide on a course of action too early or too narrowly. A liberal education can include not only a strong grounding in English but also college-level studies of some Asian languages. Even future scientists and engineers can benefit professionally and personally by broad exposure to the great works of Eastern as well as Western civilization. Increasingly, the United States economy will be influenced by the Pacific rim nations. Asian Americans with appropriate professional credentials and familiarity with an Asian language and culture will hold an advantage in the job market.

Finally, the diversity among Asians, increasingly foreign born, means that members of each ethnic group will have to work against historic prejudices and cultural differences to develop a sense of being Asian Americans as well as Asian Indians, Koreans, or Vietnamese. The shared belief in educational achievement through hard work and family solidarity is a good starting point for the thousands of ethnic organizations to begin building coalitions, developing a common agenda, and making plans for social and political action to the benefit of all Asian Americans. With the exception of Japanese Americans, Asian Americans have been approaching occupational and economic parity while avoiding full participation in the nation's political and economic life. The aggregated efforts of individuals, their families and ethnic communities have improved Asian Americans' standard of living with each generation. The next level, genuine equality, will be impossible without greater unity among Asians, alliances with other minority groups, and political and economic integration with mainstream American society.

IMPLICATIONS FOR POSTSECONDARY EDUCATION

There will be more Asian Americans applying to all types and levels of postsecondary institutions. Increasingly, they will be from immigrant or refugee backgrounds. There will be greater variations in ethnicity, English language proficiency, and prior educational experience. Students from poor immigrant and refugee families will be more likely to consider college than other disadvantaged Americans. Asian American students typically apply to the best institutions they can afford because they are aware that as a visible minority, they will only be able to enter desirable occupations and make a decent living by overinvestment in higher education.

There will be growing numbers of students whose mother tongue is some language other than English. Disadvantaged applicants will include a substantial proportion of recent refugees. Many will have had very limited exposure to formal education before landing in this country. Community colleges and other 2-year institutions in metropolitan centers already serve many adult and college-age Asian immigrants and refugees. These institutions will receive more applications as the young Asians grow up. For most of these newcomers, theirs will be the first generation to attend college. They need to improve their English and to acquire other basic skills, prepare to earn a living, and to cope with an alien, multicultural, and multiethnic society. Some students may not know how to go about finding a job after completing a course of studies. Others may want help in making the transition to a 4-year institution. These new Americans will be turning to the community colleges for help not readily available from their families, their immediate ethnic communities, local Asian American organizations, or social welfare agencies.

Other recent immigrants, who had acquired a sound knowledge base before emigrating, may be hampered by a limited command of English. The immigrant families often expect their young to attend a 4-year public institution and then find a good job. These students are expected not only to contribute in the future to the education of younger siblings but also to the well being of the whole family. The burden to finish college in good time and with a strong academic record may lead some students to the use of strategies that run counter to their own long-term interests. Getting by with the minimum of required humanities and social science courses in order to concentrate on scientific or technological specialties with high labor market potential may result in a degree. However, the graduates may not be able to produce a clearly written letter or report, nor to speak English coherently and comprehensibly. A program of academic support and counselling for these students with limited English proficiency can ensure the acquisition of crucial communicative skills during their undergraduate years.

Students who have resided in the United States for 6 years or more can generally be considered academically competitive with the majority of their classmates. More recent arrivals, even the best prepared academically, must devote all their efforts to learning English and keeping up with their studies. This is the group least likely to have the extracurricular credentials or acculturated personal qualities considered important by admissions officers. For applicants whose best language is not English, standardized admissions test scores will likely underestimate students' true developed mathematical abilities. Their high school English grades and test scores on indirect measures of writing, on the other hand, may overestimate their capability to communicate in English. Despite general language handicaps, otherwise qualified recent immigrants and refugees usually turn out to be better-than-average student in selective institutions. If given the chance, these highly motivated students will be the most likely to major in intellectually demanding physical sciences and engineering fields or in applied and performing arts and more than return institutional investments by future contributions to American society. They will be better integrated in campus life and more versatile in future jobs if some time is invested in improving English speaking and writing skills.

The Asian immigrant focus on sciences, engineering, and the health professions has been influenced by a desire to capitalize upon strengths in quantitative abilities while minimizing the adverse influence of limited ability to communicate in English. These fields are also likely to lead to jobs that impose the least cost, in terms of lower income, even for the native born. When institutional policies discourage well qualified, motivated Asian Americans from specializing in these fields, or deny them access solely on the basis that there are too many Asians in these specialties already; the policies in effect perpetuate discrimination on the basis of race alone. A selection policy that assigns greater weight to ascriptive criteria than to merit has the potential for diminishing departmental and institutional integrity and vitality in the long run. In the end, the nation may be the loser because talented and motivated individuals would not be encouraged to develop their abilities to the fullest in order to contribute to the nation's needs in education, health, economy, and national defense.

Native-born or long-term resident Asian Americans no longer need to be treated as underrepresented minorities by most higher education institutions. This is an occasion that calls for celebration on the part of the people and the institutions, it should not remain a bone of contention. Among the most selective institutions, Asian American applicants who are fluent in English should be evaluated by the same set of criteria as general applicants. Verifiable academic and nonacademic credentials, not physiognomy or ascribed ethnic traits, should be the primary factors considered in admissions decisions. If equality of educational opportunity means full opportunity to compete on the same terms, then ethnicity per se should not be at issue in evaluating the academic or personal qualities of individual Asian American applicants. The distribution of Asian American talent in the right tail may be somewhat skewed, but numbers are and will remain small compared to other minorities and to the majority. American higher education has successfully embraced previously excluded groups of students, minorities and women, and can undoubtedly accommodate the growing, but finite number of Asian Americans. Higher education is not a zero sum game. Neither institutions, nor society, nor Asian American students need be the loser.

The United States population is changing, and the growth of Asian Americans is an integral part of that evolution. Higher education will also have to change in order to keep pace. There has been a great deal of public discussion about the importance of reaching for excellence in higher education in order to keep United States competitive economically. Asian Americans, particularly the first and second generations, will play a pivotal role in our common pursuit of excellence.

LABOR MARKET IMPLICATIONS

In the past, Asian sojourners and immigrants accommodated to legal, economic, and social sanctions by restricting themselves to less competitive trades and personal services in the secondary labor market. As a result, Asian American groups' occupational structures developed in lopsided ways that skirted sectors and occupations dominated by whites and other minorities (King & Locke, 1980). As second and later generations obtained college and professional degrees, and barriers to the primary labor market have gradually fallen away, Asian American occupational patterns changed in response. The native born typically hold jobs high up in occupational scale. They concentrate in professional and technical occupations but are not as likely as white peers to move up via the fast track to managerial or executive positions. Recent immigrants and refugees cluster toward the bottom of the job market.

Well qualified, United States educated, Asian immigrants still face bleak employment opportunities compared to immigrants from the Western hemisphere and the native born majority (Parlin, 1976). Asian immigrants or refugees educated abroad must settle for jobs at levels far below their training and experience. Immigrants or refugees with limited education and few marketable skills are only a little better off than 19th century coolies. Unskilled labor is being increasingly replaced by machines, and access to many union-controlled, skilled crafts training programs remains closed to Asian Americans. These realities belie the principles and flout the laws of a democratic nation.

Labor policies and industrial, government, and academic hiring and promotional practices can forstall potential problems that could arise from perpetuating the current maladaptive Asian American occupational structure. As the numbers of Asian Americans increase, the gulf will widen between the well-educated, high socioeconomic level, native-born and acculturated immigrants, and disadvantaged, new immigrants and refugees. The native-born and long-term residents hold predominantly American values, and have English as a common language. Newcomers will be increasingly polyglot and balkanized. Bridging the gap will require training and employment policies and career counseling programs that open a wide range of educational, training, and employment opportunities for newcomers across all sectors. Access to the entire spectrum of American occupations can foster among all Asian ethnic groups the sense that each has the potential for full economic and political participation in their new country.

Any widespread limitations in numbers trained or hired in an occupation category, by specific sectors, or by an employer; observable ceilings in job levels or salary grades, or devaluation of occupations due to substantial participation by Asian Americans, on the other hand; would rightly be regarded as signs of inequality in employment despite above average educational attainment, zeal for work, and productivity. Such acts would also send a message to other American minority groups that obtaining a better education may not mean better jobs. The long held suspicion among United States minorities that pursuit of excellence does not necessarily yield the same rewards to all Americans will continue to be reinforced.

As Asian Americans increase in visibility in the job market, Pacific rim nations will continue to monitor the progress of their emigrants. Those who leave their native lands to seek better opportunities in American, particularly sciences and technology experts, no longer limit themselves to a single labor market. They are elite members of an international corps. Perceived inequalities in the career paths of international professionals will lead to more reverse brain drain, and to other unlooked for international repercussions.

RECOMMENDATIONS FOR FUTURE RESEARCH

In order to track major subgroups of Asian Americans as they make progress in education and work, accurate and comprehensive data bases need to be maintained. Research on Asian Americans as a group, on ethnolinguistic subgroups, by generational status and by levels of English language proficiency can elucidate the web of relationships among nativity, length of residence in the United States, culture, language, values, socioeconomic status, and other characteristics; and how these factors relate to education, occupation, and· imcome. These kinds of data may also be generalizable to other United States minorities with similar historical experiences. The design of a forthcoming longitudinal study of the National Center for Education statistics, the National Education Longitudinal Study of 1988 (NELS: 88) promises for the first time to survey over 1,000 Asian American eighth grade pupils. It is a hopeful symptom of better research information bases for the 21st century (Owings, 1987).

Research on Higher Education

Understanding complexities of Asian American access to higher education requires data from representative national surveys such as the National Education Longitudinal Study of 1988 (NELS: 88), now under development; from national admissions testing programs such as the College Board's ATP, ACT, the Medical College Admission Test, and the Graduate Record Examinations; and from case studies of selective institutions that use test data and other academic and personal information to make admission decisions.

Whereas earlier national longitudinal studies sampled a few hundred Asian Americans and seldom included them as a separate category in summary statistics of ethnic groups, NELS: 88 holds considerable promise as a significant future source for developmental information on major Asian ethnic groups and Asian and Pacific Islands Americans. National surveys of minorities in higher education in recent years have published few if any details on Asian Americans. Because Asian Americans are now a significance presence on major United States campuses, it seems reasonable to include Asian Americans as a separate category in the future. Separate analyses by major Asian ethnic groups would be desirable. Asian Americans have made substantial socioeconomic gains through investment in higher education. Reports on minorities in higher education that exclude them draw a biased portrait of minorities in America.

Routinely published summary statistics from national admissions testing programs, such as the College Board's *College-bound Seniors* and American College Testing Program's *College Student Profiles,* could expand the information currently available on Asian and Pacific Island Americans by including items about detailed ethnic group membership, language use and English proficiency. Although the numbers each year may be limited, aggregated data collected over several years could identify issues that need in depth study. For example, English proficiency trends over time by subgroups, and the relationship of communications ability with academic achievement and extracurricular participation, could lead to changes in high school curricula or counseling outreach in school districts that serve specific populations. Continued differences in quantitative aptitude between the native and foreign born in favor of the latter may suggest the need for curriculum reform, or at least some topics that deserve more attention in precollege mathematics and science courses. The absence of linkages between diverse admissions testing programs and national higher education data bases require some leaps of faith in following cohorts in higher education. Development of such links could do much to improve current understanding about precollege preparation, access, and progress in higher education.

Validity studies of admission testing programs are important for interpretation and use of test scores in making admissions decisions about Asian American applicants. There is some evidence of slight underprediction of grades among Asian American groups. Test takers whose first or best language is not English should be analyzed separately because there is mounting evidence of item and test bias for their test performance. It is possible that many admissions officers are not yet aware of recent research findings in this area. Decisions about Asian immigrants should be tempered by validity studies that have reported standardized norms-referenced tests to consistently underpredict their academic performance.

Institutional research that can be shared with the interested public, or case studies of institutions, faculties, or departments that serve significant proportions of Asian American students can also do much to diminish student and parental concerns about limited access to specific institutions or fields. Widely disseminated information about access can, in fact, contribute to improving patterns of applicant and student distribution across institutions and faculties.

The role played by nonacademic credentials and personal qualities in admissions decisions for different Asian American groups is becoming increasingly important. The weight given to these factors, and how they are evaluated in the admissions process, deserve more research attention. For Asian Americans, these appear to be the most difficult hurdles. How can high schools, students, and their families work together with high schools and colleges to address these intangibles? How can institutions prevent deeply ingrained ethnocentrism of students, faculty, and administration from adversely affecting equality in opportunities for access to all aspects of higher education institutions?

Personal, Social, and Intellectual Growth in College

Particularly in the case of recent immigrants or refugees, college may be the first time an Asian American student leaves his or her ethnic community. Foreign-born students, and even some native born, arrive on campus with limited command of the English language. The less acculturated also lack general communications skills important for campus life. Research at the institutional or system level is needed to identify areas that require academic support or outreach and counselling. Research findings can also support specific recommendations to feeder schools for strengthening precollege social, personal, and academic preparation. Asian newcomers may suffer from severe language and cultural handicaps in coping with the college environment. Their risk adverse strategy of burying themselves in the library or the laboratory leaves little time for extracurricular activities that could integrrate them into the university community. How can institutions encourage such students to enrich their own lives by sharing a variety of social, athletic, and intellectual experiences with other students? How can they be motivated to consider majoring in the humanities and social sciences as well as sciences, mathematics, engineering, and business? Asian Americans are particularly strong in mathematics and sciences. Can some be encouraged to go into elementary and secondary education, which have a great need for more teachers and strength in these areas?

Higher education does not only provide students with a knowledge base for their future careers. The college experience also prepares young adults to become participants and leaders of social, economic, and political affairs of a democratic society. Research is needed to improve our understanding of how Asian immigrant students develop interest in and understanding of democratic processes in this country. These new and future citizens will remain on the fringes of American society unless they acquire the knowledge, abilities, and interest in participating in the mainstream.

Research on Asian Americans need not be limited to study of Asian ethnic groups isolated from their peers. Indeed, a useful research agenda should consider similarities and differences across groups in institutional settings. Members of several American minority groups encounter similar academic and social problems due to limited English proficiency. Research studies across linguistic groups can improve English instruction for all. Because Asian Americans are such a heterogeneous population, research on academic progress, values, interests, and motivation in higher education settings may be more meaningful when comparisons are made with other groups that share common historical or educational experiences. For example, Pacific Islands Americans may have more in common with members of American Indians, Alaskan natives, and Aleuts than with other ethnic Asians. Filipino Americans share common historic, cultural, and religious characteristics with Hispanic American groups. Recent Southeast Asian refugees are living in the same center city neighborhoods and attending schools with recent Ethiopian refugees and other disadvantaged minorities. Advantaged, suburban, native-born Asian Americans' comparison group would be their white counterparts. At the institutional level, it is important to look for common human experiences shared by all ethnic groups. Now that the long-feared eventuality of nonhispanic white students becoming the minority group at selective institutions has already come to pass in Hawaii and California, research on Asian Americans and other minorities can no longer be considered esoteric, but central issues that must be addressed by policymakers in government and in many higher educational institutions.

Finally, national data bases and institutional research should contribute to better understanding of the roles and progress of Asian American and other minority faculty and staff in higher education. This study has reported some evidence that Asian immigrant students feel diffidence in approaching white faculty and staff whom they respect and like. Some university faculty and staff have also expressed degrees of discomfort or distaste with the increasing proportions of Asian American students. There was also documentation that Asian American faculty, mostly foreign born, do not receive rank and pay commensurate with their credentials, experience, and productivity. Periodic reports on institutional trends in recruitment, hiring, and promoting of Asian American faculty and staff would alleviate any concerns that discriminatory practices are being deliberately perpetuated. Particularly in fields that have attracted relatively few Asian Americans in the past, augmenting Asian American faculty members and administrators could be instrumental to recruiting more Asian American students, who in time, will balance the occupational structure of Asian American groups.

Higher Education, Occupation, and Income

The gap between white and Asian American achievement in higher education has been widening in favor of Asian Americans. Except for the most recent groups of refugees from Vietnam and other Southeast Asian countries, more Asian Americans are graduates of selective 4-year colleges, postgraduate, and professional schools. The gap between white and Asian American occupational status has also closed. Typical Asian American occupational status is on a par with whites'. Still, occupational structures of Asian American groups remain less flexible than whites'. The gap between white and Asian American individual earnings is closing as well, but white men retain an advantage in individual earnings. Asian American families, except the Vietnamese and other recent immigrants and refugees, earn higher median incomes than white families. Higher family income is obtained by overinvesting in higher education to gain occupation status, by pooling family and household resources, by having more members of the family participate in the labor force, by working longer hours on the job on the part of blue-collar workers and the self-employed, and as a result of their concentration in metropolitan areas and states with relatively high wages.

Jencks et al. (1979) concluded that family background; academic ability; non-cognitive traits such as leadership, industriousness, and executive ability; and higher education all influence occupational status and economic success, particularly of minorities. According to a number of recent studies, the benefits of more schooling, in essentially the same or better schools, are still not the same for whites and Asian Americans. The latter incur greater economic costs by overinvestment in human capital and through earning opportunities foregone. Asian immigrants, in particular, bear greater psychological as well as economic costs for remaining in school to college graduation and beyond. Incentives for Asian Americans to invest in education go far beyond the expectation of fair monetary returns.

Continued research on the variables that influence detailed occupation category, individual earnings and family income of diverse Asian American groups can shed light on whether ethnicity per se continues to be a significant independent variable in estimating typical occupational status and earnings, or whether some as yet unidentified determinant of earnings should be included in the regression model. Are Japanese American men approaching white earnings because they possess traits in common with white men that other Asians have yet to acquire? Standardization of units of measure and methods of analysis would provide findings that could be compared directly across groups and years without equivocation. Focusing studies on states or SMSAs with large Asian populations for the time being would seem most efficient. Monitoring Asian American ethnic groups' structural changes in occupations over time can provide information about promising fields and careers. Occupational structure changes in the direction of a more normal distribution would represent signs of progress towards economic integration with the mainstream.

If some of the current earnings differential observed among Asian Americans is attributable to employers' lack of perfect information about the relationship between Asian American ethnicity, ability, education, and productivity, that ignorance should be remedied. This study is a beginning. Information costs are one source of labor market imperfection for Asian Americans and their employers in academe, government, and industry. It is not only the responsibility but also in the interest of Asian Americans, individually and together through their organizations, to improve communications with their fellow Americans.

References

Adelman, C. (1984, December). *The standard test scores of college graduates, 1964–1982.* Washington, DC: National Institute of Education. (ERIC Document Reproduction Service No. ED 248 827)

Advanced Placement Program. (1984). *1984 Advanced Placement Program national summary reports.* New York: College Entrance Examinations Board.

American Bar Association. (1984). *A review of legal education in the United States, Fall, 1983: Law schools and bar requirements.* Chicago: Author.

American College Testing Program. (1972). *Assessing students on the way to college* (Vol. 2). Iowa City, IA: ACT Publications.

American College Testing Program. (1983a). *College student profiles: Norms for the ACT assessment.* Iowa City, IA: ACT Publications.

American College Testing Program. (1983b). *ACT high school profile report, students tested 1982–83 school year.* Iowa City, IA: ACT Publications.

American Council on Education. (1984). *Minorities in higher education: Third annual status report.* Washington, DC: Author.

American Council on Education. (1985). *Minorities in higher education: Fourth annual status report.* Washington, DC: Author.

American Medical College Application Service. (1979–1984). *American Medical College Application Service admission action summary, 1979–1980 entering class through 1984–85 entering class.* Washington, DC: Association of American Medical Colleges.

Anderson, N. (1985, August 12). *Letter to health profession advisors in U.S. undergraduate institutions.* Baltimore, MD: Johns Hopkins University School of Medicine, Office of Admissions.

Anrig, G. R. (May, 1985). A challenge for the states: Protecting minority access within systemwide admissions standards. *AAHE Bulletin,* 1–5.

Arbeiter, S. (1984). *Profiles, college-bound seniors, 1984.* New York: College Entrance Examination Board.

ARTS Program. (1980–1984). Applicants semifinalists and finalists. Unpublished tabulations.

Asian American Law Students' Association. (1978). Report of the Boalt Hall Asian American Special Admissions Research Project. *Amerasia Journal, 3*(1), 21–38.

Asian American Student Association, Brown University. (1983, October 11). *Asian American admission at Brown University.* Providence, RI: Author.

Asian American Task Force on University Admissions. (1985, June 17). *Task Force Report*. San Franscisco, CA: Asian Incorporated.

Association of American Medical Colleges, Division of Educational Measurement and Research. (1977, 1978, 1979). *New Medical College Admissions Test. Percentile rank ranges for new MCAT areas of assessment 1977, 1978 and 1979 summary of score distributions*. Washington, DC: Author.

Association of American Medical Colleges, Division of Educational Measurement and Research. (1981). *Medical College Admission Test: Percentile rank ranges for MCAT area of assessment, 1981 summary of score distribution*. Washington, DC: Author.

Association of American Medical Colleges, Division of Educational Measurement and Research. (1980, 1981, 1982, 1983, 1984). *Medical College Admission Test. Percentile rank ranges for MCAT areas of assessment, 1980–84 summary of score distributions*. Washington, DC: Author.

Association of American Medical Colleges, Division of Student Services. (1974–75 through 1984–85). *Annual AAMC fall surveys of U.S. medical school enrollments*. Washington, DC: Author.

Association of American Medical Colleges, Office of Minority Affairs. (1985). *Number of students repeating the academic year for 1973–74 through 1983–84 for selected ethnic groups*. Washington, DC: Author.

Astin, A. (1985). *Achieving educational excellence*. San Francisco, CA: Jossey-Bass.

Backman, M. E. (1972). Patterns of mental abilities: Ethnic, socioeconomic, and sex differences. *American Educational Research Journal, 9*(1), 1–12.

Bagasao, P. Y. (1983, September). Factors related to science-career planning among Asian and Pacific American college-bound high school seniors. *Clippings*. New Orleans: National Association for Asian and Pacific Students.

Baird, L. L. (1982, December). *An examination of the graduate study application and enrollment decisions of GRE candidates* (GRE Board Research Report 82–53).

Baird, L. L. (1984). Relationships between ability, college attendance and family income. *Research in Higher Education, 21*, 373–395.

Becker, G. S. (1971). *The economics of discrimination* (2nd ed.). Chicago, IL: The University of Chicago Press.

Bell, D. A. (1985, July 15 & 22). The triumph of Asian-Americans. *The New Republic*, 24–31.

Berger, J. (1987, March 4). Excellence and Equality: A Conflict? *The New York Times*. pp. B1, B10.

Berryman, S. E. (1983, November). *Minority and female attainment of sciences and mathematics degrees: Trends and causes. Who will do science?* New York: Rockefeller Foundation.

Biemiller, L. (1985a, November). At College Board's meeting: Applicant pools, SAT role. *The Chronicle of Higher Education*.

Biemiller, L. (1985b, May 22). Johns Hopkins Medical School abandons test. *The Chronicle of Higher Education*.

Biemiller, L. (1986, November 19). Asian students fear top colleges use Quota System. *The Chronicle of Higher Education*.

Blalock, H. M. (1967). *Toward a theory of minority-group relations*. New York: Wiley.

Bleistein, C. A., & Wright, D. (1985, August). *Assessing unexpected differential item performance of Oriental candidates and of White candidates for when English is not the best language on SAT Form 3FSA08 and TSWE Form E47* (Unpublished statistical report No. SR-85-123). Princeton, NJ: Educational Testing Service.

Boardman, A. E., Lloyd, A. S., & Wood, D. (1978, July-August). The process of education for twelfth grade Asian American students. *Journal of Public Policy and Multicultural Education, 1*(4), 338–353.

Bonacich, E. (1972, October). A theory of ethnic antagonism: The split labor market. *American Sociological Review, 37*, 547–559.

Bonacich, E. (1980). Small business and Japanese American ethnic solidarity. In R. Endo, S. Sue, & N. Wagner (Eds.), *Asian-Americans: Social and psychological perspectives* (Vol. 2, pp. 122–131). Palo Alto, CA: Science and Behavior Books.

Bonacich, E., Light, I., & Wong, C. (1976). Small business among Koreans in Los Angeles. In E. Gee (Ed.), *Counterpoint: Perspectives on Asian America* (pp. 436–449). Los Angeles, CA: Asian American Studies Center.

Bonacich, E., & Modell, J. (1980). *The economic basis of ethnic solidarity: Small business in the Japanese American community.* Berkeley, CA: University of California Press.

Boston Public Schools, Office of Research and Development. (1986a, May). *A working document on the dropout problem in Boston public schools, 1.* Boston, MA: Author.

Boston Public Schools, Office of Research and Development. (1986b, October). *A working document on the dropout problem in Boston public schools 1986 Update, 2.* Boston, MA: Author.

Braun, H. I., & Jones, D. H. (1985). *Use of Empirical Bayes methods in the study of the validity of academic predictors of graduate school performance* (GRE Board Professional Report GREB No. 79–13). Princeton, NJ: Educational Testing Service.

Breland, H. M. (1985, January). *An examination of state university and college admissions policies* (Research Report 85-3). Princeton, NJ: Educational Testing Service.

Breland, H. M., & Griswald, P. A. (1981). *Group comparisons for basic skills measures* (College Board Report No. 81-6, ETS RR No. 81-21). New York: College Entrance Examination Board.

Breland, H. M., Wilder, G., & Robertson, N. J. (1986, Novemver). *Demographics, standards, and equity: Challenges in college admissions.* AACRAO, ACT, College Board, ETS, and NACAC.

Bridgeman, B., & Carlson, S. (1983). *Survey of academic writing tasks required of graduate and undergraduate students* (TOEFL Research Report No. 15; ETS RR No. 83-18). Princeton, NJ: Educational Testing Service.

Brown University, Office of Undergraduate Admissions. (1986). [Unpublished figures of applicants, acceptances and enrollment figures for the entering classes of 1988 and 1989].

Browne, M. W. (1986, March 25). A look at success of young Asians. New York: *The New York Times* (C 3).

Butterfield, F. (1984, June). Havard's 'core' dean glances back. New York: *The New York Times.* p. 8.

Butterfield, F. (1986, August 3). Why Asians are going to the head of the class. New York: *The New York Times* (Education, pp. 18–24).

Campbell, J. R., Connolly, C., Bologh, R., & Primavera, L. (1984, April). *Impact of ethnicity on math and science among the gifted.* Paper presented at the Annual Meeting of the American Educational Research Association, New Orleans, LA.

Caplan, N., Whitmore, J., Bui, Q., & Troutman, M. (1985, October). Study shows boat refugees' children achieve academic success. *Refugee Reports, 7*(10), 1–6. Washington, DC: American Council for Nationalities Service.

Carliner, G. (1977, October). *Final report: Ethnic in American labor markets.* Washington, DC: National Institute of Education (DHEW). (ERIC Reproduction Document Reproduction Service No. ED 161 788)

Cass, J., & Birnbaum, M. (1983). *Comparative guide to American colleges.* New York: Harper & Row.

Centra, J. A. (1979, December). *The graduate degree aspirations of ethnic student groups among GRE test-takers* (GREB No. 77-7P). Princeton, NJ: Educational Testing Service.

Chan, S. (1981). *Contemporary Asian immigrants and their impact on undergraduate education at the University of California, Berkeley* (Occasional paper No. 17). Berkeley, CA: University of California Center for Studies in Higher Education.

Chan, S. (1985a, May 15). *They shall write!* Unpublished paper distributed at a conference: Perspectives: Asian Standards in Higher Education. University of California, Santa Cruz and the Western Regional Office of the College Board. Quoted with permission of author.

Chan, S. (1985b, October 30). A comparison of Asian-ancestry undergraduates at UCB and UCLA. *East/West, 19*(44), 6.

Chan, S. (1985c, October 30). Study reveals Asian immigration and its impact on higher education, Part I. *East/West, 19*(44), 6.

Chan, S. (1985d, November 6). Study reveals Asian immigration and its impact on higher education, Part II. *East/West, 19*(44), 7–8.

Chang, L. S. (1985, November 15). Yale dean defends policy on Asian admissions. *Black Issues in Higher Education,* 6.

Chao, R. (1977). *Chinese immigrant children*. New York: The City College, City University of New York, Department of Asian Studies.

Cheng, L. (1984, September 20–25). *The new Asian immigrants in California*. Paper presented at the Conference on Asian-Pacific Immigration to the United States, East-West Population Institute, Honolulu.

Chi, P. (1972). *Inter- and intra-group inequalities of the racial and ethnic groups in the United States*. Doctoral dissertation, Brown University, Providence, RI.

Chira, S. (1986, April 7). Wages, discipline give Korea an edge. *The New York Times*, D1, 5.

Chiswick, B. R. (1978). The effect of Americanization on the earnings of foreign-born men. *Journal of Population Economy, 86*, 891–921.

Chiswick, B. R. (1979). Immigrants and immigration policy. In W. Fellner (Project Director), *Contemporary economic problems 1978*. Washington, DC: American Enterprise Institute for Public Policy Research.

Chiswick, B. R. (1980, October). Immigrant earnings patterns by sex, race and ethnic groupings. *Monthly Labor Review*, 22–25.

Chu, A. (1986, December). Asian Americans build a history, *Wellesley College Realia, 5*. 2–3.

Coleman, J. S., Campbell, C. J., McPartland, J., Mood, A. M., Weinfeld, F. D., & York, R. L. (1966). *Equality of educational opportunity*. Washington, DC: U. S. Government Printing Office.

College Entrance Examination Board (1980). [unpublished ATP data tabulations].

College Entrance Examination Board (1982). *Profiles, college bound seniors, 1981*. New York: Author.

Commission on Human Resources of the National Research Council. (1974). *Minority groups among United States doctorate-level scientists, engineers and scholars, 1973*. Washington, DC: National Academy of Sciences.

Commission on Human Resources of the National Research Council. (1980). *Science, engineering, and humanities doctorates in the United States: 1979 profile*. Washington, DC: National Academy of Sciences.

Committee on Undergraduate Admissions and Financial Aids. (1986). *Annual Report, 1985–86*. Unpublished report, Stanford University.

Connolly, C., & Primavera, L. (1983, April 7). *Characteristics of gifted students enrolled in horizontal enrichment programs*. Paper presented at the Annual Meeting of the National Association for Research in Science Teaching, Dallas, TX.

Cookson, P. W., Jr., & Persell, C. H. (1985). *Preparing for power: America's elite boarding schools*. New York: Basic Books.

Cordes, C. (1984, October). School debate too often ignores effect of culture. *APA Monitor, 15*(10).

Crosswhite, F. J., Dossey, J. A., Swafford, J. O., McKnight, C. C., & Cooney, T. J. (1985). *Second International Mathematics Study summary report for the United States*. Champaign, IL: Stipes.

Crouse, J. (1986, January). Should a million and a half students be required to take the SAT next year? *Phi Delta Kappan*, 346–352.

Daniels, R. (1976). American historians and East Asian immigrants. In N. Hundley, Jr. (Ed.), *The Asian American: The historic experience* (pp. 1–25). Santa Barbara: Clio Books.

Daniels, R., Taylor, S. C., & Kitano, H. H. L. (Eds.). (1986). *Japanese Americans from relocation to redress*. Salt Lake City: University of Utah Press.

Darsie, M. (1926). The mental capacity of American-born Japanese in California. *Comparative Psychology Monographs*, No. 15.

de la Croix de Lafayette, J. (1984). *National register of social prestige and academic ratings of American colleges and universities*. Washington, DC: The National Association of State Approved Colleges and Universities and the American Council for University Planning and Academic Excellence.

Donlon, T. D. (Ed.). (1984). *The College Board technical handbook for the Scholastic Aptitude Test and Achievement Tests*. New York: College Entrance Examination Board.

Dowd, M. (1986, March 19). Day of reckoning: Picking the Class of '90. *The New York Times*, B1, 8.

East/West. (1985, June 12). UCLA's Asian Enrollment Declines; Admissions Discrimination Charged. *East/West, 19*(25), 1.

East/West. (1985a, October 30). US Ed. Secretary Bennett warns against Asian quotas in colleges and universities. *East/West, 19*(44), 3, 6.

East/West. (1985b, October). New UC application system begins Nov. 1. *East/West, 19*(44), 8.

Endo, R. (1974, March). *Asian Americans and higher education.* Paper presented at the Annual Meeting of the Southwestern Sociological Association. (ERIC Document Reproduction Service No. ED 089 610)

Faculty and Student Committees on Undergraduate Admission and Financial Aid. (1985). *Report on Admission of Asian-American applicants to Princeton.* An unpublished report. Princeton, NJ: Princeton University, Office of Dean of the College, J. S. Girgus.

Feagin, J. R., & Fujitaki, N. (1972). On the assimilation of Japanese Americans. *Amerasia Journal, 1,* 13–30.

Feinberg, L. (1984, July). Asian students excelling in area, U. S. schools—Asian students proving to be top scholars in area, nation. *Washington Post,* pp. Al, A10.

Foell, E. W. (1984). The new Horatio Algers: Why Asian Americans stay at school. *The Christian Science Monitor,* July 2, 1984.

Fogel, W. (1966, Fall). The effect of low educational attainment on incomes: A comparison study of selected ethnic groups. *The Journal of Human Resources, 1,* 22–39.

Freeman, R. B. (1978). Discrimination in the academic marketplace. In T. Sowell (Eds), *Essays and data on American ethnic groups* (pp. 167–202). Washington, DC: The Urban Institute.

Friedling, C. A., Aveilhe, C. C., & Travina, J. D. (1985, November). *Talking points, Asian Americans as minorities, Title III of the Higher Education Act* (draft). Washington, DC: Federal Liaison Office, California Community Colleges.

The Gallup Organization, Inc. (1983, October). East Asia: The views of the American People. *Gallup Report International, 1*(7).

Gamarekian, B. (1986). City student in tie for science prize. *New York Times,* March 4, 1986, B3.

Gardner, J. W. (1984). *Excellence.* New York: W. W. Norton

Gardner, R. W., Robey, B., & Smith, P. C. (1985). *Asian Americans: Growth, change and diversity.* Washington, DC: The Population Reference Bureau, Inc.

Gee, E. (Ed.). (1976). *Counterpoint: Perspectives on Asian America.* Los Angeles, CA: University of California, Asian American Studies Center.

Gilford, D. M., & Snyder, J. (1977). *Women and minority Ph.D.'s in the 1970's: A data book.* Washington, DC: National Academy of Science.

Gilliam, D. (1987, February). A new restrictive quota. *The Washington Post.*

Givens, R. (1985). Who gets in? *Columbia Magazine, 10,* 21–25.

Goldman, R. D., & Hewitt, B. N. (1976). Predicting the success of Black, Chicano, Oriental, and White college students. *Journal of Educational Measurement, 13*(2), 107–117.

Grandy, J. (1984a). *Profiles of prospective humanities majors: 1975–1983. Final report. A study of students taking the College Board Scholastic Aptitude Test and the Graduate Record Examinations.* Princeton, NJ: Educational Testing Service.

Grandy, J. (1984b). *Profiles of prospective humanities majors: 1975–1983. Final report. A study of students taking the College Board Scholastic Aptitude Test and the Graduate Record Examinations. Supplement 1: Tables of trends in data from the College Board Scholastic Aptitude Tests: Humanities majors, 1975–1983.* Princeton, NJ: Educational Testing Service.

Grant, W. V., & Eiden, L. J. (1982, May). *Digest of education statistics 1982.* Washington, DC: Superintendent of Documents, U. S. Government Printing Office.

Grant, W. V., & Snyder, T. D. (1984). *Digest of education statistics 1983–84.* National Center for Education Statistics. Washington, DC: U.S. Government Printing Office.

Greenhouse, L. (1980, August 7). Bar unit spurs minority enrollment law schools. *The New York Times,* A13.

Gross, A. L., & Su, W. (1975). Defining a "fair" or "unbiased" selection model: A question of utilities. *Journal of Applied Psychology, 60,* 345–351.

Harmon, L. R. (1978). *A century of doctorates: Data analyses of growth and change.* Washington, DC: National Academy of Sciences.

Harmon, L. R., & Maxfield, B. D. (1979). *Career patterns of doctoral scientists and engineers, 1973–1977: An analytical study.* Washington, DC: National Academy of Sciences.

Hassan, T. E. (1986–87, Winter). Asian-American Admissions: Debating discrimination. *The College Board Review, 142,* 18–21, 42–46.

Hechinger, F. M. (1987, February 10). The trouble with quotas. *The New York Times,* C1, 10.

Hilton, T. L., & Schrader, W. B. (1986, April 18). *Pathways to graduate school: An empirical study based on National Longitudinal data.* Paper presented at the 1986 American Educational Research Association Annual Meeting, San Francisco, CA.

Hirschman, C., & Wong, M. G. (1984). Socioeconomic gains of Asian Americans, blacks and Hispanics: 1960–1976. *American Journal of Sociology, 90,* 584–607.

Ho, D., & Chin, M. (1983, Summer). Admissions impossible. *Bridge,* 7–8, 51.

Hodgson, T. F., & Lutz L. (1975, March). *A study of the academic records of all students enrolled in the University of Washington Educational Opportunity Program: Autumn 1969 through Summer 1973.* (ERIC Document Reproduction Service No. ED 104 223). Seattle, WA: University of Washington Institutional Research Report 142.

Hsia, J. (1983). Cognitive assessment of Asian Americans. In M. Chang (Ed.), *Asian and Pacific-American perspectives in bilingual education comparative research* (pp. 123–153). New York: Teachers College Press.

Hu, A. (1986, February). The changing face of MIT. *The Tech.* 4–5.

Hutchinson, S., Arkoff, A., & Weaver, H. B. (1966). Ethnic and sex factors in classroom responses. *Journal of Social Psychology, 69,* 321–325.

Indochinese Refugee Panel. (1986, April). *Report of the Indochinese Refugee Panel.* Washington, DC: U. S. Department of State.

Isaacs, H. R. (1958). *Images of Asia-American views of China and India.* New York: Harper & Row.

Jencks, C., Bartlett, S., Corcoran, M., Crouse, J., Eaglesfield, D., Jackson, G., McClelland, K., Mueser, P., Olneck, M., Schwarz, J., Ward, S., & Williams, J. (1979). *Who gets ahead? The determinants of economic success in America.* New York: Basic Books.

Jennifer, F. G. (1984). How test results affect college admissions of minorities. In C. W. Daves (Ed.), *The uses and misuses of tests* (pp. 91–106). San Francisco: Jossey-Bass.

Jiobu, R. M. (1976, October). Earnings differentials between Whites and ethnic minorities: The cases of Asian Americans, blacks, and Chicanos. *Sociology and Social Research, 61*(1), 24–38.

Jones, R. F., & Mitchell, K. (1986, April 17). *Racial/ethnic differences in the predictive validity of MCAT scores.* Paper presented at the 1986 Annual Meeting of the American Educational Research Association, San Francisco.

Kempner, B. (1985, October 30). Jewish college applicants: A history of quotas. *East/West, 19*(44), 4.

Kim, B. C. (1980). *The Korean-American child at school and at home: An analysis of interaction and intervention through groups* (Project report September 30, 1973–June 30, 1980 (Grant NO. 90-C-1335(01) funded by Administration for Children, Youth, and Families). Washington, DC: U.S. Department of Health, Education, and Welfare.

King, H., & Locke, F. B. (1980). Chinese in the United States: A century of occupational transition. *International Migration Review, 14*(1), 15–42.

Kitano, H. H. L. (1976). *Japanese Americans: The evolution of a subculture* (2nd ed.). Englewood Cliffs, NJ: Prentice-Hall.

Klitgaard, R. (1985). *Choosing elites.* New York: Basic Books.

Kulick, E., & Dorans, N. J. (1983, August). *Assessing unexpected differential item performance of Oriental candidates on SAT Form CSA6 and TSWE Form E33.* (Unpublished statistical Report No. SR-83-106). Princeton, NJ: Educational Testing Service.

Law School Data Assembly Service. (1975–1979). [Unpublished national application and acceptance data.] Princeton, NJ: Author.

Leary, L. F., & Wightman, L. E. (1982, June). *Estimating the relationship between use of test-preparation methods and scores on the Graduate Management Admission Test* (GMAC Research Report 83-1, ETS Research Report RR-83-22). Princeton, NJ: Educational Testing Service.

Lee, J. (1985, August 16). National study launched on Asians' verbal skills. *Asian Week, 6*(51), 1, 19.

Leong, F. T. L. (1984, July). *On the hidden cost of being a Chinese-American.* Paper presented at the Summer Institute for Educational Research on Asian and Pacific Americans, Honolulu, HI.

Lesser, G. S. (1976). Cultural differences in learning and thinking styles. In S. Messick (Ed.), *Individuality in learning* (pp. 137–160). San Francisco: Jossey-Bass.

Lesser, G. S., Fifer, G., & Clark, D. H. (1965). *Mental abilities of children from different social-class and cultural groups* (Monographs of the Society for Research in Child Development, Serial No. 102, 30(4)).

Li, P. S. (1977, Autumn). Occupational achievement and kinship assistance among Chinese immigrants in Chicago. *The Sociological Quarterly, 18,* 478–489.

Light, I. H. (1972). Business and welfare among Chinese, Japanese, and blacks. In I. H. Light (Ed.), *Ethnc enterprise in America.* Berkeley, Los Angeles, & London: Universityof California Press.

Light, I. H., & Wong, C. (1975). Protest or work: Dilemmas of the tourist industry in American Chinatowns. *American Journal of Sociology, 80,* 1342–68.

Light, R. J., & Pillemer, D. B. (1984). *Summing up: The science of reviewing research.* Cambridge, MA: Harvard University Press.

Lindsey, R. (1987, January 19). Colleges accused of bias to stem Asian's gains. New York: *The New York Times* (A, 10).

Linn, R. L., & Hastings, C. N. (1984, Fall). A meta analysis of the validity of predictors of performance in law school. *Journal of Educational Measurement, 21,* 245–259.

Low, V. (1982). *The unimpressible race: A century of educational struggle by the Chinese in San Francisco.* San Francisco: East/West Publishing Co.

Lynn, R. (1977). The intelligence of the Japanese. *Bulletin of the British Psychological Society, 30,* 69–72.

Macaranas, F. M. (1979, April). *Education and income inequality among Asian Americans.* Paper presented at the April 1979 National Association of Asian American and Pacific Education Conference.

Maeroff, G. I. (1985, Feburary 10). Enrollment in professional schools declining. *The New York Times,* 1, 50.

Manning, W. H., & Jackson, R. (1984). College entrance examinations: Objectives selection or gate-keeping for the economically privileged. In C. E. Reynolds & R. T. Brown (Eds.), *Perspectives on bias in mental testing* (pp. 189–220). New York: Plenum.

Mathews,J. (1985, November 14). Asian students help create a new mainstream. *The Washington Post,* A1, 6.

Maxfield, B. D. (1981). *Employment of minority Ph.D.s: Changes over time.* Washington, DC: National Academy Press.

Maykovich, M. K. (1972). *Black, Asian, and white students in the Educational Opportunity Program.* Sacramento, CA: Sacramento State College. (ERIC Document Reproduction Service No. ED 073 220)

McKnight, C. C., Crosswhite, F. J., Dossey, J. A., Kifer, E., Swafford, J. O., Travers, K. J., & Cooney, T. J. (1987). *The underachieving curriculum: Assessing U.S. school mathematics from an international perspective.* Champaign, IL: Stipes.

Meredith, G. M. (1965). Observation of the acculturation of Sansei Japanese Americans in Hawaii. *Psychologia, 8,* 41–49.

Messick, S. (1983, June). *Assessment in context: Appraising student performance in relation to instructional quality* (Research report). Princeton, NJ: Educational Testing Service.

Minami, D., Gee, J., Lee, L., Wey, N., Kubota, A., Himel, Y., & Kong, C. (1979, April). *Confrontation with racism: The Asian Pacific American faculty member and job discrimination.* A symposium presented at the National Association of Asian American and Pacific Education Conference.

National Center for Education Statistics. (1984a). *Digest of education statistics, 1983–84.* Washington, DC: Author.

National Center for Education Statistics. (1984b). *High School and Beyond tabulation: Mathematics course-taking by 1980 high school sophomores who graduate in 1982 and High School and Beyond tabulation: Science coursetaking by 1980 high school sophomores who graduated in 1982.* Washington, DC: Author.

National Commission on Excellence in Education. (1983). *A Nation at risk: The imperative for educational reform.* Washington, DC: U.S. Department of Education.

National Merit Scholarship Corporation. (1984). *Annual report 1983–84*. Evanston, IL: Author.

National Merit Scholarship Corporation. (1985). *Annual report 1984–85*. Evanston, IL: Author.

National Science Board Commission on Precollege Education in Mathematics, Science and Technology. (1983). *Educating Americans for the 21st century: A plan of action for improving mathematics, science and technology education for all American elementary and secondary students so that their achievement is the best in the world by 1995*. Washington, DC: National Science Foundation.

National Science Foundation. (1981a, September). *Foreign participation in U.S. science and engineering higher education and labor markets: Special report* (NSF 81-316). Washington, DC: Author.

National Science Foundation. (1981b). *Young and senior science and engineering faculty, 1980* (NSF 81-319) Washington, DC: Author.

National Science Foundation. (1982a). *Characteristics of doctoral scientists and engineers in the United States: 1981. Detailed statistical tables* (NSF 82-332). Washington, DC: Author.

National Science Foundation. (1982b). *Characteristics of recent science/engineering graduates: 1980. Detailed statistical tables* (NSF 82-313). Washington, DC: Author.

National Science Foundation. (1983, February). *Science and engineering doctorates: 1960–81: Special report* (NSF 83-309). Washington, DC: Author.

National Science Foundation. (1986, January). *Women and minorities in science and engineering*. (Washington, DC: Author.

Nee, V. (1986, October 1). *Bringing the family back in: The limits of ethnic solidarity for new Asian immigrants*. Paper presented at the East Coast Asian American Scholars Conference, Cornell University.

Nee, V. G., & Nee, B. D. (1972). *Longtime Californ': A documentary study of an American Chinatown*. New York: Pantheon Books.

Nee, V., & Sanders, J. (1985, January). The road to parity: Determinants of the socioeconomic achievements of Asian Americans. *Ethnic and Racial Studies, 8,* 75–93.

Neidert, L. J., & Farley, R. (1985). Assimilation in the United States: An analysis of ethnic and generation differences in status and achievement. *American Sociological Review, 50,* 841–851.

Oltman, P. K., & Hartnett, R. T. (1984, May). *The role of GRE General and Subject Test scores in Graduate Program Admission* (GRE Board Research Report GREB No. 81-8R, also ETS RR-84-14). Princeton, NJ: Educational Testing Service.

Oren, D. A. (1985). *Joining the club: A history of Jews and Yale*. New Haven, CT: Yale University Press.

Owings, J. A. (1987, April). *Persistence and course taking behavior of Asian-American students*. Paper presented at the annual meeting of the American Educational Research Association, Washington, DC.

Parlin, B. W. (1976). *Immigrant professionals in the United States. Discrimination in the scientific labor market*. New York: Praeger.

Peng, S. S. (1983, November). High school dropouts: Descriptive information from High School and Beyond. *NCES Bulletin*. (NCES 83-221B). Washington, DC: U.S. Department of Education.

Peng, S. S. (1985, April). *Enrollment patterns of Asian American students in postsecondary education*. Paper presented at the Annual Meeting of the American Educational Research Association, Chicago.

Peng, S. S., Owings, J. A., & Fetters, W. B. (1984, April). *School experiences and performance of Asian American high school students*. Paper presented at the Annual Meeting of the American Educational Research Association, New Orleans.

Perrucci, C. C. (1973). Minority status and the pursuit of careers: Women in science and engineering. In B. T. Eiduson & L. Beckman (Eds.), *Science as a career choice* (pp. 79–587). New York: Russell Sage Foundation.

Petersen, N. S., & Livingston, S. A. (1982). *English Composition Test with Essay* (Statistical Report No. SR-82-96). Princeton, NJ: Educational Testing Service.

Petersen, W. (1971). *Japanese Americans*. New York: Random House.

Podeschi, R. L. (1987, April). *A case study of Hmong adolescents in community context*. Paper presented at the annual meeting of the American Educational Research Association, Washington, DC.

Presidential Scholars Program. (1980–1985). *Unpublished tabulations*. Princeton, NJ: Educational Testing Service.

Racial and ethnic makeup of college and university enrollments. (1986, July 23). *The Chronicle of Higher Education*, p. 25.

Rafferty, C. (1984, April 15). New academic elite keeps up old tradition. *New York Times*, 12, 44–45.

Ramist, L., & Arbeiter, S. (1984a). *Profile, college-bound seniors, 1982*. New York: College Entrance Examination Board.

Ramist, L., & Arbeiter, S. (1984b). *Profile, college-bound seniors, 1983*. New York: College Entrance Examination Board.

Ramist, L., & Arbeiter, S. (1986). *Profile, college-bound seniors, 1985*. New York: College Entrance Examination Board.

Randlett, R. R. (1982). *National applicant pool entering class statistics 1978–1982*. Washington, DC: AAMC, Division of Student Services.

Randlett, R. R. (1984). *National applicant pool entering class statistics 1980–1984*. Washington, DC: AAMC, Division of Student Services.

Roark, A. C. (1986, November 23). UCLA to alter student admissions policy next fall. *Los Angeles Times* (Part 1, p. 3).

Rock, D. A., Ekstrom, R. B., Goertz, M. E., & Pollack, J. M. (1985). *Determinants of achievement gain in high school* (Briefing paper prepared under Contract No. 300-83-0247 for the U.S. Department of Education, National Center for Education Statistics). Princeton, NJ: Educational Testing Service.

Rock, D. A., Ekstrom, R. B., Goetz, M. E., Pollack, J., & Hilton, T. (1984, June). *Study of excellence in high school education. Cross-sectional study, 1972–1980: Background and descriptive analysis sections* (draft technical report). Princeton, NJ: Educational Testing Service.

Rock, D. A., & Werts, C. E. (1979, April). *Construct validity of the SAT across populations—An empirical confirmatory study* (College Entrance Examination Board Research and Development Report No. 78–79, No. 5, ETS Research Report RR-79-2). Princeton: Educational Testing Service.

Rokter, L. (1986, January 26). 15 from New York are among finalists for science awards. *New York Times*, 33.

Rolph, J. E., Williams, A. P., & Lanier, A. L. (1978). *Predicting minority and majority medical student performance on the National Board exams*. Santa Monica, CA: Rand Corporation.

Roos, P. A. (1977, September). *Questioning the stereotypes: Differentials in income attainment of Japanese, Mexican-Americans, and Anglos in California*. (ED No. 148 651). Rockville, MD: National Institute of Mental Health (DHEW).

Rossi, A. S. (1965). Barrier to the career choice of engineering, medicine, or science among American women. In J. A. Mattfeld & C. Van Aber (Eds.), *Women and the scientific professions* (pp. 51–127). Cambridge, MA: MIT Press.

Rothman, R. (1986, December 10). Record number of schools join Advance Placement Program. *Education Week*.

Salholz, E., Doherty, S., Tran, D. (1987, February 9). Do colleges set Asian quotas? *Newsweek*, p. 60.

Sawyer, R. (Summer, 1986). Using demographic subgroup and dummy variable equations to predict college freshmen grade average. *Journal of Educational Measurement, 23*, 131–145.

Schmidt, S. (1986, May 12). Medical schools, seeking diverse students, study Hopkins change. *The Washington Post*.

Science Service. (1978–1985). *Washington trip winners of the thirty-seventh to forty-fourth Annual Science Talent Search for the Westinghouse Science Scholarship and Awards*. Washington, DC: Author.

Sege, L. (1987, March 29). Failure and success for Asian students. *Boston Sunday Globe, 233*(88), 1, 38.

Sherman, B. (1986, January 5). Asian-Americans turn to private schools. *New York Times*, 12, 63.

Sinnott, L. T. (1980, March). *Differences in item performance across groups* (ETS Research Report RR-80-19). Princeton, NJ: Educational Testing Service.

Sjogren, C. (1986). Additional measures in the admissions process. *Proceedings of College Board Colloquium on Measures in the College Admissions Process*. New York: College Entrance Examination Board.

Smith, H. R., III. (1984, June). *A summary of data collected from Graduate Record Examinations test takers during 1982–1983* (Data Summary Report No. 8). Princeton, NJ: Educational Testing Service.

Smith, H. R., III. (1985, April). *A summary of data collected for Graduate Record Examinations test takers during 1983–1984* (Data Summary Report No. 9). Princeton, NJ: Educational Testing Service.

Smith, L., & Billiter, B. (1985, December 19). Asian Americans emphasis on education paying off. *Los Angeles Times,* 1, 33–34.

Soo Hoo, E. (1986–1987, Winter). An honored profession attracts Asians. *Ward Rounds.* Chicago, IL: Northwestern University Medical School.

Sowell, T. (1975). *Affirmative action reconsidered.* Washington, DC: American Enterprise Institute for Public Policy Research.

Stevenson, H. W., Lee, S. Y., & Stigler, J. W. (1986). Mathematics achievement of Chinese, Japanese and American children. *Science, 231,* 693–699.

Stevenson, H. W., Stigler, J. W., Lee, S. Y., Lucker, G. W., Kitamura, S., & Hsu, C. C. (1985). Cognitive performance and academic achievement of Japanese, Chinese, and American children. *Child Development, 56,* 718–734.

Sue, S. (1983, May). Ethnic minority issues in psychology. *American Psychologist, 38,* 583–592.

Sue, S. (1985). Asian Americans and educational pursuits: Are the doors beginning to close? *Asian American Psychological Association Journal,* Spring, 16–19.

Sue, S., & Morishima, J. K. (1982). *The mental health of Asian Americans.* San Francisco: Jossey-Bass.

Sue, S., & Zane, N. W. S. (1985). Academic achievement and socioemotional adjustment among Chinese university students. *Journal of Counseling Psychology, 32,* 570–579.

Sung, B. L. (1977). Employment policy recommendations: Looking to 1980. *Occasional Papers/Reprints Services in Contemporary Asian Studies No. 12.* College Park: University of Maryland, School of Law.

Sweet, D. A. (1983). How well do high school graduates of today meet the curriculum standards of the National Commission of Excellence? *National Center for Education Statistics Bulletin* (NCES 83-223). Washington, DC: U.S. Department of Education.

Syverson, P. D. (1982). *Summary report 1981 doctorate recipients from United States universities.* Washington, DC: National Academy Press.

Takeuchi, S. M. (1974). *Verbal skills of the Asian American student.* (ERIC Document Reproduction Service No. ED 097 395) Boulder, CO: University of Colorado.

Tang, N. M. (1983, March 22). *Immigrant and Refugee Student Project. Report and recommendations: 1982– 1984.* An unpublished report of the Immigrant and Refugee Students Project, Berkeley, CA: University of California, Berkeley.

Taylor, M. E., Stafford, C. E., & Place, C. (1981). *National longitudinal study of the high school class of 1972. Study reports update: Review and annotation.* Washington, DC: National Center for Education Statistics.

Thomas, G. E. (1984, December). *Determinants and motivations underlying the college major choice of race and sex groups.* Washington, DC: National Academy of Sciences, Office of Scientific and Engineering Personnel.

Toupin, E. A., & Son, L. (1985, October 15). *Preliminary findings on Asian Americans the model minority in a small private east coast college.* Paper presented at a Conference on Perceptions, Policies and Practices: Asian and Pacific Americans in the 1980s. Sponsored by Minority Rights Group (NY) Inc. and Columbia University.

Travers, K. J., & McKnight, C. C. (1985, February). Mathematics achievement in U.S. schools: Preliminary findings from the Second IEA Mathematics Study. *Phi Delta Kappan.*

Turner, W. (1981, April). Rapid rise in students of Asian origin causing problems at Berkeley campus. *The New York Times,* A-16.

UCLA Asian American Studies Center. (1984). Unpublished figures of UCLA ethnic survey of new students, fall, 1984 and related correspondence. Los Angeles, CA: Author.

U. S. Commission on Civil Rights. (1986, April). *Recent activity against citizens and residents of Asian descent.* Washington, DC. AUthor.

U. S. Department of Commerce, Bureau of the Census. (1980a, November). *1977 Survey of minority-owned business enterprises.* Washington, DC: U. S. Government Printing Office.

U. S. Department of Commerce, Bureau of the Census. (1980b, November). *Selected characteristics of persons in physical science: 1978* (Special Studies Series P-23, No. 108). Washington, DC: U.S. Government Printing Office.

U. S. Department of Commerce, Bureau of the Census (1983a). *General population characteristics United States summary: 1980 Census of population.* Washington, DC: U.S. Government Printing Office.

U. S. Department of Commerce, Bureau of the Census. (1983b). *General social and economic characteristics United States Summary.* Washington, DC: U.S. Government Printing Office.

U. S. Department of Commerce, Bureau of the Census. (1983c). *General social and economic characteristics: California: 1980 Census of population.* Washington, DC: U.S. Government Printing Office.

U. S. Department of Commerce, Bureau of the Census. (1983d, March). *1980 Census of population supplementary report. Detailed occupation and years of school completed by age, for the civilian labor force by sex, race and Spanish origin: 1980* (PC 80-51-8).

U. S. Department of Commerce, Bureau of the Census. (1983e, June). *1980 Census of the population. General social and economic characteristics-Hawaii* (Vol. 1). Washington, DC: U.S. Government Printing Office.

U. S. Department of Commerce, Bureau of the Census. (1983f, December). *Asian and Pacific Islander population by state: 1980—1980 Census of population.* Washington, DC: U.S. Government Printing Office.

U. S. Department of Commerce, Bureau of the Census. (1986, January). *Enrollment in institutions of higher education by sex, race/ethnicity and attendance status of student and control and type of institution: 50 states and D.C.: Fall 1984.* Washington, DC: Author.

U. S. Department of Education, Office for Civil Rights. (1986a, March). *Bachelor's degrees conferred by institutions of higher education by race, ethnicity and sex: State and national 1982–83.* Washington, DC: Author.

U. S. Department of Education, Office of Civil Rights. (1986b, March). *Degrees conferred by institutions of higher education by race,e thnicity and sex: State and national 1982–83.* Washington, DC: Author.

U. S. Department of Education, Office for Civil Rights. (1986c, March). *Master's degrees conferred by institutions of higher education by race, ethnicity and State and 1982–83.* Washington, DC: Author.

U. S. Department of Education, Office for Civil Rights. (1986d, March). *Doctor's degrees conferred by institutions of higher education by race, ethnicity and sex: State and national 1982–83.* Washington, DC:

U. S. Department of Labor. (1974). *Immigrants and the American labor market* (Manpower Research Monograph No. 31). Washington, DC: Author.

Vernon, P. E. (1982). *The abilities and achievements of Orientals in North America.* New York: Academic Press.

Wainer, H. (1984, Summer). An exporatory analysis of performance on the SAT. *Journal of Educational Measurement, 21*(2), 81–91.

Walberg, H. J., & Tsai, S. (1983, Fall). Matthew effects in education. *American Educational Research Journal, 20*(3), 359–373.

Wang, L. (1985, October 30). Anti-Asian exclusivism at University of California, Berkeley. *East/West,* 7–8.

Watanabe, C. (1973). Self-expression and the Asian American experience. *Personnel and Guidance Journal, 51,* 390–396.

Weitzman, R. A. (1982, Fall). The prediction of college achievement by the high school record. *Journal of Educational Measurement, 19*(3), 179–192.

Werner, E. E., Simonian, K., & Smith, R. S. (1968). Ethnic and socioeconomic status differences in abilities and achievement among preschool and school age children in Hawaii. *The Journal of Social Psychology, 75,* 43–59.

White House Commission on Presidential Scholars. (1985). *The 1986 United States Presidential Scholars Program fact sheet.* Washington, DC: U. S. Department of Education.

Wilber, G. L., Jaco, D. E., Hagan, R. J., & del Fierro, A. C., Jr. (1975). *Orientals in the American labor market—Minorities in the labor market* (Vol. II). Lexington, KY: University of Kentucky.

Wild, C. L., Swinton, S. S., & Wallmark, M. M. (1982, November). *A summary of the research leading to the revision of the format of the Graduate Record Examinations Aptitude Test in October 1981* (GRE Board Research Report GREB No. 80-1aR, also ETS Research Report 82-54). Princeton, NJ: Educational Testing Service.

Williams, D. A., McDonald, D. H., Howard, L., Mittlebach, M., & Kyle, C. (1984, April). A formula for success. *Newsweek*, 77–78.

Willingham, W. W. (1985). *Success in college: The role of personal qualities and academic ability.* New York: College Entrance Examination Board.

Willingham, W. W., & Breland, H. M. (1982). *Personal qualities and college admissions.* New York: College Entrance Examination Board.

Willingham, W. W., & Breland, H. M. (1977). The status of selective admissions. In *Selective admissions in higher education* (A report of the Carnegie Council on policy studies in higher education). San Francisco: Jossey-Bass.

Wilson, K. M. (1982). *A study of the validity of the restructured GRE Aptitude Test for predicting first-year performance in graduate study* (GRE Board Research Report GREB No. 78-6R, also ETS Research Report 82-34). Princeton, NJ: Educational Testing Service.

Wilson, K. M. (1984, September). *Foreign nationals taking the GRE General Test during 1981–82: Highlights of a study* (GREB No. 91-23aR). Princeton, NJ: Educational Testing Service.

Winerip, M. (1985, May 30). Asian-Americans question Ivy League's entry policies. *The New York Times*, B1,4.

Wollenberg, C. M. (1978). *All deliberate speed: Segregation and exclusion in California schools, 1855–1975.* Berkeley, CA: University of California Press.

Wong, C. (1985, October 30). Asian Americans rise to the top echelon in higher ed, but advances are too few. *East/West, 19*(44), 1–2.

Wong, M. G. (1980). Model students? Teachers' perceptions and expectations of their Asian and White students. *Sociology of Education, 53*, 236–246.

Wong, M. G. (1982). The cost of being Chinese, Japanese and Filipino in the United States, 1960, 1970, 1976. *Pacific Sociological Review, 25*, 59–78.

Young, J. J. (1977). *Discrimination, income, human capital investment, and Asian-Americans.* San Francisco: R & E Research Associates.

Yu, W. (1985, September 11). Asian-Americans charge prejudice slows climb to management ranks. *The Wall Street Journal*, 35.

Yun, G., & Nishi, S. M. (1986, April 18). *The Academic careers of Asian American University faculty.* A paper presented at the Annual Meeting of the Asian Educational Research Association, San Francisco.

Zak, P. M., Benbow, C. P., & Stanley, J. C. (1983). Several factors associated with success as an undergraduate chemistry major. *College and University, 58*, 303–312.

Author Index

Subject Index